ROCKY COMFORT
Wayne Holmes

ROCKY COMFORT

Wayne Holmes

Leonard Press
Bolivar, Missouri
2009

Leonard Press
Bolivar, MO 65613-0752

For other titles, prices, and order information:
www.leonardpress.com

ISBN 978-1-934223-00-0
Library of Congress Control Number: 2009929528

Cover design by Kaitlyn Ramsey
Author photograph on the cover by Bruce Trimble
Other photographs provided by the author

Contents

ONE

THE JILL-FLIRTED MARE

"Here she is, Packsaddle Bridge," Dad announced, and as I looked down through a knothole in the bridge floor I caught a glimpse of a narrow stream far below. "Right down there," he said, "is where your Uncle Cager lost a team of horses in the quicksand before the bridge went in." Almost three in the spring of 1933, I was sitting in the back of Dad's lead wagon looking out over the tailgate when I heard the distinctive clip-clop of the horses' iron shod hooves striking the heavy wooden timbers on the nine-tenths of a mile long arching span over the South Canadian River in western Oklahoma. This, my first memory, is the only part of our four hundred mile trek from northern Kansas to the Needmore community in western Oklahoma that I can attest to.

I remember nothing about the following year when we lived in a tent, and almost nothing of our six month stay in an old abandoned schoolhouse after we came home from town to find the tent torched by a man Dad had got the best of in a trade. But getting ready to move to the Missouri Ozarks, "the land of a million smiles," and "the land of milk and honey," as Dad described where his folks lived, made a strong impression on me.

The best part of preparing to move was butchering day when the women and girls were herded inside Grandpa and Grandma Green's house, where they stayed until the yearling steer had been killed, skinned, and gutted. Four, going on five, I was plenty big enough to stand with my older brother Fred, eight, and hang on to the fence outside the barn lot and watch while Dad and Mama's three teenage brothers did the job that women and girls were not permitted to see.

Clay Holmes where we lived in Needmore, Oklahoma before moving to Missouri in February, 1935

Instead of dropping dead when Dad shot him, the dazed steer shook his head, raised his tail high and raced wildly around the enclosure. "Catch him! Catch him!" Dad yelled, and the long legged, high stepping middle boy managed to over-take the bawling wide-eyed animal and hang on to its tail while it pulled him around and around the lot before it collapsed in a corner where the boys held it, and Dad cut its throat with the heavy curved butcher knife Fred handed him. As I

8

craned my neck to get a good look at the gushing bright blood and the animal's dying spasms, Dad said, "I hope all that excitement didn't taint the meat."

After Mama's brothers helped Dad hoist the steer to a limb on a nearby scrub oak with wire stretchers and a singletree off Grandpa's garden plow, they watched as he carefully skinned the animal, tied a stout string around its asshole, then split the pelvis with an ax before plopping the guts into a washtub. Following Dad's directions, the big boys carried fresh buckets of water from the cistern and sloshed out the still steaming carcass. Mama's tedious job of cutting up the meat before packing it in half gallon jars in Grandma's pressure cooker failed to hold my attention. Nothing I'd seen in women's work excited me anything like seeing the botched killing of the steer.

* * *

Before we moved to Missouri, Dad and Uncle Homer—named Oklahoma Territory Green in honor of his birthplace after the family migrated from Texas, where his nine older siblings were born—rode west into Texas, where Dad traded his two well broke teams for a blemished bay mare and a spoiled paint bronc, drawing seventy-five dollars to boot.

The new horses, one gentle, the other spooky, were jumped into the back of the one ton Ford truck from the pond bank, then tied to the front rack and penned with wooden panels. A jumble of things followed, including Dad's square wooden box filled with the beef Mama had canned, a four foot long narrow pine box containing its cargo of perishables, several backless chairs, and two sets of iron bedsteads and springs. Two thin, straw filled mattresses covered with comforters were placed in the left hand corner behind the horses as far away as possible from the truck's exhaust. There we, the four youngest, Joyce six, I four, Wanda three, and Jay one, huddled under the gray tarpaulin safe with Mama. The three men got to ride in the cab. There was Uncle Calvin, the drinking driver, owner of the truck, and Dad, of course. Fred, snug and smug in the middle, had earned his honored spot almost two years earlier by driving the second team pulling a faded blue circus wagon across Kansas and half of Oklahoma.

The trip to Missouri took a lot of the starch out of the snorting bronc, Old Casey. Crowded in her corner, Old Bird, the small bay mare, barely moved. After the twenty hour February ride under the flapping tarp, accompanied by a tailwind and a skiff of snow, a sudden rush of warm air, heavy with the smell of burning coal oil and peach pie juices, spilled out of the open door where Grandpa and Grandma Holmes lived.

We soon moved to the Wise Place, a half mile east, where Dad worked his mismatched team daily. He constantly curbed the plunging walleyed outlaw while clucking approval to the steady mare. Reliable and good as she was, I wondered how the mare was blemished. Closemouthed, Dad wouldn't say. Finally, too curious to keep quiet, I risked his anger: "What's wrong with Old Bird?"

Redder in the face than ordinary, Dad ignored my question. Then it hit me. It's her farting. She farts too much, especially when we go to town. Out on the farm where rude noises abounded nobody minded, but the closer we got to town the louder she sounded, bringing grins and snickers from perfect strangers. Meanwhile I, sitting on a tomato crate in the back of the wagon, acted hard of hearing as I stared straight ahead.

On the way home from town once, foolhardy, I asked, "What makes her do that?"

Dad's sharp glance and curt, "She's been pasture bred and she's jill-flirted," told me nothing but shut me up. More questions would have brought a whipping.

Months later a strange wagon pulled up in the barn lot. "Mr. Holmes?"

Wary with strangers, Dad nodded. "Call me Clay."

"We're the Gilhams, father and son, from up on the county line. We heard you're a trader."

"I've been known to trade. What's on your mind?"

"You got any horses you'd swap?"

10

"I doubt it. My team inside the barn there suits me pretty good."

The older Gilham's eyes brightened when he saw Old Casey. "Would you trade your spotted horse?"

"No, he's my ridin' horse."

"What about the little mare? Would you trade her?"

"Oh, I don't know, I might if I thought it was a fair trade," Dad answered in a flat voice.

"Bring her out here in the light so I can see her better. But before you do there's something I need to say. Mr. Holmes, we're Gilhams, and we're Christians. If there's any cheatin' to be done, we'd rather be cheated than cheat."

"I'm just like you, only different," Dad said. "If there's any cheatin' to be done, I'd rather cheat than be cheated."

Dad brought the mare out, farting every step, where Mr. Gilham looked her over but didn't raise her tail.

"How does she work?"

"She's a good worker. You can put her anywhere."

"How would you trade her for my offside gelding?"

Dad examined the scrawny horse with care, taking special pains with his mouth, feet, and legs as he asked, "How does he work? Is he sound? Will he balk?" Assured, Dad continued, "I'll tell you what. With a little extra feed I think your horse will match my paint better than the little mare does. I'll trade with you, even up, and you can change them right here."

"You've got yourself a trade," said Mr. Gilham, smiling broadly as he stuck out his hand.

Dad shook, limp handed, and the Gilhams quickly exchanged the two animals and drove off. That fart, fart, farting fading into the far distance was the sweetest sound I'd ever heard.

Within the week a tight faced set of Gilhams announced by familiar sounds drove up in the yard. The older man sputtered: "Mister, you – you – you didn't tell us that mare was jill-flirted."

"No," Dad replied evenly before waving them off. "I didn't. The man I got her from didn't tell me, and I thought he wanted it kept a secret."

Clay Holmes
before he sold his saddle for 5 dollars and
turned into a dirt farmer

TWO

MILK SNAKES AND GOAT SUCKERS

When dry, hot weather hung on that summer, causing our drinking water in the cistern to run low and taste brackish, we hauled water in two fifty gallon barrels, one wooden and the other metal, from Wilkin Spring about a mile away. Dad laughed when I said "that's dange'us, Dad, that's dange'us," as we rolled down an especially steep hill in the wagon pulled by the green broke paint bronc and the steady bay gelding Dad got when he skinned the Gilhams. By the time we got home from the spring half of the water we'd started with had leaked and sloshed out.

Dad increasingly preferred doing business at Osie rather than at either of the two stores at Sage Hill, even though it was twice as far away. I never knew for sure what accounted for his preference, but he liked the owners, Emmit and Beulah Hilton, as well as Beulah's tongue-tied sister, Marie, and he seemed more comfortable about asking them for credit than he did from the people who ran the other stores.

On our way to Osie, not more than a half mile from home, Watermelon Charley Smith often hailed us from where he sat on the front porch of the first house on the north side of the road. "Git down and come on over," the hearty old man would yell.

"We don't have much time," Dad would holler back, but he'd stop the team and step down while making sure he carefully tied Old Casey to a tree before he motioned Fred and me out of the wagon and over to the porch where we sat and listened. Like us, the talkative man's big boy, Eddie the Little Booger, sat silently in the background.

I didn't understand much of what the two men said, but they often laughed and slapped their legs as they carried on. Once, after we'd left and were out of hearing, Dad said, "Now boys, there's no need to worry your mother with what you've heard at Watermelon Charley's. Okay?"

Another time after Dad and Fred and I got home from the store later than usual, Mama's dark eyes flashed as she sharply asked Dad: "What was you up to all afternoon? There's work to do around here and you know it."

"Any fool can work," Dad angrily retorted, and he banged out the door toward the barn and waiting chores.

Another problem surfaced after Wilma Wilkin, who lived across from the Smith Place, told Mama that we often stopped there on our way to Osie. "Wilma says old man Smith is a windbag," Mama said.

"He may be a little windy," Dad grinned, "but he sure can tell a good story."

"Good story, my foot," Mama said. "You know I don't want our boys gittin' the idy that storyin' of any kind is all right. Another thing," she went on, "Wilma said she thinks Watermelon Charley is an old infidel."

"Old infidel? What does she know about what he believes? He hasn't said a word to me about bein' an infidel."

"Wilma says there's drinkin', fiddle playin', and who knows what else goin' on across the road lots of nights, especially when a man named Randolph with his big contraption is there collectin' dirty songs and stories."

"I don't know a thing about what goes on at Watermelon Charley's at night," Dad said. "But what the boys and I've heard is harmless. Don't worry about it."

Mama also was concerned about what kind of company we kept at the store. She said little, but from the frown on her face and the set of her jaw I could tell she disapproved of anything Buck Reavis said and Dad repeated. "Where does the Reavis family go to church?" she asked Dad. "I haven't seen anyone by that name at White Oak or either one of the Osie churches."

"I don't know where they go to church, or if they go," Dad said. "The subject hasn't come up."

Around the middle of June Grandpa and Grandma Holmes came to our house after church to help celebrate my fifth birthday. Birthdays generally went by with little notice at our house beyond the mock spankings Dad gave us. Holding us gently but firmly, he'd deliver soft pats, one for each year, punctuated with a concluding sharp tap, "And one to grow on!" before turning us loose. Dad's birthday ritual was all the more surprising because he studiously avoided touching any of us except the latest baby

Wayne, Wanda, and Jay at
the Wise Place

15

during the rest of the year. Mama didn't play games of any kind, not even once a year, and when she spanked or whipped us, she meant business.

Fred had run me down and hit me on the hindend with his open hand as hard as he could several times before Grandpa and Grandma arrived, and I was still crying when they came in the back door.

"Dry that up, young man," Grandma told me, "I've made you something for your birthday," and she pulled out a jaunty blue cap with a red bill. "Oh dear, it's too little," she said, as she tried to force the cap over my head. "Here, if it'll fit Wanda you'll have to be a big boy and give it to her."

Seeing Wanda wear my pretty cap caused me to start crying again. "Now dry up," Grandma repeated. "Remember, the Lord loves a cheerful giver, and He says it's more blessed to give than receive."

Unconsoled, I went outside and searched for the dead copperhead Mama had killed the day before while looking for ripe blackberries. As for the cap, I never saw it again. Mama may have thrown it in the cookstove after Grandma and Grandpa left, especially considering how angry she became later on when Jay and Lottie Jean, grinning and giggling, emerged outside the toilet wearing one another's clothes, only to be jerked up and blistered for their innocent derring-do. Mama knew that even the slightest appearance of evil was wicked.

* * *

We were at the breakfast table one morning when Dad told Mama: "I'm gonna get rid of that spotted horse."

"Why, what's wrong with him?"

"He can't be trusted. After all this time he still flinches and lays back his ears when I step behind him or touch him. I'm afraid he'll cripple or kill one of the kids."

Dad didn't mention how Old Casey had suddenly unloaded him in the middle of the rocky road a few days earlier in front of Loy Burbridge's house, something Fred and I heard Loy laughing about at the Sage Hill store. "It was better than any rodeo I ever saw," Loy said, and he described how funny it was to see the slim cowboy turned dirt farmer with his high crowned felt hat and patched overalls sitting on a folded tow sack instead of a saddle astride the loud paint. Loy said the best part was when the horse threw Dad sky-high and left him stranded in the middle of the road holding the sack.

"When I asked Clay if he was hurt," Loy said, "he grinned and said it hurt his feelings pretty bad, but he guessed he'd live. I offered to take him home, but he said he needed the exercise."

Dad remembered that Carson Shockley, who lived a mile south and a little west of us, had often admired Old Casey. As we headed toward Carson's, Fred and I pulled back on the brake pole with all our might as we went down the steep red hill south of White Oak. The tall man hailed us as we pulled in where he was busy shooing an old sow and her litter out of the front yard: "Howdy," he said. "Git out. What are you men up to?"

"Not much," Dad said, "I thought we'd come over and see if you're still interested in my paint horse."

"I'd about given up on ever ownin' him. The last time we talked you said he wasn't for sale at any price. What changed your mind?"

"He's still not for sale, but I might trade him."

"Why do you want to git rid of him? If that's a fair question."

"He's too much horse for me. I need somethin' with a little less piss and vinegar."

"I just may have what you need," Carson said. "See that smooth bay mare out there in the pasture?"

"Yeah, I see her. She's awful small."

"She is small, but she's an easy keeper, she's kid broke, and you can catch her anywhere."

17

"Let me tie up my team so I can see her better," Dad said, and we walked out to the horse pasture. When we returned, Dad said, "She's not a bad lookin' little mare, Carson, but from the looks of that hollowed out place on her right hip and the stutter step she takes when she walks, I'd bet money that hip's been knocked down."

"You're a good judge of horseflesh," Carson said. "I was about to mention that hip. And there's one other thing you need to know. Besides favorin' that leg, when you first hitch her up she can be a little cold shouldered."

"You mean she'll balk?"

"I wouldn't go so far as to say balk, but on a heavy load she's been known to rare up or plunge before she gits warmed up. Start her out slow and easy and she's just fine. Now tell me more about why you're in the notion of gittin' rid of your bronc."

"You've seen me work and ride him right along," Dad said. "Like I said, he's just a little too hot-blooded to suit me."

"How'll you trade him for my mare?"

"I'd have to have considerable boot. You and I both know your mare's not half the horse Old Casey is."

"He's worth more than she is, all right, but not twice as much. What if I threw in a right good yearlin' calf?"

"No, that wouldn't be enough," Dad argued. "But I might consider a fresh cow. I don't drink milk myself, but it takes a lot for Geneva and the kids."

"Let's go out to the cow pasture," Carson said. "We're gittin' more milk around here than we know what to do with, and now I've got to fool with a two year old heifer that lost her calf."

After we circled the young Jersey cow, Dad exclaimed, "Why, her bag's not much bigger than mine. How much milk does she give?"

"Oh, I'm not sure, my wife milks her, but she gives a right smart."

"Hmm, a right smart," Dad mused, as he looked the cow over. "It's against my better judgment, but I'll trade horses with you if you'll throw in the cow and that ruptured runt pig I saw in the yard when we first drove up. And I'll need to borry a stout rope."

"I'm gonna trade with you," Carson said, "but that cow's not broke to lead."

"I don't aim to lead her. If you'll help me, after I rope her we'll ease her up on the pond bank, throw her and hog-tie her, then after we've changed horses I'll drive up close and we'll roll her into the wagon and I'll take her down the road."

"I wouldn't a thought of that," Carson said.

"There's more ways than one to skin a cat," Dad replied, and he quickly adjusted the harness to fit the mare.

"Good luck with Old Casey," Dad said as he prepared to drive off. "Oh, I forgot to ask about the mare's name."

"Old Bird."

"Well, I'll declare. The last mare I owned had the same name," and he made a click-click sound in the corner of his mouth and slapped the lines as we started home.

The new Old Bird reminded me of the earlier one, but as bad as the constant jiggling motion caused by her knocked down hip was, it wasn't anything like as embarrassing as the sound the jill-flirted mare made. "Hang on tight to that pig, boys," Dad told Fred and me as we neared the bottom of the hill, and he popped the mare's butt hard with his whip and spoke sharply as he urged the team up the steep incline.

Dad was upset that evening over how little milk the new cow gave.

"She's prob'ly still excited and hasn't let her milk down," Mama said.

When the next day's attempts brought no better results, Dad was furious. "It looks like Carson Shockley give me a good skinnin'," he announced at the supper table. "I'm goin' to Osie tomorrow to see if anyone down there can tell me what to do."

* * *

By midmorning the next day Fred and I were sitting on sacks of feed in the far end of the country store while Dad visited with Buck Reavis and other men in the community who congregated there. "Buck," Dad said to the friendly livestock dealer: "Remember me askin' about certain words and sayin's I'd heard since movin' to Missouri?"

"Yeah, I recall you had trouble figurin' out how far a fur piece was."

"Well, I still don't know the answer to that, but a couple of days ago one of my neighbors give me a lesson in the meanin' of another sayin' I hadn't heard."

"What's that?"

"A right smart. I was dickerin' for one of his cows and when I asked him how much milk she gives, he said he didn't know for sure, but it's a right smart."

Buck laughed, "And you bought her."

"No, but I traded for her," Dad admitted. "And now I know how much a right smart is: It's about half a teacup full."

After the laughter in the store died down, Buck took out a sack of Bull Durham tobacco, filled and tamped his short stemmed pipe, then struck a kitchen match across the tight hindend of his overalls and sucked noisily before he spoke. "Have you been seein' any milk snakes or goat suckers around your place?"

"What are you talkin' about?"

"You know what king snakes and bull bats are, don't cha?"

"Sure."

"They're called milk snakes and goat suckers around here, and they've got a reputation for suckin' cows and nanny goats and dryin' 'em up."

"Maybe that's it," Dad said. "How can I put a stop to it?"

"Given all the huntin' and trappin' you've done, you ought to be smart enough to figure out somethin'."

"I just might," Dad replied. "Much obliged."

20

Instead of turning the new cow out of the stall into the lot with the rest of the cows that evening, Dad left her locked in a stanchion. The next morning he opened the barn door, smiled, and motioned Fred and me over. "Come here," he said. "I want to show you boys somethin'."

Fred, ahead of me, started running. "What is it, Dad?"

"Look at that cow. I believe the mystery's solved."

"What mystery?"

"The mystery of the disappearin' milk. Remember all of Buck's talk at the store yesterday about milk snakes and goat suckers?"

"Yeah."

"And what he said about how a hunter and trapper like me ought to be able to figure out a way to catch whatever was suckin' the cow?"

"Yeah, I remember."

"Well, that stanchion's the trap I set, and the cow herself's the guilty party."

"I don't understand," I said.

"I've been keepin' a close eye on her, and I've noticed she curls up in a tighter knot than most cows do when they lay down."

"I still don't understand."

"Look at how plump her bag is. We haven't seen that before. She couldn't turn around far enough to reach her bag in the stanchion last night, which means she's been suckin' herself, just as I suspected."

When he'd finished milking the cow Dad tipped his bucket towards us. "That's not hardly a gallon," he said, "but it sure beats half a teacup full."

After we'd finished chores and breakfast Dad was in a hurry to get to Osie where several men, including Buck, got a big kick out of his account of how he'd set and baited traps for milk snakes and goat suckers, but caught a cow instead. When he'd finished explaining, Dad turned to Buck. "Now that I've caught her, what do I do next?"

"You can build a box yoke so she can't bend her neck around to suck herself, or you can hire me to haul her to the stockyards."

Although Dad's cumbersome yoke worked, it was so heavy it dragged the ground when the cow grazed, and he ended up hiring Buck to take her to the Saturday auction at the Monett sale barn.

As the cow entered the sale ring Fay Cisco, sale barn owner and auctioneer, set her in at fifteen dollars, but when nobody bid he paused and worked the crowd. "You boys better pay attention here," he said. "This is a right good first calf Jersey heifer and she's worth a whole lot more than fifteen dollars. Who'll give me seventeen and a half, seventeen and a half, seventeen and a half?" Stopping again, Fay asked, "Whose cow is this, and how much milk does she give?"

Expressionless, Dad stood and said, "She's my cow, and she gives a right smart."

When the chant resumed a hand went up and Fay Cisco yelled "Sold." After Dad got his check, Fred and I climbed in to the back of Buck's truck and we were on our way home.

THREE

THE BOWERS PLACE

Within six months after we'd moved to the Wise Place, the owner stopped and told Dad he had a buyer for his farm, "And if you folks'll move right away I'll give you back the two hundred dollars you paid me for the year's rent."

"I don't care," Dad told him. "My tomato crop's already burnt up. We'll be out of here as soon as I can locate another place."

Dad learned at the store that the eighty acre Bowers Place atop a long hill a couple of miles east could be rented for half what he'd paid for the same sized Wise Place. He looked it over on his way home, and he told Mama: "It don't have much in the way of outbuildings—I could throw a grown cat through any side of the barn—but the three room house is tight and you'll be glad to know there's a cellar out in back."

"Good," Mama said. "Is it big enough for a bed? You know how scared I am of cyclones and thunderstorms."

"Yeah, it's a regular size cellar."

"I've prayed about it, and I think we better take it," Mama said. "What do you think?"

"It's likely as good as we're gonna git," he replied. "The boys can help me haul water until I can build a windlass so we can git started on diggin' a cistern."

"We'll make do," Mama said. "The Lord will provide."

* * *

In early February, on the coldest and worst night of the year, Dad unexpectedly put all five of us kids in his and Mama's bed in the bedroom, while Mama slept in one of our beds in the front room. "Now behave yourselves and be quiet," he told us. "Your mother's sick and I'm goin' to the Old Lady Johnson's for help. I'll be back as quick as I can."

We knew from the few times we'd been in bed with the boys at one end and the girls in the other that we could have a lot of fun tickling and goosing one another, but Dad's fierce look scared us. Besides, all thoughts of under the covers shenanigans vanished when we heard the unmistakable cry of a baby. Unbeknownst to us, Mama had got up to use the slop bucket, and when she grunted the newborn baby fell head first into it.

The mingled sounds of the baby and Mama's crying confused us; we hadn't known she was pregnant, and we'd never before heard her cry; but after Dad and the old granny woman finally got up the ice covered hill to the house the sniffling sounds subsided, and Dad came in and told us we had a new baby sister named Lottie Jean.

Afterwards, I wondered if the baby had cut her upper lip on the sharp bail of the slop bucket, but Mama said that wasn't it. "I marked her months ago when I hit my upper lip on the doorjamb," she insisted. Later, when she was taken to Children's Hospital in Kansas City to have her lip and palate repaired, doctors explained that a harelip was a congenital defect, but Mama still maintained she'd marked the baby.

Dad never said whether he was afraid they'd have another disfigured child—Mama's youngest brother's wife bore two sons with cleft palates—or whether he simply thought six kids in twelve years was enough. Whatever the reason, he started practicing a form of birth control Mama and all her family strongly opposed. "The Bible plainly says that spilling a man's seed upon the ground is an abomination unto the Lord," Mama argued, and she and Dad fought pitched battles night after night. One morning, following an especially bitter exchange, Dad split a bigger than usual pile of wood for the cookstove, then marched stiffly off to the barn where he bridled Old Bird, grabbed a tow sack to sit on, and mounted up. "Mind your mother," he told us kids before he turned to Mama and said, "I don't aim to come back."

"Suit yourself," she said. "If you're not back in a week, I'll put the kids in an orphans' home and leave too."

The instant Dad was out of sight down the hill, I ran to the barn and climbed up in the loft where I waited and watched until I saw him far below on the crippled mare headed west and then north over Crane Creek near the canning factory and out of sight beyond where the one armed Hutchinson and his family lived.

Although I didn't expect to ever see Dad again, near the end of the week Wanda first heard and then saw him coming up the hill swinging a hand bell announcing his arrival. "Dad's home! Dad's home!" she yelled, and all of us except Mama ran out to meet him.

"Here," he said, handing down a sack from the mare's withers. "It's a little late, but better late than never." Inside the sack were tiddlywinks for Joyce, rag dolls for Wanda and Lottie Jean, and rubber balls for Fred, Jay, and me. He also had oranges for everyone, including Mama and himself. Best of all, shortly after he got home Dad caught the mumps, they went down on him, and he no longer had a reason to spill his seed upon the ground.

* * *

Then another big change occurred. I was asleep in the brooderhouse where Fred and I slept in all but the coldest weather when he roused me to announce that Dad had just been saved at the Osie revival. As Fred told it, Brother Keith and Brother Ericson had taken turns preaching until Dad finally relented and went forward. "And I got saved, too!" Fred crowed. "Mama thinks from the way I shouted I got the Holy Ghost!"

"What's the Holy Ghost?"

"I'm not sure, but Mama said that lots of times people who git it end up preachin'."

"You're too young to preach."

"I'm not either," Fred said. "I'm 'leven, goin' on twelve, and I'm gonna go to Africa and save the heathens." As he babbled on about his new plans and I drifted off, I hoped he'd go the next day. But even if he didn't leave, now that he was saved he'd surely quit grabbing my little fingers and bending them all the way back. Fred didn't say a word about Africa the following morning, and he was as mean as ever.

Dad was more subdued than usual, and when we sat down to eat breakfast, instead of Mama's short, "Bless this food for the nourishment of our bodies, in Jesus' name, Amen," Dad stumbled through a longer prayer that sounded like he was thinking out loud.

After several such halting attempts, Dad deferred to Mama. "You go ahead," he told her, and I never saw him pray again. He sometimes attended church, and he bowed his head and closed his eyes when others prayed, but he didn't take to religion the way Mama had hoped he would. To hear Mama tell it, Dad was in danger of backsliding when he started slipping off in the evenings and visiting with Buck and Thelma Reavis and other godless people in the community who never attended church.

26

"Birds of a feather flock together," she'd mutter as he headed out.

"Maybe so," Dad once answered, "but at least we laugh and enjoy ourselves."

* * *

Following Lottie Jean's birth, Mama lost considerable weight. I didn't realize how serious the situation was until years later when Joyce told me Mama had taken her aside and told her if something bad happened she should run up the road a half mile away and get Joe Madewell.

"Why Joe Madewell?" the baffled nine year old girl had asked.

"'Cause he'll know what to do. Nothin' scares Joe Madewell. He ain't afraid of the Devil himself."

During the worst part of her illness Mama often lifted the lid on the off-limits to us kids wooden box with its six coffin handles behind the kitchen table where three of us sat at mealtime. She often counted her ever dwindling Indian head penny stash she used for once a week postcards to Grandma Green in Oklahoma, and she sometimes fondled the pearly white face of her bodiless porcelain doll, but she spent most of her time flipping through the family snapshot album, blotting or scratching out her face with a fountain pen in picture after picture, then placing the album in the bottom of the forbidden box.

All of us kids were afraid to open the box when the folks were around, but when Dad was gone to the store and Mama was visiting May Phillips, one of her few friends, we'd open the box and look at the album.

We didn't discuss Mama's strange behavior, nor that the several shots with her obliterated face turned up missing. After Mama got better she sold enough popcorn seed and white cakes to WPA workers who parked in our front yard to send off to Sears and Roebuck for a severe off white dress. When she'd altered the dress and put it on, Dad asked, "Is that your new dancin' outfit?"

Mama in her preaching outfit with Jay and Wanda on her left and I, in my soiled Sunday overalls, at her right.

"Dancin' outfit my foot," she growled. "It's my preachin' dress."

"Preachin' dress? Since when?"

"Since right now. I've felt the call for a long time, but I didn't do anything about it until Brother Keith encouraged me to fill in for him on fifth Sundays and other times when he can't make it."

"You know how I feel about preachers," Dad said, "Especially women preachers."

"I aim to do the Lord's will," she replied. "And if you don't like it you can lump it."

* * *

Mama ordinarily hated to have her picture taken, but she posed proudly, if self-consciously, holding her Bible in her left hand, before setting out on foot wearing her new white ready-made dress on her first preaching assignment. Sallow faced and skinny as a shikepoke, Mama's glistening black hair and

28

hooded eyes, her prominent nose and cheekbones, and her
tightly compressed gash of a mouth betrayed the one eighth
Indian blood she'd inherited from her papa's full-blooded
Creek grandma, Narcissa, an early transplant from Alabama to
Indian Territory.

Acutely aware of how she looked, Mama had improvised a
strip of leftover material into something resembling a scarf to
help hide the goose egg sized goiter growing off center at the
base of her long neck. I halfway expected the goiter to disap-
pear after she went forward and got prayed for at a special
healing service, but it kept right on growing. Maybe Mama's
faith wasn't as strong as I'd thought it was. But if she didn't
have enough faith, who in the world did?

In the evenings, after the rest of the family had gone to bed,
Mama spent long hours reading her Bible on the kitchen table
with its faded red and white checkered oilcloth. Any time one
of us kids got up to use the slop bucket in the front room, or to
get a drink out of the long handled dipper in the water bucket
on the washstand in the kitchen, we'd see her hunched over
next to the dim coal oil lamp, slowly tracing the strange sounding words she muttered as she committed long passages to
memory. As for Dad, whether asleep or awake behind the
closed door in the bedroom, he was bound to be in his usual
fixed position, face up, stiff and straight as a board on the far
side of the cold bed.

In the irregular times when Mama got to preach, never
enough to suit her from her feverish, dissatisfied look, Dad
stayed home with the baby, but the rest of us kids went to
church with her. Many of her sermons followed a grim and
predictable routine of describing sinners caught in the clutches
of an avenging God, but at her best and scariest she put aside
her anger and gradually worked herself into a joyous and ecstatic state marked by outbursts of whooping and hollering
and even speaking in tongues, something entirely too rich and
out of control for most of the staid churchgoers. Only two or
three women in the congregation, including Dollie Fenton who

later preached on the radio, tried to match Mama's shouting, but they couldn't hold a candle to her carryings-on.

When it came time for the altar call, Wilma Wilkin pounded on the piano and led the congregation in singing "Come Home" or some equally doleful hymn while Mama searched out the worst sinner she could find. When she was lucky the two dyed-in-the-wool old infidels in the community, Amos Shockley and Chesty Earnhart, were present, and she, fearless in her righteousness, would march back and take on first one and then the other.

Once when she had Amos cornered on the back row, I was turned around watching him shift back and forth on his gimp leg when, to my surprise, someone took hold of my hand. Faye Hilton, our nearest neighbor woman, stood in front of me, crying. "Don't you want to come forward and be saved?" she asked. "Your dad and brother got saved at the revival. Now it's your turn."

"No, I'm not old enough."

"How old are you?"

"Eight."

"The Lord said to suffer the little children to come unto Him. Besides, your mother was five when she got saved. Don't you want to be like her?"

"I don't think so."

By slipping up on me, Faye had caught me before I'd had time to think out my objections. All I could do was shake my head, hang on to the school desk, white knuckled, and think that I hadn't had enough fun, hadn't sinned enough to warrant giving it up forever. But I was weakening and would likely have given in had I not suddenly remembered: Jesus didn't start His Father's work until He was twelve. I didn't have to become a Christian yet. I had four more years to sin and have fun. This time when I said no, Faye believed me.

Shortly after I escaped salvation, Fred was tormenting me, grabbing my little fingers and twisting them all the way back, as he often did; but this time instead of running from him

30

when I pulled loose, I grabbed him and shoved him down on the rough wooden floor in the front room as hard as I could. Before he could get on his feet I had him in a tight armlock around his skinny neck, an armlock which, for the first time, he couldn't break. As he bucked and twisted I held on in desperation while Dad and Mama, their eyes averted, said nothing.

At last Fred pleaded, "Turn loose. You're hurtin' me."

"You've got to say 'Calf Rope' first."

"Okay, 'Calf Rope,'" he whispered, and when I turned him loose I felt better than when I'd got out of being saved.

FOUR

MAKING THE
GRAVY STINK

One old saying, "the closer to the bone the sweeter the meat," meant a number of things when I was growing up, but the most common had to do with trying to justify eating half grown wild animals. When my two brothers and I quizzed Dad about how big young rabbits or squirrels should be before we killed them for the dinner table, he always had the same response: "The bigger the better, but anything out of the nest is fair game. Don't let anything git away if you can help it. Even the littlest squirrel or rabbit will make the gravy stink."

As we raced through the woods following the sounds of the treeing dog, Old Tuffy, part Beagle, part farm shepherd, few squirrels escaped us. Almost any rainy day when there wasn't a downpour we were in the woods exulting in our respite from hoeing, pulling weeds, cutting sprouts, plowing, putting up hay, and all the other endlessly boring and repetitive jobs the folks had lined up for us. By the time we were five, nine, and thirteen—I was the middle one—we scanned the skies for promising rain, not for the good it would do the crops, but because we would likely get to go squirrel hunting.

Dad would take the single shot twenty-two down from the nails where it hung over the front door, ration out a short handful of shells in Fred's eager hand, and off we'd go. At the sound of Old Tuffy's treeing we ran as fast as we could, fanning out on opposite sides of the tree the dog was barking up in order to keep the squirrel from jumping to other trees and escaping.

As we looked upward, each of us tried to spot the squirrel first, but sharp-eyed Fred almost always won the prize of getting the first shot. Lucky for me, Fred often missed and Jay was still too young to take his turn. Steady, I generally hit what I aimed at. When the squirrel came tumbling down Old Tuffy grabbed and shook it, Jay got to carry it, and away we went again.

Red or fox squirrels and their gray cousins, smaller and more active, populated about equally the roughly square mile wooded area where we hunted. The reds hugged the tree trunks; but with the three of us slowly rotating around our quarry, we could generally get off a good shot. Anytime a flighty gray squirrel started jumping our chances of getting it diminished when it headed for a den tree. Fred could climb any tree he could get a hand and toe hold on, and he was often successful in scaring a squirrel out of a hole in a tree. Once, perhaps twenty feet up in a big black oak, he foolishly reached into an oversized pileated woodpecker hole where he'd spotted a squirrel. Screaming, he jerked out his bleeding hand and dropped from limb to limb to the ground like a monkey.

When a squirrel or rabbit escaped into a hole in the base of a tree, one of us would run to the house for Dad's chopping ax which we used to cut a hole higher up on the tree, giving us a better chance to reach the trapped animal. We learned to thread a hickory sprout with a fork at the end or, better, a length of barbed wire up into a hollow tree and then twist it until it caught in the trapped animal's fur or asshole. After a few high-pitched screams the stick or wire usually brought forth a dead rabbit or squirrel, but sometimes the first twist and pull brought out little more than a tangle of hair or a string of warm guts.

Old Tuffy and Me

Ordinarily nothing so nightmarish took place. Instead, we depended on twenty-two short bullets to put a quick end to the hapless animals' lives. Anytime it came to risky shots or when we got low on shells Fred, who understood need's claim over fairness, handed the gun and remaining shells over to me. Using his still, bony shoulder as a rest, I carefully squeezed off the final shots.

Back at the house, we threw the dead animals onto a table on the screened in back porch, where Dad inspected them. As he carefully checked them out, he scowled at a gut shot, frowned at an upper body shot, nodded approvingly at a head shot, and actually smiled at the sight of a popped out eye.

Each hunter was responsible for skinning and cleaning his own game. Dad was as persnickety about what he ate as he was about what he drank, and we made sure there wasn't a single hair left on the carcass, no easy task when cleaning a squirrel. Mama rolled young squirrels in flour and fried them in lard in a heavy cast iron dutch oven she'd ordered from Montgomery Ward for a dollar. Tough old sow squirrels with wrinkled black tits or old boar squirrels with big black balls were parboiled and left simmering on the back of the cookstove up into the night, then fried the next day. Rabbits, young and old, got the same treatment. Of all the meat dishes I've ever had, nothing matches Mama's fried squirrel and squirrel gravy. Nothing at all.

We heard recurring stories about how fiercely territorial old boar squirrels were, and how they would invade nests or simply run down and attack young males, castrating them with their long, sharp incisors. I heard a version of this story from a man who often spoke of liking to go after a mess of young stag squirrels. The hotheaded long time native of the area would have fought anyone who doubted his veracity. Although I tended to be skeptical about these stories I heard about squirrels, I am inclined to think that old tomcats sometimes stalk and kill young toms who show up in their territory.

* * *

Dad rarely accompanied us when we hunted in the daytime (if it was rainy he might mend harness or do what he liked best, go to the store where he'd whittle and swap stories with his friends), but he often went with us when we hunted at night for possums, occasional skunks, and a rare civet cat. As we headed out, cross country, Dad took the lead; I followed closely behind him with a kerosene lantern to light his way; Fred came next with the twenty-two and a three cell flashlight; and Jay followed in the half light carrying a tow sack. Sometimes Dad was grouchy, as he always was when we were working, but most of the time he was in a good mood, much as he was at the store or when company came. He liked to tell stories about cowboying in northern Kansas and western Oklahoma when he was young, of camping out and trapping on the Cimarron River and, most of all, of hunting with his prize coon dog Old Lead in northern Kansas. As we walked briskly along single file through the woods dodging rocks and brush, Dad's quiet voice took on an incantatory quality as he reminisced about happier times. It seemed as if he was talking to himself while I, right on his heels, tried to light his way and at the same time hear everything he said. Sometimes I'd ask him to repeat something, but any interruption brought a brusque response

35

that broke the flow of his story. All the while Fred and Jay heard little more than a prolonged mumble.

When Old Tuffy treed a possum, we shook it out when we could to save shells and prevent skin damage. But ordinarily the possum was up a good sized tree and shooting was the most expedient means of getting it. Dad, an excellent shot, always did the shooting at night. When Old Tuffy's rapid barking told us he was baying something on the ground, we ran toward him because he was bad about tearing the skin on anything he got hold of. A few holes or tears in a good sized possum hide would cause it to be docked from, say, fifty cents to a quarter.

When the dog bayed a skunk, more often than not some of us got sprayed before Dad shot and killed it. Much rarer was the treeing of a civet cat when the spotted little animal's eyes could be seen shining brightly twelve or fifteen feet up a small tree. Although some people refused to believe that civet cats could climb a tree, the shy little creatures managed it when hard pressed.

Dad's reverie

Much of our reason for night hunting was for the fun of it, but on extra cold nights when nothing was stirring we got little more than exercise for our efforts. Of course, even in bad weather there was an outside chance Old Tuffy would run across a fresh trail and we'd make another fifty cents or so to add to the few extra dollars the dried and stretched hides brought at the end of the season when fur buyers came through the country.

We also ran a trap line during hunting season. As Mama built the morning fire in the cookstove, she'd yell up the stairwell to roust us out. Slipping on our shirts and overalls over long handled underwear, and putting on our heavy shoes, we were ready in a hurry. Fred and I usually alternated, one running the trap line and the other going to the barn to help Dad and Jay with the chores.

We'd set Victor steel traps in likely looking smooth holes under banks, trees, or rockpiles, but after several predawn empty-handed forays we took up the steel traps and concentrated on running our rabbit gums in a nearby abandoned vineyard. Most mornings found at least one rabbit secure in a gum, a small wooden box or a section of a hollow tree fitted with a trap door. Getting the trapped rabbit out of the gum was difficult in the early dawn's half-light, even with the aid of a flashlight or lantern. The trick was to quickly turn the rabbit around in order to prevent it from scratching or screaming for more than an instant as it was dragged out and given a quick and lethal rabbit punch.

Before heading off to school, we carefully gutted the dead rabbit then dropped it into a wooden barrel with a weighted lid to keep it out of reach of hungry cats or dogs. On Saturday mornings we took the few rabbits we'd trapped that week to the store where we got anywhere from five to fifteen cents each, depending on the market and an animal's size, freshness and general condition. We heard that the gutted rabbits with the fur still on were salted down in barrels and shipped to Chicago, Atlanta, or New York City, but we never really knew.

By the time we'd run our trap line and skinned and gutted what we'd caught, Mama always had breakfast ready. She made biscuits from scratch, she and the girls made gravy, and until the meat ran out in late winter we had either sowbelly or spicy sausage along with hard fried eggs to go with our biscuits and gravy. In addition, Joyce or Wanda cooked a big bowl of oats which we ate with plenty of Jersey cream and sugar. Everyone except Dad drank fresh whole milk, all we wanted, still warm from the cow. No thin blue john for us. Dad put cream in his oats, but he never drank milk of any kind, not even goat's milk. Jay liked milk, but he was finicky, and he refused to drink the last inch of milk in his glass for fear of finding dregs of manure, hair, hay and who knows what else might have slipped through our makeshift dishtowel strainer. Anytime a cow stepped into a bucket of milk, instead of risking rejection of an entire ten gallon can full of milk at the cheese factory, Dad brought the tainted milk into the house for Mama and us kids to drink, something Jay never forgot.

* * *

Some men in our community kept running dogs, hounds they used for chasing red and gray foxes. There was a definite social stigma associated with fox hunting, but I never understood exactly why; no doubt an occasional empty half-pint whiskey bottle left near the dead campfire had something to do with it. The fox hunters built a small fire in the middle of a crossroads near where hunting was consistently good; then as their hounds sniffed and whined through the nearby woods searching for a recent trail the few men, sometimes only two or three, sometimes as many as six or seven, sat around the fire for hours on end as the dogs, perhaps eight or ten in all, joined and chased the circling fox. Sometimes the sounds of the race stopped abruptly as the swift dogs ran a fox to ground, signaling the end of the chase for that night. The fox hunters never dug up their quarry, and on the rare occasion when the dogs caught and killed a fox, the hunters were upset. Sportsmanship and camaraderie was their game.

During the four years we lived at the Snuffer Place and the adjoining Brechbuhler Place, two years at each, my favorite late night activity was listening to the sounds of hounds yelping, bawling, chopping, sometimes alone and sometimes in concert, each with his or her own distinctive mouth, until I fell asleep. The only prettier sound than the medley of sounds the hounds made at night was the music heard the next morning before any one else stirred. One of the hunters, Arthur Jay, an Indian, gathered his hounds early with his own special plaintive call produced by a cow horn fitted with an organ reed.

Not that everyone in the community appreciated hearing the urgent clamor of the hounds chasing a fox at night, or, for that matter, Arthur Jay's early morning wake-up call, however moving and superior it was to the ordinary toot-toot-tooting of his fellow hunters' horns. Yet, like it or not, most people tolerated fox hunting with the same uneasy acceptance they accorded a pastime such as cockfighting. But not Logan Baxter. Word was out that Logan, who lived a mile north of the fox hunters' favorite encampment, often lay stretched out in the south window of his hayloft waiting to take potshots at hounds he sighted in the moonlight through the scope on his high powered rifle equipped with a silencer.

One Saturday night, while listening to a hot race from where I lay stretched out against the wall next to the open upstairs window, I noticed that the full cry of the hounds abruptly ended, and none of the dogs picked up the trail, making me wonder if the fox had been driven into a hole, or even overtaken and killed.

* * *

I dreaded going to church the next morning, as always, but I relaxed when I remembered that Pony Ross, the new preacher, never raised his voice, and unlike many other preachers, he always finished his sermon on time. As I studied Pony behind the podium after Sunday school, I thought he looked nervous, which might have explained why he was in such a hurry to finish his message and go outside to smoke. After Bon Eubanks, one of the regular fox hunters, shook out his cigarette and joined Pony on the porch, I overheard him say, "We had as good a fox race goin' last night as I ever heard. But all of a sudden somethin' scared the dogs and they didn't hit another lick."

"What do you think spooked 'em?" Pony asked.

"I don't know," Bon said. "After while they started slinkin' back to camp, one or two at a time, whinin', with their tails tucked tight between their legs. They was scared to death."

"Did all of 'em show up?"

"All but two, and you might know the missin' ones was the leaders of the pack, that good pair of Walkers Silas Cunningham paid big money for when they was pups."

"Did Silas blow his horn?"

"No, he started to, but then he thought better of it. He said if they didn't show up by mornin' he'd look for 'em then."

"Well," Pony said, "I sure hope he finds 'em. Nobody's crazier about his dogs than Silas Cunningham."

When Mama and all of us kids straggled into the clearing at home, we were surprised to see Dad and Silas sitting in Silas's black Model A Ford pickup parked on the side of the road in front of our house. We couldn't tell for sure what was going on, but it looked like Dad was trying to calm Silas down. Mama shooed the girls inside to help fix dinner, but Fred and Jay and I eased out onto the side porch where we watched and listened.

"Them dogs was valuable and I know you thought a lot of 'em," Dad said. "But if I was you I wouldn't risk bein' sent to the pen over a couple of dogs."

"I'll git that son of a bitch if it's the last thing I do," Silas yelled, and he started his truck.

As Dad got out and slammed the door, he hollered through the pickup window: "Now don't do nothing you'll regret!" The husky young man looked dazed as he drove off. His pale, clammy face set off by his red hair made me think of a ghost Wanda had recently drawn and colored with crayons.

"What was that all about?" Mama asked Dad when he stepped up on the front porch.

"Silas found his two hounds gutshot south of Logan Baxter's haybarn, and he's foamin' at the mouth and threatenin' to gutshoot Logan."

"You think he'll do it?"

"I don't know, he might. He's crazy enough to do anything. Remember me telling you he was crazy the last time I rode to town with him?"

"Crazy? No, I don't remember you sayin' he was crazy."

"I most certainly did. I told you he drove in spurts all the way to town and back. First he drove way too fast, then way too slow, back and forth time after time. I told you I'd ride shank's mare before I'd ride with a crazy man again."

"Now I remember," Mama said.

We wouldn't have been surprised to hear about a shooting in the neighborhood, but we weren't prepared to see the headlines and the pictures in the paper the Old Lady Parvin loaned Mama describing and showing how Logan Baxter had found his small herd of milk cows dead from eating a mixture of arsenic and salt. Some of the neighbors whispered that Silas likely had a part in the poisoning of the cattle, but no one who knew him well thought he masterminded the crime.

Shortly after the cattle killing episode, instead of going to Osie for necessities on Saturday, Dad hooked the team to the wagon and took Fred, Jay, and me with him to Buster Shoemaker's Sage Hill store on the county line. After he tied the team to the fence in back of the small building cocked cattycornered at the crossroads, we walked around to the front where he stopped and delivered his usual warning: "Remember, you boys are to be seen and not heard." He forgot to remind us that the first step into the store went down, and when we stumbled and made a racket behind him, he turned and glared at us.

41

"Howdy, Clay. Howdy, boys," Buster said, "Watch that first step."

"Howdy, Buster," Dad said, then smiled and nodded to Burt Fenton, a reformed fox hunter and friend of his who lived nearby.

"Howdy, Clay," Burt said in his low voice, "Me and Buster have been talkin' about the recent cattle killin'. Guess you've heard about it."

"Yeah, nobody's been talkin' about anything else," Dad said.

"Ever'body I've talked to here in the store seems to think Silas Cunningham had somethin' to do with it," Buster said, "That is, ever'body but Burt. Tell Clay what you told me, Burt."

"Silas is the logical suspect," Burt said in his quiet way, "but my wife's folks think the same man the sheriff pays to do his dirty work in the south part of the county prob'ly poisoned Logan's cattle."

"Why's that?" Dad asked him.

"A while back my wife's brother, Truie, said that the sheriff and some of his fox huntin' buddies lost several dogs in a pasture where a big man in town kept gaited horses. He said it was common knowledge that the hunters chipped in and the sheriff paid his man a hundred dollars to kill the high mucky-muck's stud horse."

"Does Truie know the particulars about how the stud horse was killed?"

"Yeah, he heard the owner rarin' about how he'd found the horse snubbed tight to a post in his stall with his throat cut, and when he got to searchin' for evidence he found a twitch and an open straight razor covered with blood."

"I don't s'pose he had any idy who owned the twitch and razor?"

"I don't think so. He said when he called the law out the deputy told him a twitch and razor would be hard to trace."

"So your wife's people think the sheriff slipped the horse killer another hundred dollars to poison Logan Baxter's cattle?"

42

"They sure do," Burt said. "And so do I."

Burt didn't say whether the killing of the high dollar stud horse stopped the killing of the fox hounds in the south part of the county, but after no one was charged in the poisoning of his cattle, Logan soon sold his farm and moved his family several miles away to another county.

It was hard to know how much the trauma and uproar over the dead dogs and cattle had to do with driving Silas over the edge. All we knew was what we heard secondhand about how, after Silas attacked his mother with a butcher knife, she had him committed to the state hospital where he'd spend the rest of his life on a floor for the criminally insane.

Although Logan Baxter was gone from the community, so was Silas, and the small band of fox hunters abandoned their old gathering place and moved a couple of miles northeast to the high lonesome ridge above White Oak. The new spot where the men cast their hounds was almost out of hearing from our place, but at times when I heard the dogs' faint bawling, I wondered if Silas ever got to listen to hounds run from his cell in the asylum. Most likely not. Even though the hospital was out in the country, the adjoining corn and milo fields, along with the nearby busy highway, would have made a sorry place for a fox race.

I also wondered if Silas ever thought about escaping from the asylum. I figured the doors and windows were barred, but anyone as stout as Silas was could break out if he put his mind to it. Once he got away from the big brick building, he could have walked backroads and cross-country at night and then slept in barns and haystacks along the way during the daytime. With all his strength, endurance, and savvy, it would have been a snap for Silas to walk the ninety miles home in the dark. It was at this point—when he arrived home—that my fantasy collapsed. Given the trouble with his mother, it wasn't at all likely that she would have let Silas climb the steep ladder to his familiar bed in the loft of the two room log house. No, the Old Lady Cunningham wouldn't have allowed that.

43

Silas broke out of the asylum one cold winter night. Instead of heading south for the hills and home, as I'd imagined it, he went west a couple of hundred yards toward the deep pond visible from his window. A blanket of snow covered the ground, and after the guards sounded the alarm, they tracked the barefooted Silas in a straight line to the pond where he walked out on the ice until it broke and he fell in.

I never knew whether Silas was buried on the grounds of the asylum, or not. Whatever happened, it would have been better and more fitting to ship him home and let his small circle of friends bury him near the old encampment at the crossroads. I envisioned Pony Ross saying a few words over the body; then, while Bon Eubanks and the other fox hunters shoveled dirt and rocks over the wooden box, hearing Arthur Jay blow his beautiful and haunting melody 'til the dogs came home.

FIVE

THE SNUFFER PLACE

After we'd moved to the remote Snuffer place, Mama's increasing bulk made it impossible for her to continue wearing her preaching dress. With nothing else fit to wear to church, she fell into a deep funk again and let herself go. For one thing, she quit wearing her waist, a strange looking undergarment she'd made out of white cotton sugar sacks. On washday, after the girls hung the clean clothes out to dry on the top barbed wire fence separating the yard from the barn lot, I noticed Mama's waist with its long flapping strings was no longer on the line.

But the clincher came one evening when I carried an armload of wood into the kitchen where Mama, caught up in one of her reveries, stood next to the cookstove stirring the gravy. To my surprise, I clearly saw her bare left breast through a hole in her raggedy old dress. Instead of looking away, I pulled my cap bill down low and then slowly threw one stick at a time into the woodbox, all the while checking her out.

At first I was struck by the symmetry and beauty of her full breast, but as I continued to stare I felt an overwhelming and gut wrenching mix of desire and revulsion. I'd seen little pink titties before, and various shades of brown tits, much like my own, but I was shocked to see Mama's coal black nipple. I'm not sure how long I stood there watching, but it couldn't have been long because I knew Mama would have knocked me into the middle of next week with a stick of wood if she'd had any inkling that I'd turned into a Peeping Tom—and she was the one I was watching.

Mama's increasing size and shabbiness not only kept her from going to church; according to her bitter account she didn't step foot off the place for over a year. That's not quite true, because when she and Dad were having a particularly hard time getting along, she sometimes left the house in a huff and walked a mile north to the Old Lady Parvin's where she stayed several hours or even overnight until things cooled off.

Later, when Dad took off, supposedly for wheat harvest, there was a freer than ordinary atmosphere around our place. Mama let us make tunnels by putting the bedcovers over the kitchen chairs, she jacked up the potato soup with onions, something Dad never allowed, and we could smile and laugh as we worked, again something strictly taboo when Dad was there.

While he was gone we sometimes went overboard, ripping and tearing around in our new found freedom until Mama lost patience. When she corralled us she tended to become harsh, too harsh, reaching for the razor strap hanging behind the kitchen stove. If we felt especially daring when she overreacted we circled her, dancing around and around, making certain we were out of reach, singing in unison, over and over: "She's a mean old sow, she eats her pigs. She's a mean old sow, she eats her pigs." Our outlandish chant often caused Mama to laugh, after which she'd throw down her strap and the dangerous situation would be averted. We never rubbed it in or pushed our luck after she'd conceded. We knew better than that.

Dad was still gone the last of November. Few neighbors were brave enough to question Mama about his whereabouts, but when the Old Lady Parvin asked, Mama glared and mumbled something about him following the wheat harvest all the way to North Dakota. Although everyone knew wheat harvest was over, no one dared dispute Mama's word. Maybe she didn't know where he was. She rarely mentioned him and when one of us kids returned from the mail box she didn't seem to be expecting a card from him. Naturally, none of us had enough nerve to come right out and ask: "Where's Dad? When's he comin' home?"

Since Fred didn't have to work on Thanksgiving, and I didn't have to go to school, he and I were free to take Old Tuffy and the single shot twenty-two and go hunting. "We'll try to kill somethin' special for Thanksgiving supper," Fred said.

"All right," Mama replied. "I'll have the potatoes on."

Fred carried the gun and because he was older he got to take the first shot any time we had plenty of shells. But because I was the better shot, he often deferred to me. We were on Efton and Carrie Robbins' place where Fred cut sprouts for a dollar a day when he hissed, "Listen, Old Tuffy's hit a trail."

"Yeah," I whispered, "and it sounds like he's circlin' this way." Shouldn't I take the gun?"

"Not yet," was hardly out of his mouth when a large jack-rabbit, something we'd heard of but never seen in Missouri, hopped into a small clearing and stopped. Quickly, shaky as always, Fred raised the gun and fired. To my amazement, the rabbit fell over dead.

"How about that?" Fred crowed. "You thought I'd miss him, didn't you?"

"Yes, and so did you," I answered.

"Here you go," Fred said. "You can carry him. Won't Mama be proud?"

"Yes, she will," I answered, and I gladly carried the jackrabbit, two to three times the size of a cottontail, more than a mile home.

We were barely in the front yard when Wanda shouted, "Look, Mama, look! "

Mama busted out laughing, "Why, it's a jackrabbit, the first since we left Oklahoma! You boys clean it while I heat up some water. We'll have ourselves a feast!"

Fred held the rabbit spraddle legged while I skinned it. But something was wrong. Big worms as long as my little finger and fat in the middle worked alive in the rabbit's upper legs and back.

"Mama, come quick!" I yelled, pointing at the wrinkled grubs.

"Throw that nasty thing away," she said. "No self-respecting family eats meat with warbles in it."

That evening we ate potato soup, with onions, as usual. For anyone still hungry, there was plenty of cornbread and milk. Next morning Old Tuffy's belly bulged. He'd eaten our Thanksgiving treat, worms and all.

* * *

In addition to willingly handing over to Mama the dollar a day he made cutting sprouts, Fred came up with the idea of making some extra money for the family by getting a head start on other hunters and trappers in our area. Some six weeks or so before hunting season opened, Jay and I helped him dig a round pit, a holding pen about six feet in diameter and right at three feet deep, with walls sloping back at the bottom to prevent possums from climbing out.

Although Jay and I helped, it was Fred who best remembered where all the likely looking hollow trees were located in various nearby stands of timber, and it was mainly Fred who shinnied up the trees and stirred the dens in search of the grinning, hissing creatures. Fred was adept at tormenting the possums with a stick until they rolled up into balls and pretended to be dead, after which he'd grab them by their rough hairless tails, pull them out of their holes, and drop them on the ground below where Jay and I quickly put them in a tow sack so Old Tuffy wouldn't damage their hides.

After one especially good Saturday afternoon haul, we had dropped several possums into the crowded pit when Mama came out to watch. "Whatever you do, don't tell anybody about this," she told us. "We sure don't want the game warden slippin' up here and arrestin' you boys." I didn't know what a game warden looked like, but the thought of being on the bad side of the stocky, unsmiling constable who sometimes showed up at local pie suppers made me uneasy.

The mighty possum hunters

The evening before hunting season officially opened, Jay and I had watered the possums and fed them a big bait of ripe persimmons when we decided to have some fun by poking them with long poles to make them hiss and growl, bare their white teeth dripping with spit, then sull up and play dead.

Fred was up early the next morning helping Mama do chores before going to work when we heard him yell: "The possums are gone! The possums are gone!" Sure enough, the pit was empty of everything except one of the poles that Jay and I had been playing with the previous evening. One end of the pole was in the center of the pit and the other lay on the upper edge. "I bet one of you boys left that pole there," Fred said.

"We did not," I argued.

"You boys shut up," Mama said. "What's done's done. Ever since we started breakin' the law I've been afraid somethin' like this might happen. We need to start renderin' unto Caesar what's Caesar's, like Jesus said."

That night, the first legal night of hunting season, we heard Efton Robbins' good spotted hound barking treed time after time in the woods west of our house on the tract of land old-timers called The Nine Forties. Not long after that Efton, who had got wind of Fred's escaped possums, walked the mile and a half to our house carrying a tow sack filled with stretched hides. "Here," he said to Fred as he emptied the sack on our front porch. "From what I've heard, I figure I owe you at least half of what I caught across the road from your house."

"You don't have to do that," Fred said, but I could tell from the way he looked at the six pelts on the thin, curved pine boards that he was gong to accept Efton's offer.

"Just be sure you bring my boards back after the hides cure out," Efton said. "By the way, have you heard from your dad lately?"

"No, not lately," Fred said. "Much obliged, Efton."

After Efton left, Mama gathered the six of us around the kitchen table. "I think the Lord knows that from now on we aim to obey the laws of the land," she said, "and He sent Efton over here with them possum hides as a sign. Let it be a lesson to us all."

Before I dropped off to sleep, I wondered if Jesus kept as close a watch on possums as He did on people and sparrows.

*   *   *

A few days after Dad showed up in December, he and Fred and I removed the box from the wagon and went to the timber where we worked hard cutting and piling red and white oak poles for firewood between the bolsters of the running gears.

We had the poles piled high and were ready to start to the house when Dad's normally red face turned gray and he slumped to the ground, moaning. Way back in the woods, Fred and I hardly knew what to do, but we improvised a pallet of sorts with our denim jackets, then helped Dad climb up on the poles, and as I walked alongside the wagon trying to make sure Dad didn't fall off, Fred skillfully maneuvered the team and its load through the narrow trail. Once when he miscalculated and hubbed a tree, the load shifted, crushing the rifle's walnut stock, but Dad wasn't hurt and we made it home safely.

We helped Dad inside the house where he stayed in bed week after week. There was no talk of seeing a doctor, just as Mama said there hadn't been a few years before in northern Kansas when he was bedridden all winter. The doctor he'd seen as a child in the state of Washington where he'd been sick with rheumatic fever had told his folks that he would have recurring spells with his heart which only bed rest might help.

Joyce cheerfully ran errands and did the major part of caring for Dad after school and on weekends, but Mama, hard faced and capable, did the most of it. We especially dreaded the nights when Dad screamed and cried out: "It wouldn't hurt any worse if someone stabbed me in the back with a knife!" Scared and confused, I wondered why I never heard Mama praying for Dad. Dad was gruff and hateful, but did that mean he had backslid and couldn't be healed? Or had Mama herself lost faith because her goiter had kept growing at an alarming rate since she'd twice proclaimed it healed before she quit attending church?

Maybe it was my fault. I knew that God worked in mysterious ways; perhaps He was punishing me because I'd refused to go up front at altar call on the night Mama thought I was under conviction. The rest of the kids were saved early, but I wanted to do some serious sinning before I became a Christian, even if it did mean jeopardizing Dad's health.

* * *

The holiday season looked bleak before Grandpa and Grandma Holmes showed up with toys a week before Christmas in Grandpa's black '34 Chevrolet coupe. I especially remember the Chinese Checkers. After noticing soft blobs of fresh paint clinging to the holes on the underside of the board, I guessed that Grandma, resourceful and upbeat as ever, had managed to find secondhand toys which she'd painted in her slapdash way with her favorite colors, lavender and purple. Even more exciting than the Chinese Checkers were the gaudy red and green popcorn balls piled high in Grandma's gleaming copper boiler. The sticky balls, hard and knobby as Fred's fists, were just the ticket, even if some of us kids did make ourselves sick by eating too many before dinner.

Mama had announced ahead of time that since the Snuffer Place was too far out of the way for Santa Claus to find, there was no point in putting up a tree, but she changed her mind after Joyce said she thought it would be nice to have a place to put our unexpected gifts from Grandma. Finding a cedar tree wasn't easy, but after Fred finally spotted a scraggly three foot tall specimen, he and I took turns carrying it home. The hardest part was making a cobbled up stand for holding the prickly tree in place in the empty closed off dining room.

Mama was in charge as the seven of us strung buckbrush berries and popcorn on alternate rows of sagging strings. Idiot faced paper dolls, cutouts from the previous year's wish book retrieved from the toilet—now masquerading as angels—added their comic effect to the gaily decorated juniper. By the time we were finished only an occasional glimpse of green showed where the sharp smell came from as the transfigured little tree with its rough triumphant star fashioned from crinkled tinfoil leaned cockeyed against the east window.

Mama's high Christmas Eve spirits were greatly subdued the next morning, and when I opened the door between the kitchen and the front room to look at the tree, it was gone.

Whether she and Dad had gotten locked into one of their late night arguments, or she simply couldn't bear to continue the subterfuge, I never knew. She'd thrown the tree and its trappings into a snowbank on the east side of the house where drifting snow soon covered it. There it rested until spring, when chirping English sparrows announced its resurrection.

All of us kids were subdued as we ate breakfast Christmas morning, but afterward, when Mama opened the long mouse proof wooden box we used as a bench behind the table, our bitterness over the banished tree disappeared. Even Grandma's wonderful red and green popcorn balls the week before took a back seat to the huge white cake overflowing with coconut frosting. Mama had saved up almost enough money to buy ingredients for a coconut cake, and when the Raleigh Man had come by, despite Dad's angry protest from his bed, she'd traded an old hen for what she lacked, a small brown bottle of pure vanilla.

* * *

The weather turned bad after the first of the year, and a winter storm dropped eighteen to twenty inches of snow, with waist high drifts in places. Unlike most winters in the Ozarks when warm spells tended to quickly melt whatever snow fell, cold weather hung on and additional snow built up, making going to school impossible.

At first it was fun to keep all the stock confined. All the stock included half a dozen Jersey cows, with three or four half Guernsey yearling heifers, plus two small, perhaps eight hundred pound mares and two half Percheron colts which might eventually weigh eleven hundred pounds each. In addition, there were game chickens and guineas, as well as various goats and pigs to care for. Dad's four horses tied fast in the shed next to the hay barn barely tolerated the nanny goats which crowded around and underneath them, and the nervous horses trampled and killed several new born kids. Although I was too big and too tough to cry over a dead goat, it was never easy for me to pick up a frozen kid and toss it over the hill out of sight far enough away so the bleating nanny couldn't smell it and continue her grieving. Our nannies, part Toggenburg, part Angora, weren't heavy milkers, but I preferred the sweet tasting easily digestible goat milk with its ever so faint billy goat smell over cows' milk any time. My preference for goats' milk likely came, as Mama thought, from way back when, as a baby, after I couldn't tolerate either her milk or cows' milk, she'd switched me to goats' milk.

The novelty of caring for the beleaguered animals wore off quickly, turning into drudgery. As the bad weather hung on our scant feed supplies shrank at an alarming rate. The mixed timothy and lespedeza hay packed in the haymow was most easily accessible, but following Dad's warnings, we doled it out a few pitchforks at a time. When Mama countermanded Dad's instructions, it was hard to know which one to obey. We knew that a man was supposed to be head of his household, but sometimes Mama's judgment seemed better than Dad's.

After milking the cows in the stanchions, Fred and I often hung our buckets on nails and then searched along the sides of each cow's backbone for boil like swellings, sure signs of warbles, maggots half as big as a man's little finger which infested the animals. With practice we became adept at pressing firmly downward with our thumbs and popping the grubs out of the cows' backs.

"I get dibs on Old Pet," I told Fred when we first started looking for warbles, and since she was special I always saved her for last. The first calf in a string of extra good muley heifers out of Old Frankie, who herself was out of Wiley Wise's naturally polled Jersey bull, Old Pet was the best cow Dad ever owned. Heavier boned, deeper bodied, and straighter backed than most Jerseys, she was cream colored all over. Old Pet's bag was extra big, her tits were just right, not too big nor too little, and she could be counted on to give twice as much milk as any of the other cows except for Old Frankie.

The prize cow had a couple of drawbacks. She was reluctant to let her milk down, and once she let it down she was hard to milk. Dad's technique of milking, using forefinger and thumb, was slow and ineffectual, and Fred, too fidgety to sit still for the few minutes it took to milk a cow, couldn't be depended on, leaving Mama, the best milker of us all, to do the job. Later, when I'd mastered Mama's furiously thorough style of milking, the folks relaxed and let me milk my favorite cow.

I became immensely fond of Old Pet. While I was both intrigued and repulsed by the increasingly numerous and colorful accounts of fellow farm boys who more or less openly admitted and even bragged about their exploits with animals, I was in a bind. As long as Dad was bedfast I didn't worry about him, but Mama was nosey, and she was capable of slipping around and spying on Fred and me and then beating us with Dad's leather horsewhip if she thought we were up to something she and Jesus didn't approve of. More than once she had described how her mother had thrashed her brother Reuben with a braided blacksnake whip, "within an inch of his life," as she approvingly put it, for some awful unnamed but presumably sexual transgression.

Prepubescent, and ignorant past belief or understanding, what finally scared me away from Old Pet was my fear of monsters. After a long stay alone with Old Pet in the barn one night, on the way back to the house I saw what looked like a witch wearing a cape perched on top of a blackjack tree at the edge of the barnlot.

Inside the house, I asked Mama, "Do you believe in witches?"

"I most certainly do," she replied. "Don't you?"

"Maybe. I think I saw one tonight. Where do witches come from?"

"They come from the Devil. Witches do the Devil's work, and angels work for the Lord."

"Was Jesus an angel?"

"In a way He was," she said, "but He was more than an angel. He was flesh and blood."

"And God's a spirit?"

"That's right, the Holy Spirit. Why do you ask?"

"I just wondered."

"You're asking entirely too many questions, young man."

Mama would have skinned me alive if I'd asked her what I most wanted to know: If a cross between a human and an animal was bound to be a monster, as I feared, and a cross between the Devil and a human was a witch, as Mama had said, what about a cross between the Holy Spirit and a human? Or could Mama's sweet Jesus be just another boogerman grownups had made up to scare kids and keep them in line, something like a full-time, high-powered Santy Claus?

* * *

Early in the spring after the weather broke, but before Dad was able to be up and around, his rich sister Anna and her husband George from western Oklahoma came bearing two cans of chop suey which they insisted we have for supper. Mama heated it up, and we all tried it, but it wasn't fit to eat. Mama's leftover fried mush tasted much better. After supper George and Anna loaded us kids in their shiny new black '41 Ford club coupe and took us to the Princess theater in Aurora, where they treated us to our first picture show, "Tombstone, the Town Too Tough to Die." It was a grand experience, marred only by Mama's disapproving looks upon our return. Mama knew that picture shows were the work of the Devil.

Next morning after chores and breakfast Mama, George, and Anna stood by Dad's bed in the downstairs bedroom where the four of them held a lengthy, whispered discussion. From our vantage point outside the open door we, the four oldest kids, gleaned from bits of conversation that George and Anna, childless, were bent on trying out two of us kids with the idea of adopting if everything panned out. It sounded as if they were leaning toward picking Wanda and me. Fred, their first

56

choice, was immediately vetoed, and Joyce was soon out of the question. Quick to please and hardworking, they would have been anyone's pick, but they couldn't be spared. The folks sounded reluctant to part with Wanda and me, but they were weakening when Anna, eager to head home, said, "With four kids left, you surely wouldn't miss two of them." Outraged, Mama ran George and Anna out of the house and off the place.

After they'd left Dad cried great heaving sobs, as if he were a big, hurt baby. That was the first time I knew that a grown man could cry. Mama didn't cry, not then or later when we overheard Dad and her agreeing that it looked as though they'd have to give up all six of us. I wondered how living in an orphanage would feel, and whether the authorities might send Fred to reform school where older and meaner kids went.

* * *

By late spring Dad was able to help with the big garden the rest of us had put out. Before the garden started producing, he traded a ruptured shoat he'd sewn up to Clovis Friend for a big rank billy goat with huge swinging balls that we butchered but couldn't stand to eat. We'd eaten possum with sweet potatoes earlier—the sweet potatoes tasted better than the greasy possum—and Mama had boiled five fledgling screech owls Fred and I shot. Although they were young, the owls were stringy and tough. Even Old Tuffy turned up his nose at the prospect of eating screech owl.

The folks heard there was relief for the poor at the county court house in Cassville. At Mama's urging, Dad reluctantly hired Joe Madewell, who took us in his touring car through the open range on a good gravel road to the square where we lined up with many others needing help. I remember feeling small and ashamed, but I dared not say anything. Our round of cheese, big as a washpan, looked and tasted good, but I ate too much and puked out the back of the open car on the way home. Grapefruit, oversized pale oranges, I mistakenly thought, were bitter as gall. The stiff, dark blue chambray shirts doled out to each boy and man were just fine, but the work shoes had dead giveaway toes, and the overalls had stripes wide as a convict's. At school Monday morning everyone would know. Oh well, who cared? Some of the other students would be wearing the same clothes.

Just as I hoped, some of the other kids in the community also wore their telltale new relief overalls to school on Monday. The homely good-natured and lanky teenaged Jenkins boys, Willie and Wilbur, stuck out like sore thumbs in their new outfits, especially when the teacher called them to the front of the room where they reluctantly joined their second grade classmates on a bench and haltingly recited from their Dick and Jane readers. But after Willie and Wilbur were chosen first by the softball captains at recess, their skills at batting and fielding lessened the stigma I felt.

Anna's picks

Three Smith boys, new in the neighborhood from up on the county line, also wore their new handouts. The oldest boy, with his powerfully built upper body and long arms, wore his usual heavy, built-up work shoe on his right foot while going barefoot on his left. He was in a particularly black mood as he struggled up the steep concrete steps to the cloakroom. Once inside, he slowly clunked to his seat near the back, ready to explode at anyone foolish enough to make fun of his stiff new ill fitting rolled up government overalls with their damning inch wide stripes.

58

One cold and windy early March Saturday, after Dad felt well enough to harness the team for the first time since early winter in preparation for plowing the garden, the horses were acting up, as they often did after a long layoff, and Dad was having a hard time hooking their tugs to the singletrees.

"Go git me that clevis on the turnin' plow," he yelled to Fred. "Run!" When Fred came running back empty-handed a few minutes later, Dad flew into a rage and took the doubled ends of the leather lines to him. There in the middle of the un-plowed garden the horses plunged wildly, Old Tuffy barked and lunged at Dad as he sought to protect Fred, while Dad rained down blow after blow on Fred's skinny back and shoul-ders. Finally finished, Dad hissed: "If you can't do what I say, young man, then you can just go to the house. Go on, git outta my sight!"

Spent and trembling, Dad turned to me. "Take that team to the barn and don't give 'em a bite to eat before you let'em out. You understand?"

I nodded and did as he said.

Late in the night Dad slipped up the creaky stairs and climbed in bed next to Fred. "Will you forgive me?" he asked.

"Yes," Fred quickly replied, "I forgive you."

While the two lay there hugging and making up, I thought: "Not me. I won't ever forgive him."

* * *

After the weather had moderated and Dad had gained addi-tional strength, I became increasingly aware of how severely limited my opportunities for sinning were. I might have prac-ticed my lying since I was so poor at it, but the returns looked slim. Not that I had reservations about lying. It just didn't seem to pay.

But then the combs of the old hens started getting red, a sure sign they'd soon be laying. Although some of the hens re-turned to the henhouse to lay, most hid their nests in the barns, either under the mangers in the milk barn or in the hayloft of the log barn. I left the eggs alone in the henhouse, that kind of stealing was too obvious, but I searched out every hidden nest I could find and soon had a full bucket of eggs stashed under loose hay.

It would be a long walk to Osie, three miles each way, but maybe I could go on Saturday when Dad would ride Old Barney to Aurora. I could give Fred and Jay the slip, as I sometimes did when I hid out and read a book instead of going hunting with them. As I uncovered the milk bucket, I saw with horror that a hard freeze the night before had cracked every last one. Emmitt Hilton wouldn't buy cracked eggs, so what was I to do?

A few days earlier I'd heard the folks discussing how few eggs the hens were laying. Later, Dad heard a racket in the henhouse, after which he chased off Mart Johnson's redbone hound. Dad said little, but he picked a tiny hole in each end of an egg, sucked out the white, then carefully blew arsenic through a straw next to the yolk in the shell. Finished, he sealed the holes with paraffin and placed the altered egg in the nest where the broken shells lay.

While Dad kept vigil, the hound returned. There was a commotion in the henhouse, but Dad quietly waited until the dog left before he examined the disturbed nest. "I think that'll break him of suckin' eggs," he said.

A couple of days later Mart told Dad that he'd found his dog dead in a manger.

"What do you reckon happened to him?" Dad asked.

"I don't know," Mart answered. "He was a young dog."

"That's too bad," Dad said.

As I looked at my bucketful of ruined eggs, I thought about Mart's dead dog. Dad surely wouldn't kill me if he found out, but he would likely give me a terrible whipping with the leather plow lines doubled the same way he'd whipped Fred. I thought about hiding the damaged eggs in the woods. But then, remembering that Mama sometimes cooked with cracked eggs, I trudged to the house, bucket in hand, practicing the lies

I'd been neglecting. "Look, Mama," I said. "I found a big nest in the loft. Last night's freeze must have broken the eggs. Can you still use 'em?" From her narrowed eyes I could tell that she and God knew. But they didn't have proof.

"Yes, I can use them."

After this narrow escape I backed off, but I still needed money. Then good luck came, and I didn't have to steal or even lie this time. I was in the brooder house checking on a hen with a clutch of eggs Mama thought was overdue when, sure enough, baby chicks peeped out underneath her. When I lifted the hen I saw that all the eggs, perhaps ten, were hatched except for a big, odd shaped one resembling double yolked eggs I'd seen.

Hurrying to the barn where I quickly threw hay to hungry animals, I shirked other chores and raced back to the brooder house. As I lifted the hen off the chicks again, the big egg moved and I saw that the last chick had almost finished pipping. Suddenly the shell split and there lay an awkward, struggling, spraddle legged, two headed baby chicken. Strictly speaking, it had just one oversized head but two beaks and four eyes. As I watched, astounded, the grotesque creature gained strength. Soon it pecked at crushed oats and drank from the upended glass jar, first with one beak and then the other.

By midday the rest of the kids had come to see my odd find. They all wanted to hold it but I, remembering the fates of earlier handled chicks, wouldn't allow it. Even Dad and Mama took time to look. With nightfall approaching I left my post, confident that the clucking hen would take good care of my prize.

That night I didn't walk in my sleep, as I often did, but I slept fitfully and I had a dream in which I dreamt I was rich. Everyone passing down our road, whether in a car, on foot, or a horse back, stopped and gladly paid a nickel to see my wonderful two headed chicken.

Early the next morning before breakfast I raced to the brooder house where the mother hen sat in a corner with her

61

feathers fluffed out protectively over her new brood. Lifting the hen with one hand, I gently stirred the chicks as I looked for my precious freak. It was gone. Looking around, I saw it, a few feet away, flat on the floor, with dark blood oozing from a deep hole in the top of its big head. I picked it up tenderly, then ran to the house to show Mama. Mama knew everything. When I held out the limp chick, she nodded approvingly, "Mothers know when something's wrong with their babies, and they know what to do."

While I stood in front of her, shaking, Mama had the same faraway look I'd seen many a time when she stood late in the evening in the dim light watching over her brood of six. Only now, instead of lingering over the cruel scar on the baby's upper lip, she stared at my oversized head.

I dropped the dead chick and ran like hell.

SIX

THE BRECHBUHLER
PLACE

One Sunday afternoon in the middle of March, about the time when we first began to hear spring peepers and see buzzards circling again, the Old Lady Snuffer drove up for what Dad hoped would be a short dickering session over farming arrangements for the coming year. No telling what she thought when she saw Fred, Jay, and me perched like crows high in the soft maple trees in the front yard. But whatever she thought, she kept it to herself as she stepped up on the front porch and knocked.

"Howdy, Miz Snuffer," Dad said, as he stepped out. "We've been expectin' you."

"It's that time of year again, Mr. Holmes," she said. "We need to talk about next year's rent."

"Times are hard, as you know," Dad said, "and I've been in bed most of the winter. What are our chances of sharecroppin' this comin' year instead of payin' cash?"

"What kind of shares do you have in mind?"

"The usual arrangement around here: I'll pay you the goin' rate for a third of the cane, corn, and tomatoes I grow, and I'll git the rest for doin' all the work."

"I don't think Walter will agree to that," she said, "but I'll ask him," and the gray headed stocky woman walked out of hearing distance beyond the garage where she held a several minutes long discussion with her late husband. We could tell from the set expression on her face and the determined way she walked back to the porch with her hands in the pockets of her heavy winter coat that we'd soon be moving again. "Walter's afraid the drouth will hang on," she said on her return, "and he says I'd better hold out for cash on the barrelhead."

"Then I guess we'll have to move," Dad said. "Cash is hard to come by."

"All right," she replied. "I'll expect you folks to be out by the end of the month."

"Two weeks is short notice, but we'll be out of here as quick as we can," Dad told her, and he abruptly turned on his heel and headed for the barn where he bridled Old Barney and headed east. When he returned later that evening Dad was whistling a cheery tune. "After I told Ollie and Hazel Brechbuhler that we're havin' to move because of the advice of a dead man," he told Mama, "they had a good laugh, and then Ollie turned serious and asked me if we'd like to move to their place."

"Their place?"

"Yes, their place. Ever since the war started they've been talkin' about movin' to town so Ollie can git work as a carpenter and Hazel can cook or wait tables in a cafe. Ollie said if they had someone they knew they could trust to take care of the farm, they'd move in a minute."

"What did you tell him?"

64

"I told him we'd move in as soon as they move out if we can agree on terms."

"What did he say to that?"

"He said a third for them and two thirds for us suited him if it suited me, and we shook hands on it."

"You mean it'll be the same arrangement we wanted here?"

"That's right," Dad said. "And their place will produce more than twice as much as this one. Here's our chance to git ahead. "

"Praise God!" Mama shouted. "Praise His Holy Name!"

Moving was easy this time. Shortly before our end of March deadline we tolled and drove our livestock through the gate separating the two farms, loaded the wagon with farm equipment, drove back and forth several times, and then moved our meager household goods across the gradually sloping meadow that turned steep as we approached a spring near a good sized chinkapin tree at the bottom of the hill below where the Brechbuhler house and outbuildings stood. Fred and Jay and I went back for several loads of odds and ends and it was a done deal.

On our last load we'd stopped the team out of sight in the woods, and were chewing rabbit tobacco we'd picked from under a blackjack tree when Fred spotted something better, a dead grapevine, which we cut to size with our pocketknives. We were sitting on the ground enjoying smoking the wicked vine with its sharp bite to the tongue when Dad, riding Old Barney, slipped up on us. "You boys better throw them grapevines down," he said, with a grin. "Don't you know smokin' will stunt your growth and turn you black?" It was a good thing Mama hadn't caught us. She would've whipped our hindends for sure.

The well built clapboard bungalow Ollie had recently remodeled had two bedrooms downstairs, a small one for Joyce and a bigger one with enough room for Dad and Mama's bed on one side and Wanda and Lottie Jean's on the other. The single, long, upstairs room with its slanted ceiling on both sides was more than big enough to accommodate the heavy iron bed Fred and Jay and I shared.

Although Ollie hadn't quite finished his remodeling project, we didn't mind the tarpaper on the inside walls. Besides, Ollie's generous mother, who wore a long dark dress and spoke with a heavy German brogue, with the help of her chattering translating grandchildren, made sure that we understood we were welcome to use her two black walnut dressers with their mottled pink and gray marble tops and fancy glove drawers she was leaving behind. For a minute I thought Mama was going to cry when the old lady silently motioned to her that she was also free to play the imposing pump organ standing against the wall in the front room.

The best thing about the new place was its abundance of water. In addition to two reliable cisterns, one in the yard handy to the house and the other next to a concrete stock tank in the barn lot, Ollie assured us that the wet weather spring located at the bottom of the hill north of the house ran way up into midsummer in all but the driest weather, providing plenty of fresh water for bathing and even swimming at times. For the first time in five years we wouldn't be hauling household water from Wilkin Spring.

Dad and Mama were still at odds much of the time, but we all pitched in and put out an extra big garden south of the house. We planted row after row of lettuce, radishes, carrots, peas, beans, sweet corn, and Irish potatoes, and set out plenty of tomato plants and sweet potato slips. Dad even let Mama set out a short row of green onions. Later on we planted okra, peanuts, mushmelons, and watermelons and, in the fall, sowed so many turnips that even the hogs finally refused to eat the bitter, pithy surplus.

* * *

Early in the morning on butchering day, Dad asked me if I thought I could stick the old sow after he shot her. Although I wasn't sure why he was asking me instead of Fred, I guessed it

66

was because the sow was so big it would take both of them to hold the animal still while I stuck her. Since I could tell from Dad's manner that he had confidence in me, I naturally agreed to do the man sized job. After giving me instructions with a special warning to not stick the long blade into the shoulder hams, Dad took the twenty-two down from its place above the kitchen door, counted his short supply of shells, and we headed for the pig pen.

A single shot ordinarily sufficed to stun and knock down a hog. But not this time. The massive four to five hundred pound sow merely squealed and shook her head at the first shot. Three more carefully aimed shots, the last in her ear, failed to drop or stop the rampaging beast. Now empty-handed, Dad yelled at Fred: "Go get the post maul! Run!" With one mighty over his head blow Dad knocked the sow down, then he and Fred frantically turned her over and held her as best they could while I threaded the slender foot long blade down and back, doing my best to avoid the precious shoulder hams as I prodded for the heart. An extra heavy gush of bright blood, along with a final spasm, signaled my shaky success.

We quickly dipped the bubbling water in the big kettle over the fire into the canted steel barrel, after which Dad tested the temperature of the water the good old fashioned way: three swipes with his bare fingers, no more, no less, meant the hog's bristles would scrape off easily. Special care had to be taken to prevent getting the water too hot and setting the hair. If we set the hair our only option was to shave the carcass, a long and tedious process. After the water was just right, the three of us half lifted, half rolled the still twitching sow head first into the barrel where we sloshed her up and down and then pulled her out with a singletree substituted for a gambrel stick attached to her back leg tendons. After adding more hot water, we scalded the back half, using hay hooks thrust deep into her throat to jostle her up and down before pulling her out and scraping her clean. With wire stretchers already secured on a nearby limb of a blackjack tree, we hoisted the sow high enough to clear the ground before Dad cut off her head and began his pre-butchering routine.

First, he cut around and loosened her asshole so he could get a heavy cord of binder twine tied in a secure square knot near its opening. Next, he separated the pelvic girdle with his ax, which let the guts slide down while he carefully worked his knife blade between two fingers as he slit the abdomen. Whatever he did, he didn't want to bust a gut. The guts, along with the lights, liver and heart, all still attached, came tumbling out into a waiting tub. Dad cut the heart out first, then the liver, making sure he cut around the bile sack. As always, before sending the heart and liver to the house, he gave us boys a chance to cut into and taste the discarded bile. Dad seemed to think everyone needed to know what bitter as bile really meant. He let us strip the kidneys from where they hung encased in leaf fat on the insides of the carcass, and we roasted the bratwurst look-alikes over the nearby open fire. As we ate the grainy, odd tasting charred meat, I tried to not think about the kidneys' function.

While the ghostly white carcass hung high in the blackjack tree cooling out, we had fresh fried liver for dinner. A full afternoon of cutting up the meat and starting the curing process of hams, shoulders and sowbelly lay ahead, but Dad and Mama's joint efforts and expertise would take care of most of what remained to be done. Following the tiresome jobs of collecting fat for leaf lard, turning the sausage grinder, and cleaning up generally, we were rewarded at suppertime with the choicest part of a pig, fried tenderloin. Months later cured ham, a close second to the tenderloin, would be ready.

The morning after butchering day we had a big bait of scrambled eggs and brains for breakfast, the only day of the year when our eggs were scrambled instead of fried. The exotic dish was too rich for common fare, even had it been available. After finishing off his second heaped helping, Dad leaned back in his hickory chair and actually smiled as he considered the previous day's work: "I'm not sure, boys, but I think we drownded the old sow."

* * *

Despite the continuing edge and uneasiness between Dad and Mama, many things fell into place that fall. The cellar was bursting at the seams. Besides the hundreds of quart and half gallon jars of canned vegetables and fruit lining the basement cellar shelves, Irish and sweet potatoes filled the big wooden bins on one side of the cellar, with opposite bins heaped high with Jonathan and Yellow Delicious apples we'd picked at a neighbor's orchard, and several tow sacks full of peanuts hanging from the rafters. All that winter we were free to go down the steep stairs and get apples, peanuts, and our favorite treat, sweet potatoes, which we baked in the hot cookstove oven until they split open. We ate them slathered with butter, crisp peelings and all.

In addition to having all we wanted to eat for ourselves at the new place, we also had plenty of feed for the livestock. With the approach of a winter storm, it was fun and rewarding to throw hay down from the loft, without scrimping, to the various animals secure in their stanchions and stalls. Even pitching the heavy compacted manure out of the barn windows the next morning wasn't too bad. And when there was a prolonged snowstorm there was always enough waste hay and weeds left over from the previous night to provide extra bedding.

Fred, Jay, and I had to keep enough corn shelled, either by hand or with the sheller, for the chickens and guineas, but we threw shucked ears of corn to the horses and let them do their own shelling. We simply threw unshucked ears to the hogs and pigs. Smart, beady eyed, and fierce, they made short work of shucks and corn alike.

We made sure we kept Mama supplied with dry cobs in the wood box behind the cookstove so she could start a fire from scratch before anyone else got up every morning. Sometimes there would be a few live coals left in the heating stove, but the cookstove never held fire overnight.

We also kept a stock of dry cobs in the barn for when nature called. We weren't allowed to take a dump in the barn or in any of the sheds, but on our way to the woods we'd swing by the barn for cobs. In emergencies we wiped with rocks and leaves, neither altogether satisfactory. Although Ollie was a better than average jake leg carpenter, there was no sign that he'd ever built a toilet on the Brechbuhler Place. Of course, as sorry a carpenter as Dad was, it wasn't surprising he never built much of anything other than whistles out of lilac wood when the sap was up in the spring and, once, a miniature hickory oxbow fashioned to fit two adult wethers he trained to pull a little wagon. Mama finally cobbled together a ramshackle toilet that she and the girls used, but it was too near the downwind house and there was little privacy when a breeze caught the unravelled tow sack that passed for a door.

Fred, Jay, and I kept a stash of corncobs in the barn for when company came and several of us boys chose up sides for a corncob fight. Everyone in the community except the Madewell boys abided by the general ban against throwing rocks at one another, but the rest of us often participated in vicious corncob fights. After choosing up sides, we'd load our pockets with broken cobs and pelt one another, especially our older brothers, as hard as we could, preferably in the face. We weren't supposed to throw heavy manure soaked or icy cobs, but once when Fred ignored the rules he and I ended up in a fistfight.

Bobby Lynn Wilkin, who was one of the last to be chosen at school for Friday afternoon spelling or ciphering matches, would be picked first in a corncob fight. Anyone who had hunted squirrels with Bobby Lynn knew that when he ran out of twenty-two shells, any squirrel his dog had treed was still in mortal danger from whizzing rocks. Only Efton Robbins, his ambidextrous cousin, was deadlier throwing rocks, but because he was recently married he considered himself too old to have anything to do with younger boys and their squirrel hunting.

70

When Fred and Jay and I shelled corn we kept the prettiest and straightest cobs back, pretending they were horses, which we tried to match with other cobs. But hull-gully was our favorite corn game. Although Dad frowned on the girls working in the fields, he sometimes took all six of us to the barn where we'd play raucous guessing games with our allotted handfuls of kernels. I've forgotten the exact rules and details of the game, but I remember trying to fool the person guessing by acting as if I had few kernels, or many, then calling out, "Hull-gully, I've got a handful of how many?" as I shook my closed hand in front of the guesser. Of course, we couldn't think of playing such a wicked game of chance in the house.

Dad and Fred enjoyed playing checkers behind the cookstove on long winter nights. Sometimes the two of them walked a mile northwest and played checkers with Ellie Ethridge, the acknowledged champion of the whole area. Ellie liked to play with Fred as well as he did with Dad because Fred sometimes beat him. Dad and Fred also liked to show off their manual dexterity at home by demonstrating how fast they could take apart and then put back together intricate puzzles Dad often constructed out of smooth heavy wire. Meanwhile, the rest of us were totally baffled and frustrated.

Just before bedtime after a deep, fresh snowfall, the folks would let all of us run barefooted around the house a few times, screaming and yelling like the wild little Indians Dad accused us of being. He rarely passed up a chance, even in fun, of getting a dig in at Mama for being part Indian.

On the Saturday nights when we bathed Dad always seemed to be in a good mood. Some of our neighbors supposedly took a bath every Saturday night; some by their own admissions and smells didn't bathe all winter long. We bathed occasionally, depending upon the availability of wood, clean clothes and the folks' whims. The Old He got to go first, naturally. There in the front room next to the heating stove he stepped into the round galvanized tub half full of clean, warm water. Finished, he dried off with a rough towel, then paraded through the house buck naked, his privates cupped modestly in his right hand. No one dared snicker at the king's antics.

Then quickly, alternately, oldest boy, oldest girl, middle boy, middle girl, youngest boy, youngest girl, all in the same scuzzy water. Last, Mama squeezed her great folds of flesh into the tepid, overflowing tub. Nobody risked her wrath by looking, not even Dad.

* * *

In late May and early June while Fred and I cut sassafras and hickory sprouts with dull axes, Dad and Jay cultivated the field corn. The rickety old walking cultivator had no seat, and Jay had to sit all day long on a gunnysack wrapped around the butt end of the rough oak tongue while he did his best to keep the team in a straight line as Dad walked behind guiding the cultivator shovels through the rocky ground. Dad was way too uptight to actually take the Lord's name in vain, but he directed a loud torrent of abuse at the timid eight year old boy when the horses inevitably stepped on cornstalks while turning around at the ends of the rows. As the cornstalks grew, Jay had the added responsibility of trying to keep the horses from reaching down and snatching out their tops. Some farmers used checkreins or wire muzzles to help control their horses, but not Dad.

When the corn was knee high Dad left for wheat harvest in western Kansas, leaving instructions for Fred and me to cultivate it one more time before laying it by. One hot day in the middle of the afternoon as we jiggled over the badly eroded rocky hillside, Fred suddenly yelled, "Whoa! Whoa!"

"What's wrong?"

"Nothin's wrong. Look at what I just plowed up!"

Behind the cultivator on the uneven ground lay a curved, strange looking rock about the size and shape of a football cut in half lengthwise. Inside a broken cavity I saw what looked like a cluster of sparkling tadpole eggs transformed into diamonds glittering in the bright sunlight.

"Let's go show Mama!" Fred said, "We won't have to plow no more corn if we're as rich as I think we are!"

Fred didn't wait as I unhitched the team and he was way ahead of me as he headed for the house cradling his find against his belly. By the time I put the horses in their stalls and reached the front porch, Mama was bent over examining the rock.

"Are we rich?" I asked her.

"I'm afraid not," she said. "I hate to say it, but I'm afraid it's worthless."

"Worthless?" Fred said. "What makes you think it's worthless?"

"It looks just like a rock Reuben found on Indian Hill in Oklahoma," she said. "Reuben thought he was rich too, but Papa knew better. Reuben cried when Papa told him it was fool's gold."

"What's that?" I asked.

"I'm not sure, but it's worthless. Reuben later insisted that fool's gold was the wrong name for his rock. He called it a geode, but it still wasn't worth anything."

"Well, I guess we'd better git back to plowin' corn," Fred said.

"Why don't you boys unharness the horses and take the rest of the day off," Mama said. "That corn'll wait. And put your rock over there where we can see it. It'll make a pretty door stop."

Fred and Jay and I milked the cows while Dad was gone, and we helped Mama hoe and pull weeds in the garden. Although the three girls never learned to milk, and they rarely worked in the field, they helped with the housework right along. In fact, from early on Joyce did more than her share of the housework. She also carried Lottie Jean around on her left hip until she permanently disfigured her shoulder and back.

All six of us helped Mama pick wild blackberries. In addition to what she and the girls canned and we ate fresh, we sold lots of berries. Every other afternoon, three times a week, we hitched the crippled mare to a buggy the Brechbuhlers had left behind and drove three miles to Madry Store. The last mile was catty-cornered on the Old Wire Road, a road made infamous in the early 1800's by the forced Indian march known as the Trail of Tears.

At the Brechbuhler Place

Loy Boswell, always friendly and courteous, paid us the going rate for blackberries, twenty to twenty-five cents a gallon. We ordinarily bought little if anything at the store, but on Fridays Mama let us buy sugar, salt, and junket tablets, and a block of ice which we wrapped in a tow sack before going home to make ice cream. Of course we had plenty of milk and eggs. We ordinarily made a gallon of ice cream, but once when the Brechbuhlers were visiting us Fred talked Mama into letting us crank a second batch. By the time the second gallon was ready only Fred and Ollie were still hungry, and the two of them, big eyed and bigger bellied, sat and slowly ate every last bite of it.

One of the few times Mama made pancakes, Fred asked her if he could eat as many as he wanted. "As long as everyone else has had their fill, I don't care how many you eat," she said. After the rest of us had finished breakfast, Fred started in on the thin saucer sized pancakes Mama flipped off the griddle on the side of the cookstove into the platter in front of him. At first Mama had a hard time keeping up with Fred, but the second batch of eight pancakes slowed him down, and by the third and fourth time around he was way behind. But he didn't quit. Only after Mama had piled a fifth stack in front of him did he concede. "I guess forty'll have to do me," he said, as he rubbed his big belly and eased his skinny frame up from the table.

"I know where there's a feather if you need to puke," Mama said, when he headed for the back door.

Rain fell right along that summer, extending the growing season, and we sold hundreds of quarts of the free for the picking blackberries. Mama had bribed us, especially Fred and me, at the beginning of the season by telling us that if we cooperated and didn't quarrel or fight, she'd order a croquet set and the biggest and best little wagon, the one with the wooden racks, in the Sears and Roebuck catalog. Although Fred and I couldn't agree on much, we managed an uneasy truce while we all worked and saved our money.

Long sleeved shirts helped protect our arms from the sharp, curved blackberry briars, but nothing seemed to work against the ticks and chiggers. Mama used minty smelling pennyroyal on herself when she could find it, but the rest of us rubbed coal oil, or lard mixed with sulfur on our wrists, ankles, underarms, crotches, and bellies to help ward off the biting insects. Pale green, foul smelling stink bugs often fell in our buckets as we picked, and daddy-long-legs, which we sometimes bent over and asked for directions while searching for cows in the evenings, gave off an awful stench when we happened to touch one. We were wary of snakes, and we kept our eyes peeled for threatening bulls when we slipped over to pick on neighbors' places. All bulls were dangerous, but old Jersey bulls had especially bad reputations.

After we'd made enough extra money, Mama ordered our prizes and soon Tub Ellis honked to let us know there was something special at the mailbox a quarter of a mile away. Following the instructions to the croquet set, we drove the stakes and wickets in place on a level grassy spot east of the house. Fred quickly mastered the game and he delighted in driving all of our balls flying down the hill while holding his own ball in place with his foot. Although Mama disapproved of playing games of any kind on Sundays, she reluctantly allowed us to play croquet after church. Maybe she considered croquet more genteel and less worldly than some of the other sinful games we liked to play such as jacks and Rook.

We loved riding in the flashy little red wagon. By removing the wooden racks, two or three of us at a time careened wildly down the steep hill all the way through the wet weather stream. One day after dinner Mama interrupted our play with the sober reminder that, according to Dad's recent card, wheat harvest was finished and he'd be home soon. When suppertime came, all of us kids noticed that the potato soup was unusually bland, but only Fred had the nerve to ask Mama, "What's wrong with the soup?"

"You know how particular your Dad is about what he eats," Mama said. "When he gets home I don't want him throwin' a fit over the taste of onions."

The next evening Dad, thinner than ever, but still ramrod straight, came walking down the lane. When Fred, Joyce and Lottie Jean, less guarded than the rest of us, ran to meet him he greeted the girls with big hugs and then awkwardly acknowledged Fred with a limp handshake. At supper everyone except Mama sat at the table waiting for Dad to start eating. Before taking his first sip of soup, he sniffed his spoon and frowned. "That stinks like onions," he said, and he threw the offending spoon as hard as he could against the black tarpaper on the far wall before stomping out.

"Never mind him," Mama said. "That just means there'll be more soup for the rest of us."

We were still eating when Dad charged into the house, yelling, "Where'd that croquet set and little wagon out there in the shed come from?"

"From the kids' hard work pickin' blackberries," Mama said.

"Don't talk to me about hard work. The very idy of spendin' good money on toys!"

Home after harvest

Later Fred and Jay and I lay stockstill in our bed upstairs listening to the argument below through the warm air vent Ollie had cut in the floor. Dad's enraged outburst ended when Mama hissed, "You listen to me, Clay Holmes. If you're still alive when the kids grow up, I'm leavin' you."

Fred and I slipped out early the next morning and replaced the wooden racks on the new little wagon in an attempt to make Dad think it was meant to be a utility vehicle instead of a toy. Although Dad wasn't fooled, his anger gradually subsided and before long he joined us in our Sunday afternoon croquet games. When he won, most of the time, he laughed and joked and carried on, especially when neighbor kids visited. On the rare occasions when he fell behind he knocked all of our balls down the hill, the same way Fred did, and he'd cheat by moving his ball when he thought no one was looking.

Not that Dad's cheating surprised us. We'd all seen him stack a deck of cards and then deal off the bottom for himself or his partner on rainy Sunday afternoons when we stayed in the house and played Rook. I never saw him cheat when he played cards with adults, but he thought it was amusing to cheat kids. Some of us bigger boys decided if he could cheat, so could we.

Mama in her rock garden

Although Mama tolerated our Rook playing, she drew the line against Pitch and Pinochle with their wicked face cards. She never joined us in any game, inside or outside the house, not even Hide the Thimble.

Late at night while waiting to change jars in the pressure cooker, Mama continued her favorite activity, poring over her heavy, worn, fake-leather bound Bible in the dim yellow light of the coal oil lamp. Never a fluent reader, she struggled again and again with the strange words and phrases, finally mastering and committing them to memory. Increasingly self-assured, Mama made herself a pretty blue dress with tiny pink flowers out of feed sacks and commenced going to church again. It gradually became apparent at Wednesday night prayer meetings and Sunday morning and evening services that no one could hold a candle to Miz Holmes when it came to understanding the Scriptures, and more and more people in the small congregation came to depend upon her to clear up thorny questions. Although she seemed reluctant to start preaching again, her confidence grew when members of the small congregation nodded and said amen at her ability to recite verses from the Bible. When Dad attended services, it was clear that he was annoyed and embarrassed at the attention Mama got, and more often than not he was nowhere to be seen when the rest of us began our two mile walk through the woods toward church.

SEVEN

RAMONA

Although our economic situation was much improved, I continued to wrestle with my own unresolved problems. At eight, when I'd put off becoming a Christian with the silent argument that Jesus Himself had waited until He was twelve before taking up His Father's work, I'd imagined that my four year holiday would last forever. Now, one Sunday afternoon just short of my twelfth birthday, puberty, galloping, galloping, overtook me on the west side of the smokehouse. That night in bed I made up my mind. No matter what Mama said about how boys who played with themselves were in danger of going crazy and having to go to Nevada where depraved people were sent, here was something that made the risk of landing in the insane asylum, and maybe going to hell, worth taking. I decided right then and there that I wasn't about to become a Christian. No sir. I'd give myself plenty of time—four more years. If the war continued and we moved to Wichita, as the folks kept saying we might, I'd have plenty of chances to sin, and not just by myself.

* * *

J.J. Sperandio, Old Sprando as everybody called him, had over a hundred acres of ripening strawberries that year and he needed lots of workers. Several farmers in the area who owned trucks hauled pickers to and from the strawberry patches, then worked as straw bosses during the day. Vinton Hartin hauled pickers in our area. After stopping at local crossroads where he picked up young people, boys and girls mostly ten to sixteen years old eager to earn a few dollars while broadening their horizons, Vinton drove the few miles to Aurora where he filled out his load with town kids.

The kids in town differed from those of us from the country as far as I could tell only in their greater self assurance and their better attire. Not many of the town boys wore overalls, and few of the town girls wore ill fitting dresses homemade out of bright colored, print feed sacks. A handful of the worst dressed town kids, boys and girls alike, went barefooted, while only a few of the best dressed country kids still wore shoes by the first week in June.

A beautiful black headed girl was the center of attention in the crowd of town kids that first morning. About my age, twelve, going on thirteen, the dark complected girl with a wide smile for everyone strode confidently in her penny loafers to the front of the truck where she chatted easily with everyone around her. From where I stood near the back of the truck, slyly checking her out, it was obvious that puberty had caught up with her some time earlier. But unlike many of the country girls who seemed embarrassed by their rounding signs of approaching womanhood, this girl seemed charmingly aware of her curvaceous beauty. Somewhere in the four miles between Pleasant Ridge and Camp Bliss, I fell in love. Her name was Ramona.

Now don't misunderstand: I was no raw novice in matters of the heart. I'd been in love before, first with Roberta Cope when half a dozen of us boys vied for the attention of the pretty pug-nosed first grader. The trouble had been that though we traded her back and forth amongst ourselves, giving as many marbles as we could spare as boot, she never claimed a single one of us.

I'd also fallen in love with Ruth Wiley when she came to substitute teach at Osie. The tall eighteen year old with the broad face and winning smile and manner was filled out in all the right places and she was the first beautiful woman I'd seen. Maybe she loved me too, I'd thought, when she bent over and patted my head and exclaimed over how well I read, but she never returned after that one day.

Parker Cave

I'd also been struck on Phyllis Lemaster; I'd carefully carved our initials in the trunk of my favorite chinkapin tree near the wet weather spring where I often spent time alone. And for an entire day I'd pestered Irene Brechbuhler when eleven of us, six Holmes kids and five Brechbuhlers, went in a wagon for an outing and picnic at Parker Cave on the Hartin Ranch. I'd chased Irene in and out of the cave, touching and pinching her when I could catch her, but she never gave me anything more than a contemptuous look. She was foolishly agog over Fred, sixteen, who had dazzled her with a buzzard egg he'd found in the mouth of the cave.

But this was different; this was love, the real McCoy, I thought as I continued sneaking looks at the Indian princess in the front of the truck. The thirty minute ride on increasingly narrowing dirt roads gave me time to plan my strategy. Although I was quite aware of how good looking I was—any half blind fool could have seen that—I knew better than to take a chance on looks alone. Maybe I could risk going barefooted, but I couldn't think of making my move while wearing my ragged relief overalls. They'd been washed so many times the accusing wide stripes were almost invisible, but the patches, patches upon patches on the knees and hindend, were way too incriminating. The only sensible thing to do was to keep a low profile and pick as hard and fast as my naturally fumble-fingers would go so I could send off for a pair of new overalls.

At five cents a quart, it was almost the end of the week before I'd collected enough redeemable chits for overalls. On the way to the crossroads Friday morning, I placed the letter with the order blank, along with the cash, in our mailbox at the end of the lane, checking twice to make sure the red flag was up so Tub would be sure to send the letter on its way to Montgomery Ward's in Kansas City.

While picking on Friday, I allowed myself more than an occasional glance at Ramona, at the same time making sure I didn't linger too long in my fantasies. Whatever I did, I didn't want her to catch me mooning over her like some love lorn calf. The revealing peasant blouse she wore provided a hard test for me as I reluctantly looked away when she bent over while picking.

On Monday evening, a long week after I'd first seen Ramona, Mama told me my new overalls had arrived. Sometimes mail order clothes didn't fit, but after I'd adjusted the contrary galluses, these fit perfectly. They were too stiff and too blue, I knew that, but with my pale, faded blue chambray shirt as contrast, they were just fine, I saw, as I admired myself in the long mirror in the bedroom the folks shared with Wanda and Lottie Jean.

Next morning I was up early and waiting ahead of my shabby brothers and sisters at the crossroads a mile away. When Vinton stopped, I headed straight for the front of the truck bed in the corner next to where Ramona always stood. On the bumpy ride to Aurora I silently practiced my smooth remarks, occasionally reminding myself of the ace in the hole I'd packed in the bottom of my round half gallon lunch pail. Desperately shy, I knew there was a good chance I'd clam up completely. But I'd surely be able to blurt out: "Wanta see my two headed chicken?"

At home when strangers came, one of us kids would run for the pale yellow two headed chick floating in a small clear jar filled with wood alcohol resting on the Old Lady Brechbuhler's pump organ. The sight of the little monster invariably broke the ice with new visitors. Although I wasn't sure how someone as sophisticated as Ramona was would respond to a deformed dead chicken, I had it hidden in my pail as a last resort. When we got to Aurora the rowdy gang of kids climbed in the back of the truck, and Ramona headed to her usual place next to where I stood.

She smiled. "Hi, I'm Ramona."

"Howdy," I managed. "I'm Wayne."

If you've ever had a good dream or fantasy come true you can guess what happened next. Before we were out of the city limits we were talking easily and laughing. By the time we'd reached Pleasant Ridge we'd agreed to be partners, with each of us picking on the outside toward the center on the same row. And that's just what we did; hour after hour, day after day, all week long we bantered and flirted, all the while picking the Aroma berries as fast as we could. Our fingers rarely touched and then only momentarily as we uncovered hidden ripening fruit near the middle of the row. A slow and inept picker, I sweated hard in my effort to keep up.

While the week flew by Fred teased me unmercifully about Ramona. He was too caught up in playing the clown while on the truck to pay attention to me there, and he was always far ahead of me in the strawberry patch, but in the late afternoons after we were dropped off at the crossroads he'd start in, all the while making sure he was out of reach. We both knew that if I could catch him I could whip him.

In order to avoid Fred's teasing and at the same time bask alone in my lovesick state, I often cut across through the tick and chigger filled woods instead of walking the three-quarters of a mile home on the dirt road with the other kids. As I walked along through the timber Saturday evening, self-absorbed, I stumbled across a downed goat. I'd traded Bill Reavis a pocketknife for the young nanny, and she was special. Alive, but lying flat on her side, Snowball had a bad case of the scours. Hurrying to the barn, I returned with a handful of corn and a bucket of water, along with enough hay to feed her and prop her up. Sunday after church I watered and fed her again, hoping in vain to see rabbit like pellets as a sign of her improved condition.

That afternoon I checked to make sure Mama had washed my new overalls. Inevitable red stains on the knees by the end of the week were beginning to undermine my confidence. Mama assured me she'd washed them; they were drying on the clothesline even as I asked. Monday morning while it was still dark, I slipped out of the house to take a leak and retrieve my clean new overalls. After shaking them a few times to get rid of the worst wrinkles, I started to put them on. But something was wrong, bad wrong. Maybe I'd mistakenly got Jay's. No, his were still on the line. In the early light I saw that my overalls had shrunk something awful. Even by letting out the galluses as far as they'd go, the bottoms of the legs still hit me halfway up my shins, and the bib struck me well below the tits. I was undone. Although I couldn't stand the certain laughter and shame the shrunken overalls would bring, I knew I had to go pick. The money was too important. Clawing through the dirty clothes upstairs, I retrieved my old patched relief overalls.

Stone faced and unapproachable, I crawled in the truck at the crossroads, but I stayed near the back the same way I had the first week. When Vinton stopped near the deep ditch where the town kids waited, I first looked away, then looked forward long enough to see Ramona's stiff back as she looked straight ahead. At the strawberry patch, I waited until everyone else had bent over and started working, then I slowly and morosely picked on the last row, all the while falling farther and farther behind.

Late in the afternoon when Vinton stopped to let us off, I headed through the woods to check on Snowball. Hearing no welcoming bleat, I moved up close where her stiff limbs, bloated belly, and dull film on her open eyes confirmed my fears. Hundreds of buzzing bluebottle blowflies were busy depositing eggs in her ears, eyes, nose, mouth, and hindend. Then a movement on the ground caught my eye. I watched in horrified fascination while two black tumble bugs, in tandem, one pushing and the other pulling, struggled as they rolled a marble sized ball of shit toward the dark woods beyond.

EIGHT
FARTHER ALONG

After the corn was laid by, the folks sometimes let us older kids visit Grandma and Grandpa Holmes on Honey Creek. J.P. and Lottie Louisa, Pap and Lottie the family called them, were different from other kids' grandparents. Pap, like his father Nate before him, was known as gruff but kind. Fiery red faced and swag bellied, J.P. Holmes was thought to be an old beer drinker by adults who didn't know him. But he wasn't. He was a teetotaller from first to last. In fact, Pap had thought his father wasn't fit to carry the Bible for the Masons because Nate would take a nip of whisky right along.

Unlike other old married people I'd been around, Pap and Lottie often held hands and called one another darlin' and sweetheart. That was hard enough to get used to; worse and more frightening was their habit of suddenly, without warning, yelling HALLELUJAH! PRAISE THE LORD! or BLESS HIS HOLY NAME! When Grandma said this last phrase it was a drawn out BL-L-E-SS HIS HO-O-O-LY N-N-NAME! accompa-

nied by a prolonged shaking of her loose jowls and then a ringing JEE-SUS! JEE-SUS! JEE-SUS! OH! GLO-RY! Besides their
sudden outbursts, we also had to endure Pap and Lottie's
every morning prayer service. Following chores and breakfast,
we filed to the parlor where the kids sat in kitchen chairs while
Pap and Lottie sat on the hard mohair covered davenport and
Pap read from the Bible. Following his reading, we all hun-
kered down on the shiny new linoleum, and first Pap and then
Lottie prayed out loud until my knees hurt.

Pap and Lottie cavorting on the lawn

This wasn't too bad when only Fred and I visited, but when
our cousin Ben was there he often got us in trouble. Ben, an only child, stayed with Pap and Lottie for long stretches. We
didn't know for sure why he was there so much, but we'd
overheard that his dad drank and had trouble keeping a job.
Sometimes it sounded as though Ben's folks were separated.
Often alone, he had learned to amuse himself by mastering a
variety of sounds: bird and animal calls, including his special-
ty, Donald Duck's voice, and various weird words and as-
sorted whistles which he endlessly practiced and perfected.
Ben loved to utter strange under his breath sounds while Pap
and Lottie prayed, all the while maintaining his pious poker
face. Whoever else was there ended up being sternly lectured

for laughing at the little saint's odd noises. Pap and Lottie made no bones about their fears that Fred and I were hell-bent little heathens in danger of turning into dreaded old infidels later on.

Mama was worried that Ben was having a sinful influence on me because I liked to read the Captain Marvel and Green Lantern comic books he bought with the allowance his mom sent. If she had only known she'd have been much more concerned about what Ben and I did for hours on end in the slough on Honey Creek. In the warm sluggish water in an out of the way place we stripped off and played exciting games. Our favorite was something Ben dreamed up where each of us tried to beat the other by seeing how many incoming pecker gnats we could trap and kill with one swift upward stroke. I imagined that Ben had a secret cheesy formula for attracting gnats, and I knew I was at a disadvantage because his landing strip was noticeably bigger than mine, but it was great fun even if he did always win.

Our daily play in the slough was interrupted when Ben and I talked Grandpa and Grandma into letting us ride my bicycle back home. Fred and I had taken a bad spill going down a steep hill on our way to Honey Creek, and we'd snapped off the bike's right pedal, making riding difficult. As Ben and I started out on the ten mile dirt and gravel road trip, with only a few hundred yards of blacktop the entire way, I awkwardly pedalled the first mile or so, then stopped to rest before it was time for Ben to take his turn. To my surprise, he refused. Maybe he was spoiled, as Mama thought, and had never had to take turns. Whatever the reason, I toted him the entire distance.

There were three schools with wells on the playgrounds along the way. Three miles down the road, after getting our fill from the well at Mineral Point School, we entered the unlocked front door and pilfered through the scant supplies. Seeing nothing worth stealing, we soon left. Another couple of miles farther on, we stopped at Talmage School. Both doors were locked, so we went to the back where we couldn't be seen and shoved until the doorjamb gave way. Inside we found an almost new basketball. The leather punch in my pocketknife was too big for the needle hole, but I punctured the ball, forced out the air, and hid it inside Ben's shirt. By the time we arrived at White Oak, two miles from home, we'd decided the basketball was ruined, and we wouldn't be able to explain where it came from to the folks, so we threw it in the cloakroom and continued on the increasingly steep and rocky road.

We stopped at the old empty Don Brechbuhler house at the top of the last hill where we decided to make up for the long boring trip with some last minute fun. In short order we'd knocked out every glass in the windows and doors with handy roadside rocks. As soon as we got home we took Jay aside and told him how exciting our recent mischief had been. Scared, Jay told Joyce, Joyce told Mama, Mama told Dad, and Ben and I awaited our certain punishment.

Neither of us received the whipping we expected that night, but the next morning after breakfast Mama told Ben he had to leave. My punishment was that I had to take him back to Honey Creek. I don't know how Ben felt, but I'd rather have been whipped. We stopped at the schoolyards for water and rest on the long haul back, but that's all.

Instead of going straight back, we detoured to a store just east of the Cockatoo, a roadhouse outside Aurora, where Ben bought two bottles of pop with the dime he had. This, my first Pepsi, almost made the twenty mile round trip toting Ben on the damaged bike worthwhile. The lyrics and lilting tune to the jingle I'd heard on Grandma's radio stuck with me almost as well as the words and sounds of the hymns at church:

> *Pepsi Cola*
> *Hits the spot.*
> *Twelve full ounces,*
> *That's a lot.*
> *Twice as much*
> *For a nickel, too.*

Pepsi Cola is the
Drink for you.

Grandma received a scalding letter from Mama soon afterward saying Ben was a bad influence on me, and he was no longer welcome at our house, but she didn't say I had to come back home right away.

On Sunday afternoon following church at McNeill Chapel, Fred, Ben and I were headed for the slough when we heard laughter and splashing on Honey Creek. A short distance away at the swimming hole by the cottonwood, we saw two young neighbors and their friends. We knew Lucy and Lloyd Crowley who, along with Lucy's little girl, lived with the older Crowleys in the little house north of Pap and Lottie's at the top of the steep red hill. But we didn't know until later that the two strangers were the Perry boys. The older one repeatedly splashed Lucy in the face, and he sometimes grabbed her and ducked her. Lucy screamed and laughed, but I noticed that the tall, homely young man with pooched out red lips was solemn and sad looking the entire time. Ignored by the others, Fred, Ben and I soon drifted down to the slough.

That evening before we went to church, Lucy, with her little girl Patty skipping along beside her, walked into the yard carrying an empty water bucket. With no well or cistern of their own, the Crowleys depended upon runoff into a barrel in rainy weather. But in dry weather they carried drinking water from Pap and Lottie's well. Lucy was in high spirits as she told Grandma about going swimming that afternoon. When Grandma asked her if she was going to church that night, Lucy said that she was, and she'd better hurry home so she'd be ready when Oren Perry came to pick her up. But Lucy's buoyant spirits suddenly turned somber. "Lottie," she said, "Will you do me a favor? If I die will you promise that 'Farther Along' will be sung at my funeral?"

"What in the world are you talking about, young lady? Why, you're in perfect health." Grandma replied sharply.

"Will you?" Lucy asked in a stricken voice. "Promise?"

Confused, but sensing the distraught girl's urgency, Grandma said, "Well, I guess so. Yes, I promise."

Relieved, Lucy grabbed the water bucket in one hand and her daughter's hand in the other and hurried up the road.

When it came time to wash our feet before going to bed, a requirement at Grandma's, I decided to sleep on the screened in porch instead of in the back bedroom with Fred and Ben. I was a little bit scared out there by myself, but there'd be more room alone on the three quarter bed; and sometimes a cool breeze from the southwest blew in. Way late in the night I was awakened from a deep sleep by sobbing sounds coming down the road. At first I couldn't make out the strangled words. Then I heard clearly, over and over, "Lucy's dead. Lucy's dead." As I pressed as hard as I could against the wall, Lloyd Crowley stopped outside the screen door only a few feet away where he continued wailing, "Lucy's dead, Lucy's dead."

Grandpa and Grandma quickly put on their clothes and left with the big blubbering boy. Much to my relief, Fred and Ben, awakened by all the noise, joined me on the porch. They both tried to get me to give up my spot next to the wall, but I wouldn't budge. No way. If whatever or whoever killed Lucy came to kill us, at least Fred and Ben would be killed first. Maybe I could slip under the back of the bed and escape before my turn came. For the first time in my life, I was terrified. Even if I wasn't killed outright, from the pounding of my heart I was sure I'd die of fright.

My fearful feeling gradually subsided and then, after a long time, sometime after dawn, Grandpa and Grandma returned. Their drawn faces confirmed what Lloyd had said, Lucy was dead, but they refused to say what killed her. Grandpa said the body had been found a hundred yards or so down the lane west of the Crowley house, but that's all he'd say before he and Grandma went back to help with preparations for the burial.

Grandma Holmes kept her promise. She got Neal McNeill to sing a solo of "Farther Along" to his frowning wife's piano accompaniment. The sight of the slight, pale body with the odd looking scarf tucked about her neck puzzled and worried me. Why would anyone need a scarf, even a thin one, after she was dead, especially in August? I watched and listened as Neal McNeill closed his eyes, threw back his head, and sang in his deep melodic voice:

> *Farther along we'll know all about it.*
> *Farther along we'll understand why.*
> *Cheer up, my brother,*
> *Live in the sunshine,*
> *We'll understand it,*
> *All by and by.*

As I sat in the midst of the small gathering at McNeill Chapel, I studied and fretted about the contradiction between the words of hope in the song, and the hopelessly sad tone and feeling aroused by the sorry spectacle of the dead girl.

Lucy's sudden death cast a pall over what was left of our late summer vacation. Afterward, instead of ranging widely over Grandpa's farm and other nearby places, the three of us, especially Ben and I, hovered fearfully in and around the safety of the house. "Why don't you boys get out from under my feet and go swimmin'?" Grandma complained.

"We're tired of swimmin'," Ben said, and while Fred often helped Grandpa hoe cockleburs out in the pasture, Ben and I stuck close to Grandma's side. Only in the evenings when Pap made us go after the cows did we venture away from the house. We made a wide detour through the woods east of the Crowley house, then ran as fast as we could to the creek bottom where we gathered the startled cows and hazed them up the hill in a lope until they came out of the timber where Pap could see us as we followed them in a sedate walk toward the barn lot.

"Somethin's been spookin' them cows," Pap said accusingly one evening. "Are you boys sure you haven't been siccin' Old Shep on them?"

"Yes, we're sure," Ben quickly answered. "We know better than that." But he didn't mention all the sharp rocks we'd thrown, and how many tough ironweeds we'd worn out on the cows' backs and hocks before they learned to run at our approach.

Once when Fred was helping us look for a stray cow across the creek he began telling us what he thought had happened to Lucy: "Remember hearin' stories about how Indians used to kill big bunches of fish by smashin' walnut hulls and throwin' 'em in the creek?"

"Yeah," I said. "I've heard of that."

"And remember how Joe Madewell used to talk about killin' fish by puttin' carbide in a jar with a hole in the lid and throwin' it in the water where it would explode and kill a tub-full of fish?"

"Yeah, I heard him, but it didn't work the time he tried it up yonder at the sycamore. Remember, it didn't explode."

"I know, but that's not the point. I think the creek's been poisoned, and Lucy accident'ly swallowed enough to kill herself when that Perry boy ducked her."

"You may be right," Ben said. "I know I don't aim to play in the creek anymore. But there's somethin' else that keeps botherin' me."

"What's that?" I asked.

"I read in the back of a comic book about a killer on the loose who's been goin' around the country drivin' nails in people's heads and then coverin' up the nails with their hair."

"That's spooky," Fred said, "but what does it have to do with Lucy?"

"I've got a feelin' it has a lot to do with her," Ben said. " I bet nobody checked to see if she had a nail in her head."

"Prob'ly not," Fred said, and for the next few days, the rest of our vacation, Ben's suspicions fired our imaginations. We not only steered clear of Honey Creek and our slough of ecstasy, we kept a sharp lookout for a madman armed with a claw hammer and a fistful of nails.

It would be more than fifty years before I'd piece together a plausible reason as to why and how Lucy died. Perhaps pregnant a second time to a reluctant partner, Lucy may well have despaired over the prospect of trying to raise yet another child. Did the sullen Perry boy help her obtain the bottle of carbolic acid found empty near her body down the lane? I don't know, but from his hangdog look at the swimminghole, I think he knew something. As for the sweet, good-natured Lucy, could she possibly have understood it all by and by, as the words in the old hymn promised? I doubt it. I know I never could.

NINE
THE DOG CHAIN

I don't know whether the languor of dog days had anything to do with what went on that summer or not, but sometime after Ben and I broke out the window lights in Don Brechbuhler's vacant house, and about the time Lucy died, one evening about dusky dark four boys from around White Oak went on a spree that began innocently enough. Toshie Robbins, not quite ten, and his brother Newt, almost a teenager, rode their horses cat-ty-cornered across Sand Ridge where they and their cousin Jack Lemaster watched a meteor shower while lying flat on their horses' backs in the barn lot. After the dazzling display in the sky ended, the three bored boys rode a half mile south where they stopped and invited Nolan Ben Parvin to join them on a ride to Hartin Ranch a few miles away. But a scant quarter of a mile south of Parvins', past the crest of the hill, someone suggested detouring to their left where Hiram Hilton's empty old house stood.

Maybe the recent western the boys had seen in town starring Henry Fonda playing Billy the Kid corrupted them, as Mama thought, or maybe there's something compelling about window panes in a vacant house that makes boys smash them. Whatever the reason, according to Toshie's account the boys jumped off their horses, tied their shirttails tight on the outside of their overalls, and filled their billowing, unbuttoned shirts with rocks which they peppered against the house from the backs of their running horses.

Newt, in the lead astride Old Nig, the high-spirited and fastest horse in the whole country, commandeered his small band of Indians around and around the imaginary Conestoga until their ammunition ran out and every pane in the house was shattered. When their mock cries of attack subsided, Jack was the first to hear bawling hounds in the woods nearby. "We better git out of here, boys!" he yelled in his distinctive falsetto. "They've turned the dogs loose on us!" Forgetting about Hartin Ranch, the boys quickly headed home.

Before beginning her work peeling tomatoes at Dick Wiley's White Oak canning factory the next morning, Bernice Robbins collared Toshie as he started upstairs to help Newt roll cans. "Just a minute, young man," she said. "Where did you boys go after you rode over to Jack's last night?"

"Nowhere special, just ridin' around."

"Did you stop at Harm Hilton's old house?"

"Yeah, we stopped there for a few minutes to give the horses a blow after we picked up Nolan Ben."

"What else did you do?"

"Nothin' that I can think of," the trembling boy said.

"You better just own up to it, Toshie. Your Uncle Earl and Bon Eubanks was enjoyin' a fox race across the road from Harm's place last night when they heard a lot of yellin' and the sound of glass breakin'. Before they had time to git to the house, you boys had hightailed it down the road."

"Uncle Earl didn't see us, did he?"

"No, but he heard someone yell somethin' about gittin' out of there, and he told your Aunt Nellie there was no mistakin' Jack Lemaster's voice."

"That was Jack all right. When did Uncle Earl tell on us?"

"He told Aunt Nellie last night and she told me just a few minutes ago. You know I'll have to tell your dad when he gits off work tonight."

"Dad'll be awful mad, won't he, Mommy?"

"Yes, he will. I expect he'll work you boys over with his razor strap. Now git upstairs and help Newt."

When Toshie reached the loft at the top of the stairs, he blurted out: "Mommy knows about last night and she's gonna tell Dad."

"If she knows it's cause you're a tattletale," Newt said, and he backhanded his little brother across the mouth.

"I didn't tell! Cross my heart and hope to die!" Toshie said, as he rubbed his red, stinging face. "Uncle Earl heard us and he told Aunt Nellie and Aunt Nellie told Mommy. She thinks Dad'll whip us somethin' awful with his razor strap."

"He may do it," Newt said. "But if he does I don't aim to give him the satisfaction of seein' me cry. It's time somebody stood up to him."

The two boys had finished the chores that evening when their dad, ordinarily hearty and jovial, but now tired and out of sorts from his all day shift on a road grader, drove up next to the blackjack tree at the corner of the house. "What's for supper?" Howard asked Bernice as she stepped out the back door.

"I've got bad news," she said.

"More bad news from the hospital about Billy's hand?"

"No, nothin' about that, but bad enough. After Newt and Toshie left here last night them and Jack and Nolan Ben Parvin broke out all the window lights in Harm Hilton's old house."

"How'd you find out about it?"

"Earl told Nellie and Nellie told me at the fact'ry."

"How'd Earl know?"

"He was in the woods listenin' to his hounds run when he heard a big commotion and the sound of glass breakin'."

"And he caught them?"

"No, he didn't even git a good look before they tore out. But he reco'nized Jack's voice."

"Did you ask the boys about it?"

"Yes, I asked Toshie, and he admitted it. Now don't be too rough on them," she pleaded.

"Newt! Toshie! You boys git up here right now!" the big man boomed.

Toshie came around the corner of the house dragging a dog chain he'd been playing with as he popped prickly seed pods off jimsonweeds in the barn lot.

"Here, give me that thing!" his dad yelled, as he grabbed the chain.

"No, Howard! No! Not a chain!" Bernice cried.

"I aim to teach these boys a lesson," he said, and he doubled the chain and held Toshie by the shoulder while delivering several slashing blows across the bare calves of the small boy's legs. Although Toshie remembered Newt's defiant words, the searing sensation of metal on flesh was too much for him; he couldn't keep from screaming.

Finished with Toshie, Howard turned to Newt. "What have you got to say for yourself?"

"Nothin' I'd say would make any difference," Newt said, turning around to accommodate his father. Newt sucked in his breath with an involuntary "Oh!" the first time the whistling chain hit him, but he didn't cry.

"Well, well," Howard said. "Looky here. The big boy thinks he's turned into a little man. Maybe this will change his mind." To the measured rise and fall of the bloody chain, Newt's high scream led a chorus of sobs ever so long.

"Ever'body but Dad was a cryin' and a screamin," Toshie said later. "Mommy was a cryin', and Sally was a cryin', and June was a cryin', and I was a cryin', and Newt was a screamin' and a dancin' up and down. Billy would 'a been a cryin' too if he'd a been there, but he was in the hospital after his accident on the high line."

After supper Howard took Toshie and Newt over to Jake and Okie Lemaster's. "I give my boys a whippin' they won't soon forget," he told his brother-in-law. "What do you aim to do with Jack?"

"I'll talk to him and then punish him as I see fit," Jake said. Whether he whipped Jack, or knocked him down with his fists as he sometimes did when he flew into a blind rage, or didn't punish him at all, no one outside the Lemaster family ever knew.

When Howard took Newt and Toshie up the road to Lewis Parvin's, Nolan Ben was gone with his mother, but Lewis said he'd take care of the matter. Later, Lewis told Howard his boy denied having anything to do with breaking the glass, and he believed him. Howard also took his boys to see Hiram Hilton, an old skinflint with a long, pinched nose and huge ears who was hopping mad over his loss. "How much do the boys owe you?" Howard asked.

"I figure right at seventy-five dollars, including glass, putty, and labor," the skinny old man replied.

"That sounds high to me," Howard said.

"Would you rather I took 'em to court?"

"No, I guess not."

"By the way, Howard, that time you sued Ern Phariss for shootin' your stock dog, how much did you git in damages?"

"You know as well as I do, a hunderd dollars."

"That's what I thought. But about my house. I'll try to be reasonable, but I want ever' last busted glass replaced."

"I'll make sure my boys pay you what's right," Howard said. "They've still got most of what they made over the summer pickin' strawberries and tomatoes and workin' in the cannin' fact'ry. I doubt if Lewis Parvin will make his boy pay his share, but Jake Lemaster might make Jack cough up somethin'. I'll git back with you about it later in the week. All right?"

"All right. I'm dependin' on your word."

Howard watched as his two boys counted out their summer savings meant for school supplies and winter clothes on the kitchen table. Newt's stash came to a little over twenty-eight dollars, and Toshie's was almost nineteen. Later Howard took their money, along with the eleven dollars Jack had saved, and handed it over to the aggrieved old man.

"Here," he said. "This fifty-eight dollars is all the money my boys and Jack could scrape up. If you think you can git somethin' out of the Parvin boy, go ahead, but it's hard to git blood out of a turnip."

"That's not hardly enough," the old man said, after counting the money out then folding the bills tight and placing it all in the small purse he snapped shut before securing it in the bib of his overalls, "but I guess it'll have to do."

The old rascal never did replace the broken glass in the decrepit old house. Maybe he figured the compound interest he could make over the long run on the fifty-eight dollars would be more than he could get in rent. Hiram Hilton's thriftiness apparently paid off because someone looking for a well located place gave him his asking price of $500 for his forty acres with the damaged house.

Not long after Hiram's first wife died, a slim old maid who attended his church began keeping company with him and they soon got married. To many people's surprise, she moved in the rickety unpainted two room house with an unfinished upstairs on a nearby eighty acres where he lived. About midmorning the day after the marriage, the new bride walked a half mile up the road where she stopped and visited with Mama, busy with her pick and shovel planting iris in the front yard. Always abrupt, Mama didn't mince words: "Howdy, how do you like bein' married?"

"Not very good," the wrinkled old woman said.

"What's wrong?"

"Last night was bad enough," she began, "but when I got up to fix breakfast this mornin', Hiram told me he'd have to give me some direction. As if I didn't know how to fix breakfast."

101

"What kind of direction?" Mama asked.

"'First, make three biscuits,' he said. 'Two for me and one for you.'"

"You don't mean it."

"I do mean it, and so did he. And that's not all. 'Next, fry three slices of bacon, two for me and one for you.'"

"Let me guess," Mama said. "'Then fry three eggs, two for me and one for you.'"

"You guessed right," the outraged woman said. "I knew Hiram Hilton was as tight as the bark on a tree, but this beats all. I don't care if he is a preacher, I'm goin' to Cassville and get me a divorce or annulment, whichever one's the quickest."

"Well, 'bye," Mama said. "You better do it right now while you're still in the notion."

TEN

COTTONMOUTHS AND MAD DOGS

Joe Madewell, Windy Maidenhead as some of his less work brittle neighbors liked to call him behind his back, was ordinarily too busy grubbing out a living for his deaf wife and their eight scruffy children to waste time at Osie store. But on the rare occasion when he was caught up with his work, he and his five tough sons showed up.

One rainy day when Dad and Fred and Jay and I arrived at Osie, we noticed Joe's old flatbed Chevrolet truck parked east of the store. Inside, the Madewell boys, along with several others, were sitting on sacks of feed in the back part of the building where kids were expected to stay unless they had money to spend. The men sat on tomato crates or the few stools or chairs around the potbellied stove.

Most of the men wore similar clothes: solid blue denim or striped overalls, many bearing patches, faded blue chambray shirts; and badly worn ankle high work shoes. Young boys dressed much the same as their fathers, but all of them went barefooted. Older boys wore shoes, or not, according to their circumstances and aspirations. A few men wore black felt hats both summer and winter, but most of them wore cheap straw hats in the summer.

An occasional man, Buck Reavis for one, smoked a pipe. Some of the others, including Clifton Hutchinson, who'd lost an arm as a boy in a hunting accident, smoked roll-your-own Bull Durham cigarettes. It was fascinating to watch Clifton place a thin paper in a wrinkle of his overalls, shake out the loose aromatic tobacco from his sack, close the sack with his teeth, then deftly lick and twirl the perfectly made cigarette before placing it in his mouth and lighting it with a kitchen match struck against his tightly flexed hindend.

As far as I knew Dad didn't smoke. Not that he was opposed to smoking or chewing, but he'd given up his tobacco at the same time he and Mama gave up their morning coffee. I never saw him smoke or chew or take a drink, but Ed Robbins said that when Dad was off in wheat harvest, or hunting and fishing with the men, he'd use tobacco as well as take an occasional sip of whiskey.

Some boys at the store got to buy a small amount of candy, maybe a penny or two's worth. But Fred, Jay, and I knew better than to expect anything. When Dad paid off the bill he'd been running, perhaps once or twice a year, Emmit and Beulah generously filled a poke full of candy for us six kids to enjoy.

With few distractions at the store, I sat quietly on sacks of feed and watched and listened to the men. Their witty good-natured give and take as they whittled and spit out the back door or into the stove made me wonder why men enjoyed one another's company, while men and women, or Dad and Mama anyway, either squabbled or were silent when together.

Joe Madewell sat spraddle legged on an up-ended tomato crate in the middle of the room near the stove, while five or six of the regular Osie loafers gathered around him. "I don't want to interrupt anything," Dad said, as he entered, nodding to the circle of men.

"Come on over here," Joe said. "I was just braggin' about how much money I used to make in the timber. I didn't spend thirty-five years workin' in the woods for nothin'. You boys may find it hard to believe, but I used to cut and hack a hunderd railroad ties a day. At a dime a piece, that bought a lot of groceries."

"Ten dollars is a lot of money for a day's work," Buck Reavis said.

"It wasn't just one day's work," Joe said. "I'd spend one day cuttin' and hackin', and two more days haulin' and loadin' the ties in a railroad car down at the roundhouse. Even so, a little over three dollars a day is good money. It's a whole lot more than what some people I know make."

"That's right, Joe," Buck said. "I sure don't make three dollars a day haulin' livestock, but it suits me better than hackin' ties ever did."

"To each his own," Joe said. "The most money I ever made was loggin' on the Osage."

"How's that?" Buck asked.

"When I was young and stout some of us used to round up a crew and go up on the Osage and work ever' fall and winter. Up there in the middle of the state it was easy as pie to top trees and then fall 'em into the river. We'd make a big raft, then ride it downstream to the Missouri and sell the whole kit and caboodle for big money."

Jake Lemaster, a hard worker himself, spoke up: "I always wanted to fish the Osage, but I heard it's full of snakes."

"Let me tell ya about it," Joe said. "One day a new kid in the crew had just shinnied up a big red oak and was toppin' it when he must've done somethin' wrong. We heard the tree crack and him holler and it looked like he was a goner the way his belt tightened up. But all of a sudden his belt broke and he fell in the river."

"Lucky for him," Jake said.

"That's what we thought," Joe said, "but he'd no more than hit the water when the biggest snake I ever saw struck him on the neck. In less than three minutes he was dead."

"That was mighty quick," Jake said. "Wasn't you scared?"

"You bet, but the foreman always carried a twenty-two rifle, and he shot and killed the snake. We was still scared, but some of us jumped in with our cant hooks and peavies and dragged the kid and the snake out on the bank."

"Why bother with the snake?" Dad asked.

"'Cause it was so big. We stuffed it in a tow sack and weighed it with a set of stillyards. I know it's hard to believe, but it weighed a hunderd and nineteen pounds."

"A hunderd and nineteen pounds," Dad mused. "Are you sure it didn't weigh a hunderd and twenty pounds?"

"Yes, I'm sure," Joe said, shifting his weight on the wobbly crate. "I wouldn't lie for a pound."

"Hmm," Dad said. "That must have been a mighty long snake."

"No, it wasn't very long. It was five foot two. It was a chubby little thing."

After the laughter around the stove subsided, Joe stood and yelled: "You boys go git in the truck. We've got work to do."

The Madewells were barely out the back door when Dad turned to Jake: "Would your wife's grandma's madstone have saved that kid's life?"

"I doubt it," Jake answered, "especially seein' as how that kid prob'ly never existed in the first place. But if you're doubtin' the power of a madstone, you ought to ask someone who's used it."

"Someone like you?"

"No, I'm talkin' about my brother-in-law, Howard Robbins. If you've got a little extry time on your way home, drop in and see him and Bernice. They can tell you all about it."

"I just might do that. It wouldn't be much out of the way. C'mon boys, we need to git goin'." To my surprise, about halfway home we took the left hand road leading to Sand Ridge where the Robbins family lived.

"Git out and come in!" Howard yelled, when we pulled up into his back yard.

"We don't have a lot of time," Dad said, "but Jake Lemaster told me you folks can tell me all about a madstone."

"I'll be glad to tell you what happened to me," Howard said. "Tie your horses to the fence there, and make yourselves comfortable. My boys are down at the creek, but your boys are welcome to git out and play."

"They'd better just stick close to the wagon," Dad said. "It won't hurt them to hear about the madstone, will it?"

"Not a bit. See that scar on my thumb, boys? A long time ago, when I was just a boy, a stray feist showed up in our yard. I remember it was in the middle of dog days in August, when the weather's hot and close and ever'body knows to be on the lookout for mad dogs. The feist was snappin' at our dogs, and slobberin', and actin' kind of funny. I threw a rock at him, but instead of runnin' away like I expected, he dodged in and bit me right there on the thumb. Pa would 'a shot him, but he was out of shells."

"And so the dog got away?" Dad asked.

"Yeah, he crossed the field and went into the woods. I was gittin' ready to soak my thumb in coal oil when the folks insisted that I go with them over to Bernice's grandma's log cabin, you know the Old Lady Friend, and see if her madstone would suck out the poison."

"Whatta you mean?"

"Just that, stick to my thumb and draw out the poison. It works the best on mad dog bites and snake bites, but it works good on a lot of other things like wasper stings, spider bites, and blood poisonin'."

"Where'd the madstone come from?"

"You know the Old Lady Friend's a full-blooded Indian?"

"I know she sure looks like it."

"Well, when she was just a kid a stranger who was all wore out stopped at her folks' cabin on the White River and asked if he could stay a spell. After he finally got rested up and started to leave, he told her folks he was beholden, and he had somethin' he wanted to give 'em. To their surprise, he took a little rock he said had healin' powers out of his knapsack."

"Did this man say who he was?"

"No, but from his swarthy look some people thought he was a Gypsy, or maybe a Wanderin' Jew."

"Did he say where he got the madstone?"

"No, just that it came from the heart of an albino deer."

"That sounds mighty fishy to me," Dad said.

"That's what I thought when I first heard about it," Howard said, "but I ended up believin' it. The first thing the old lady did when the folks took me to see her was take the madstone out of the tobacco sack she carries on a leather thong around her neck."

"What did it look like?"

"It was three sided, somethin' like them nigger toes we buy for the kids at Christmas time, only light colored and smaller. The bottom of the rock was flat with little bitty holes in it. The first thing the old lady done was put it in a washpan half full of fresh sweet milk. Then she took it out and dried it with a dish towel before she pressed it against my thumb. It stuck to my thumb tight as Dick's hatband several minutes before it loosened up and dropped off."

"Then what?"

"She dropped it down easy like into the washpan and the milk fizzed and bubbled and turned green. Then she took it out and dried it off and stuck it to my thumb again. She did that several times 'til the rock wouldn't stick any longer."

"Well, I'll be," Dad said. "How much did the old lady charge?"

"When Pa asked her what he owed her, she said she didn't take money, but if the madstone helped me she wouldn't care if we'd give her a bucket of apples or somethin' extry out of our garden. We went home and my thumb healed up right away."

"How could you tell for sure that little dog was mad?" Dad asked him.

"I forgot to tell you that part," Howard said. "After he run out of the yard he headed west and south on the Old Wire Road in the direction of Camp Bliss. The very next day he bit one of them Marbut women down at McDowell."

"Did she go to the Old Lady Friend's?"

"No, her man said he didn't put any stock in a madstone, and he made her stay home. Here, let me holler at Bernice. She knows this part better than I do."

"Don't bother Bernice, she's prob'ly busy," Dad said, but Howard yelled in that deep voice of his, and Bernice, drying her hands on her apron, soon joined us at the wagon.

"Howdy Clay. Howdy boys," she said. "What in the world are you hollerin' about, Howard?"

"Clay wants to know about your Grandma Friend's madstone. Tell him about goin' to see that Marbut woman after she got bit by that little white feist."

"Sure," Bernice said. "After Mommy heard that the Marbut woman was in bed bad sick, she took me and Brother and we walked down the Old Wire Road catty-cornered past McDowell where the Marbuts lived. Brother stayed outside in the yard, but I hung on to Mommy's hand and we went in the house. We didn't see Miz Marbut at first – she wasn't in the front room – but when we got up to leave, one of the neighbor women said, 'Oh, she'll be disappointed if she don't git to see you'ens. Go back and see her for a few minutes.'"

"When Mommy went through the bedroom door, I was scared as could be and held back, but Miz Marbut saw me. 'Come on in here and give me a kiss, honey,' she said. 'I won't bite you.' I turned my head when she tried to kiss me on the mouth, but I give her a quick little peck on the cheek and then backed away."

"That took a lot of nerve," Dad said. "I've heard that people in the last stages of rabies are even more dangerous than a mad dog."

"Ever'body I know says that too," Howard said. "Neighbors around McDowell said before Miz Marbut died she had to be kept tied up or she'd a bit anybody she coulda got ahold of. Anyway, Clay, it was on account of Miz Marbut dyin' from gittin' bit by the mad dog, the same one that bit me, that made me believe in the madstone. Whatta ya think now?"

"It's still hard for me to imagine," Dad said, "but I have to admit you're pretty convincin'."

"Well, that's the only first hand account I have," Howard said. "If you don't believe me, let Cyril Williams or Tom Hemphill tell you what happened to them. Better yet, talk to Vinton Hartin. After Vinton went to the old lady with an infected tick bite, he offered her a hunderd dollars for the madstone—all the money he'd made from trappin' and huntin' that winter. But she told him it wasn't for sale at any price."

"Next time I see Vinton I'll ask him about it," Dad said. "Well, Howard, we've took up a lot of your time, and we've all got things to do. Much obliged, and come see us."

"All right. Come back."

On our way home Dad told us boys to remember to not tell Mama anything we'd heard at the store. "There's no point in gittin' her all worked up."

"What about Howard and Bernice's story about the madstone?" Fred asked. "Can we tell her that?"

"Maybe, but if we do, I better be the one who tells her."

By the time we got home we had to milk and do the rest of our chores by lantern light, and when we went in the house it was plain to see that Mama and the girls had already eaten their supper. "We've been worryin' about you and the boys," Mama told Dad. "Did you run into trouble?"

"No, we didn't have any trouble," Dad said. "But we come back by way of Howard and Bernice Robbins' place. We aimed to stay just a little while, but Howard and Bernice told us a

110

long story about Bernice's grandma's madstone, and first thing we knew the sun was goin' down."

While Fred, Jay, and I ate supper, Dad told Mama what we'd heard about the madstone.

"Did these boys hear all that wicked talk?"

"Wicked talk? Whatta you mean, woman?"

"Just what I said, Clay Holmes. I don't aim to have these kids of ours ruined by hocus-pocus stories and wicked talk. I've not heard of a single person named Friend ever darkenin' the door of a church. And ever'body who knows anything knows that Gypsies and Jews are in cahoots with the Devil. And let me tell you one more thing: If our kids get snake bit or mad dog bit, or anything else bad happens, I don't aim for you to be sneakin' 'em over the hill through the woods to the Old Lady Friend's madstone. If prayin' to Jesus and God Almighty won't heal 'em, then it'd be better for 'em to die than for us to have any truck with Old Satan and a bunch of old infidels."

ELEVEN
WHITE OAK SCHOOL

We attended school more regularly after moving to the Brechbuhler Place. Since Dad was feeling better, we no longer had excuses to stay home the way we had at the Snuffer Place. One of the first things Dad did after we got settled in was take his good double bit ax and walk two miles northeast through the thick woods blazing a trail on the bigger trees along the ridge leading northeast toward White Oak School. Besides shortening the distance to school, Dad said the diagonal trail was smoother than the rocky and hilly roads in the area.

For the first few days of school the four of us—Fred, Joyce, Wanda, and I—felt daring as we prepared to follow the freshly marked trail through the dark woods. "Be careful where you step," Mama warned us, "and if a copperhead bites you, remember, whatever you do, don't run and pump the poison through your system. That could kill you."

"Don't worry, we'll be careful," Joyce said, and we were more watchful than usual the first few times we walked back and forth. Instead of seeing snakes, we occasionally came across fresh signs suggesting good sized animals had been searching for acorns and nuts under oak, hickory, and chinkapin trees. From the uprooted ground and general disturbance, we guessed someone's hogs were on the loose, but we solved the mystery one cool Monday morning when we spotted a huge nest of leaves a few yards from the path. Lying in a semicircle facing us, we saw several big eared and long snouted hogs quite unlike any we'd seen before. As we drew near, the grunting and coughing animals reluctantly got up and trotted single file down a nearby draw. Instead of the chunky and uniform hogs we were familiar with, these odd looking creatures were tall and muscular in the shoulders, with small, tapering hindends, and we saw ugly patches of bristles on their shoulders and backs. Scariest of all, the fierce white tushes curling up from the older animals' lower jaws were much bigger than the ones we'd seen in mature boars. As the animals disappeared down a steep draw, I noticed tufts of coarse hair hanging from their long, straight tails.

Our schoolmates generally pooh-poohed our account of the strange looking hogs, but Bobby Lynn Wilkin, who lived nearby and often ranged over the area hunting squirrels, said he'd seen them, and he thought they were wild hogs out of Arkansas. "If I's you'ens I'd stay out of them woods," he said. "Them hogs are dangerous; they ain't afraid of nothin'."

When we told the folks about the hogs and what Bobby Lynn told us, Dad said, "They could be wild hogs out of Arkansas, but they're more likely to be somebody's tame hogs strayed from the open range a few miles south of here. It don't take long for tame hogs to turn wild."

"Are they dangerous?" I asked.

"They'd be real dangerous if you crowded or cornered 'em," he said. "But I doubt if they'll attack you for no reason, if that's what you're afraid of. Give 'em a wide berth, and you'll be safe."

Dad knew a lot, and what he said about the hogs in the woods helped lessen our fears. Anytime we came up on one of the wary animals foraging alone, we noticed it turned toward us and looked us over before turning around and trotting off in an unconcerned way. And when all of them lay bedded down in their big nest, they held their ground as they peered out at us. We could tell from their beady eyed, baleful looks that they knew as well as we did that they had their bluff in on us.

The more we went to school, the better I liked it. Occasional chinkapin trees along the new trail provided us with lots of treats to secretly munch on during class. The leathery shelled, dark brown nuts were better tasting than hazelnuts; and we could crack them silently and without fear of damaging our teeth. We also picked black haws and wild grapes along the way. Although most kids shunned the tiny possum grapes, I liked their sharp, bitter taste. They reminded me of the faint smell of a faraway skunk, the smell of boar meat frying, or the smell of my toenails when I trimmed them with my pocket-knife after washing my feet or taking a bath. All of these smells and tastes could be heavy and offensive, but I liked them in faint sniffs or small doses.

We watched for signs of a bee tree as we walked to and from school in warm weather. Fred was adept at following a beeline to a tree after he spotted a honey bee in flight. If an unmarked bee tree was found – no matter on whose property – the person who found it was free to cut his X in the tree's bark and later cut the tree down and collect the honey at his convenience. A man's or a boy's distinctive X was as good as his word or his handshake.

When it snowed, Dad ripped up gunnysacks and showed us how to wrap our shoes and fasten the strips with baling wire, enabling us to walk the two miles in heavy snow without getting our feet wet. Shortly before arriving at the schoolyard, we'd stop and sit on a downed hollow snag where we'd unwrap the burlap strips, hide them and the wire in the hollow log, then carefully walk the remaining distance through the woods, all the while hoping none of our schoolmates would notice or wonder why our feet were dry.

We, or I anyway, tried to hide the biscuits Mama wrapped in pages from last year's catalog for our lunches. By noon the same wonderful tasting sowbelly and hot biscuits we'd had for breakfast had turned into ugly, revolting slabs of congealed grease. By adroitly cupping my hands around my biscuit, I hoped to conceal my despised fare from curious onlookers. Just once I would have liked to brazenly display a sandwich made of white store boughten light bread with a thin, red slice of baloney, like most of the other kids ate for lunch.

Even so, I felt lucky I didn't have to eat my lunch the way the Brechbuhler kids did. They were the only ones who ate rice sprinkled with raisins or slimy, disgusting looking tapioca pudding. But it might have been worth the shame of eating odd food with a spoon out of a jar just to get a chance to eat one of their mother's delicious fried pies. The dried peach and apple pies Hazel Brechbuhler fried on her slick cookstove top were better by far than everyone else's food, including the candy bars the Lemaster and Shoemaker kids brought from the stores their folks ran at Sage Hill.

Before books took up, and at recesses and noon, boys and girls together played various games, including Annie Over, Blackman, and Crack the Whip. I played softball, but I didn't enjoy it. Stiff and awkward, I was picked way down the line and placed far out in the field where hardly anyone ever hit the ball.

On the rare occasion when someone did hit the ball my way, I could be counted on to fumble it. When it came my turn to bat, my vicious swing resulted in a long hit only once in a blue moon. I ordinarily struck out.

For the most part only boys played softball, but Polly Perriman played softball and other rough games as well as any boy ever could. For that matter, when the ill treated redheaded and freckle faced spitfire got in a fight with the toughest of the boys, she'd stand toe to toe, flailing away. No holds barred fighting at home with her brother Boone prepared Polly well for the rough and tumble of the schoolyard.

White Oak School

On extra cold or rainy days when we couldn't go outside at recess, some of the older boys drew big circles on the floor with chalk and played marbles, sometimes for keeps. When this happened, Fred and I made sure we didn't tell the folks, because they were dead set against gambling. The best marble players, Max and Jerry Burbridge and Bobby Lynn Wilkin, had their special taws they flipped with their cocked thumbs, beating the rest of us easily, even when we fudged. Someone occasionally brought a ball bearing, a steely, for his taw, but a steely was generally off limits because it often shattered ordinary clay and glass marbles. A few of the big boys sometimes brought wooden tops which they wound around and around with a tough string and then propelled with great force, spiking their opponents' tops with sharp metal spikes. But playing with these dangerous and destructive toys was usually forbidden.

Many boys carried nigger flippers fashioned out of a forked hickory stick, two strong red or black rubber bands cut from a discarded inner tube, and a smooth leather pouch cut from the tongue of an old pair of shoes, all put together with the strongest string we could find. Bobby Lynn Wilkin could hit almost anything with his powerful weapon, including squirrels and rabbits. At home we mostly used our nigger flippers to hurry the cows to the barn, but an occasional blue jay or chicken fell victim. We were required to keep our weapons holstered in our hip pockets at school, but the instant we stepped off the school ground we unwrapped the rubber bands and commenced firing away.

Every self-respecting boy who wasn't a sissy carried a pocketknife, and many school desks bore a boy's and his latest girlfriend's initials. Occasionally someone especially dexterous with a knife challenged another boy to play mumbly peg. Although most of us couldn't master this intricate game, it was fun to watch the loser try to pull the short peg out of the ground with his teeth, mumbling the dirty peg as he did so. Although virtually every schoolboy carried a pocketknife, most abided by the same rule Dad solemnly gave Fred, Jay, and me at home: "Don't you ever take that knife out of your pocket unless you aim to use it."

Shortly after the school term began at White Oak, the young teacher quit on short notice when it became apparent she wasn't up to corralling and instructing over sixty students in eight grades. Members of the school board talked Glen Nichols, a local farmer, into teaching while they looked for a replacement. Glen was likable, but he had little training or aptitude for teaching school.

He ordered sports equipment right away—some parents insisted the money was intended for library books—and many of us boys spent noon hours and extended recesses playing tackle football without benefit of protective equipment or supervision. I saw right away that the aggression I'd learned at home to protect myself against Fred stood me in good stead playing this new game. Instead of being reluctantly chosen, now I was the first to be picked on defense.

Billy Joe Hilton was always picked first on offense. The spoiled and sullen bully had never challenged me, but he had run over and intimidated many smaller and more timid kids for a long time. As he repeatedly insisted on carrying the ball, I slammed him down on the rocky playground so hard and so many times he became gunshy. I intentionally grabbed his khaki pants by the pockets while tackling him, often tearing them in the process. Unfortunately, Billy Joe's clothes weren't the only ones torn. Many thin chambray shirts and old overalls were ripped wide open, resulting in parents' complaints to the school board and a quick end to football. Glen was soon replaced by someone better suited for the job.

Howard Rinker was small, wiry, and young, perhaps in his mid twenties, but from day one he was the boss at White Oak. Few of us knew how hard he whipped misbehaving students with his big hickory sticks. Only the transgressors and Mr. Rinker knew for sure as he ran everyone else out of the building before he leaned the misbehaving youngsters over his desk and whipped them. From the sounds of the whacks, the desk may have absorbed most of the stick's sting. And girls weren't exempt. After someone locked Polly Perriman in the library and she took a dump in a corner before jumping out a high window, she received a hard whipping. The other kids who'd been whipped came outside red eyed and sniffling. But not Polly. "That didn't hurt," the dry eyed, gangly girl muttered as she walked out the door. After the three or four most flagrant violators in school received one or two whippings, that was the end of it. From then on everyone minded Mr. Rinker, resulting in more harmony and learning than we'd had in a long time.

Outside of school proper, I was inclined to be a little too handy with my fists. One night, when Bobby Lynn followed some of us outside at a pie supper, I stepped behind a tree and waited for his certain arrival. As he ran by, I stepped out and delivered a hard blow to his stomach, a blow that knocked the wind out of him and doubled him over, stopping his habit of tagging along.

Another time, on a Friday afternoon after books let out, but before we said so long, my favorite playmate Jimmy Hubbard and I were tensing our belly and chest muscles and daring each other to see who could inflict the most pain when Jimmy cried out and begged me to quit hitting him. Confused, since we'd played our rough hitting game many times, I quit, and he headed north humped over holding his belly as he made his way home. Monday morning I heard the bad news. Jimmy had died over the weekend with a ruptured appendix. I never told anyone what I'd done on Friday, but I felt bad about it for a long time. Maybe I'd killed him. If I did, I didn't aim to.

Guilt and grief settled over me at bedtime like a heavy blanket. With my face turned to the sloping upstairs wall, away from my sleeping brothers, I quietly wrestled with fierce, man sized questions—questions that turned into nightmares later in the night. Was Jimmy in hell? Had I sent him there? Would I go to hell because I sent him there? Would he be mad at me when I got there? I was subdued at school for some time after Jimmy died, and I tried harder than usual in all my subjects, with increasing success, especially in spelling and reading.

Many Friday afternoons we gladly put away our books for ciphering matches or spelling bees. I was better than average at ciphering, but no match at all for Max Burbridge or his cousin Jerry. When they went to the board to add, subtract, multiply, or divide, dust and chalk flew as they mowed down the opposition.

It was hard to be modest about being the top speller. Phyllis Lemaster sometimes gave me a run for my money, but not often. When one of the kids told Mama about my spelling achievements, she said it was nothing to be proud of: I'd simply inherited my ability to spell, along with my broad forehead, from Great Grandma Susan Holmes, the champion speller for many years around Gaylord in northern Kansas.

* * *

After a heavy frost in early November when I was in the seventh grade, some of us older boys spent much of our free recess time gathering huge mounds of freshly fallen oak leaves. After filling washed out places and natural draws in the schoolyard's uneven terrain with the crisp pungent leaves, we crossed over a fence into Chesty Earnhart's nearby brushy woods where we cut grapevines, buckbrush, and sassafras sprouts which we fashioned into closely knit covers for a hidey-hole. Most of our crude efforts resulted in little more than low tunnels, but we built an inner sanctum tall enough and big enough around to accommodate half a dozen of us as we sat upright facing toward the middle of our rough structure.

At first we thought we'd have a secret club with elected officials, but since we could never agree on who'd be top dog, we were glad to hear Ed Sumacher's suggestion: "This'd be a good place for a jackin' off contest. I'll bet any and all of you a quarter apiece I can come closer to fillin' a quart jar in a month's time than anybody here. Whatta ya say?"

All of us sitting in our enclosure were well into masturbating, of course, but only Ed and Houston had nerve enough to admit it. "Count me in, Ed," Houston said. "I'll be happy to take your money."

"What about you other chicken shits?" Ed asked, looking at the rest of us with contempt. "Ain't nobody else here got the balls to take me on?"

After a short silence, Ed turned to Houston. "This'll be simple. Me and you'll bring quart jars to school t'morrow mornin'. If it suits you, we'll whip off five times a day: right before books takes up in the mornin', at first recess, durin' noon hour, at second recess, and right after books let out before we head home."

"Sounds good," Houston said. "But how'll we make sure one of us don't slip back and cheat?"

120

"That's easy. We'll git somebody we can trust to be in charge of the jars at night and on weekends."

"Who'll that be?"

"I don't care. It's up to you."

"What about Boone Perriman? He lives close by. He's kinda young, but he's honest and tough enough to do the job."

"That'll work. Let's ask him."

"Okay. I bet he'll do it."

Although none of the rest of us was man enough to enter the uninhibited contest, we were invited to watch Ed and Houston. Anyone who's ever held a handful of jism can well imagine how the two boys collected their sticky, spurting seed into their cupped hands before carefully scraping it off into their open Atlas and Ball fruit jars.

Little if any difference could be seen in the slowly filling jars after the first week, causing surprise and concern among those of us who'd made nickel and dime side bets on Houston. Like most of the other onlookers, I figured that anyone who knew the pecker order around White Oak would have known that while Ed would have been unbeatable for everyone else, Houston would beat him, hands down.

But he didn't. As the second week wore on, imperceptibly at first, then gradually but clearly, Ed took the lead, and as the end of the contest approached, there was no doubt who'd win. Ed's pale green Atlas jar was filled well up into its sloping top, while Houston's clear Ball glass container with its ropy, ivory, tapioca look-alike contents fell a full inch lower.

* * *

Even though Houston got beat in the contest with Ed at White Oak, his stature steadily increased. While he'd been at least a head taller than most kids his own age for a long time, some of the shorter and more pugnacious boys had their bluff in on him. Bobby Lynn Wilkin, ordinarily not all that brave himself, had learned early on that he could whip Houston in a fist fight, even if he did have to jump off the ground in order to hit him in the jaw.

I never knew whether it was his dad's doing or not, but someone must have put a bug in Houston's ear and advised him to resort to rough tactics in order to put a stop to being picked on. Or maybe he thought of it himself. However the change came about, the next time Bobby Lynn started badgering the gentle six foot tall boy, instead of cowering and running away, Houston reached inside the bib of his overalls and unbuckled a leather belt from around his waist. He quickly wrapped the end of the belt a couple of times around his hand and began flailing away with all his might. The prospect of being badly injured by the flying, brass buckle caused Bobby to back off: "You're not fightin' fair," he screamed.

"That's right," Houston said. "You listen to me, Bobby Lynn Wilkins. Don't you ever mess with me again. You do an' I'll cut you to pieces with this here belt buckle." As Bobby Lynn slowly backed off, warily watching, Houston matter-of-factly threaded his belt inside his overalls.

The contest with the fruit jars that fall, soon followed by Houston's decision to protect himself with his hidden belt, marked the beginning of his gradual transformation from a skinny, scared mama's boy stripling into a broad shouldered, confident, fully seven foot tall cocksman, the most famous – and infamous – seducer of girls and women in the entire area.

Following the increasingly ballyhooed contest, word quickly spread that twelve year old Houston was hung like a young mule. While many of his friends and acquaintances were understandably reluctant about discussing how they measured up, Houston basked in his shiny new spotlight. Not that his improved status went to his head. He remained friendly and unassuming while his earlier whipped dog manner gradually disappeared.

TWELVE
SNAKEBIT

After Joyce and Wanda got brave enough to pass by the wild hogs' nest by themselves, they'd set off for school first. Because Dad always had early morning chores lined out for Fred and me, we were often late getting to school. One morning we were in a hurry, and he was ahead of me not far past the empty hog's nest, when he pulled up short and pointed to a jumble of Wanda and Joyce's things, including several loose pages of sheet music strewn alongside the path.

"What do you reckon happened?" Fred asked.

"I don't know," I replied. "I hope the wild hogs didn't get 'em."

"Let's look for tracks and blood," Fred said, and then yelled, "Oh no! Looky here!"

A few feet beyond the last of the scattered sheets of music lay the biggest copperhead we'd ever seen. After we'd killed it with a barrage of rocks and Fred held it up, the tip of its tail touched his chin and its smashed and bloody diamond shaped head reached the ground.

When we arrived at the school yard, our excited schoolmates told us that Wanda had been bitten by a copperhead, and Everett Ray had taken her to a doctor. "That musta been the same copperhead me and Wayne killed on the trail," Fred bragged. "It was as big around as my arm and as long as a bull whip."

After we got home from school, Mama let us go into the downstairs bedroom where Wanda, pale and listless, lay propped up with pillows in the folks' bed wearing her loose flannel nightgown instead of the pretty yellow school dress with tiny blue flowers and matching bloomers Mama had made for her out of feed sacks. Wanda's leg was swollen in such a strut Mama had to cut the new bloomers up the side in order to get them off.

"We knew the words of most of the songs we was singin' by heart," Joyce began, as she told us what happened, "but we was practicin' a new song and when we took our eyes off the path, Wanda stepped on a snake and it bit her and we started runnin'."

Wanda roused enough to correct her. "You started screamin' and cryin' and runnin' and I follered you," she said.

"That's right. I was scared," Joyce admitted, " and we run all the way to the Huse Place. Miz Huse soaked Wanda's leg in coal oil while I run on to Buck and Coleen Earnhardts'. When I asked Buck if he'd take Wanda to the doctor, he said he'd like to, but he was down in his back and maybe Everett Ray would take us."

"Was Everett still home?" Fred asked.

"Yes, and he took us to Dr. Kelsay's, Grandma Holmes' doctor, in north town."

"What did the doctor do?"

"He cut an X on the outside of both red places where the snake bit her, and then he pressed some kind of suction cup on her leg and tried to draw out the poison."

"Was the poison green?" Fred asked.

"I didn't see any poison," she said. "After the doctor couldn't suck out anything but blood, he cussed great big and said it was too late and there wasn't anything he could do for her."

"Wasn't you scared?"

Joyce and Wanda

"I sure was. When I asked him if we ought to go get the Old Lady Friend and her madstone to draw out the poison, he got madder than ever. He cussed again and said there wasn't anything to a madstone, and that people who believed in it was fools. He said Wanda's leg would swell up real big, and she would get mighty sick, but he'd never heard of anyone dyin' from a copperhead bite. 'Take her back home,' he told Everett, 'and tell her folks to take care of her the best they know how.'"

"When I asked the doctor how much we owed him, he just stared at me," Joyce said, "and then he said it wouldn't hurt to soak her foot in coal oil several times a day until the swellin' goes down."

Wanda was bedfast most of that winter, longer than Dad had been the year before, and although she finally felt well enough to be up part of the time, Dad and Mama agreed that she should stay home the rest of the school year. By the time she had recovered enough to want someone to play with, Jay and Lottie Jean were used to playing together, Joyce and I were paired up, and Fred's habit of teasing and tormenting everyone he was around left the skinny nine year old out in the cold. Once when she com-

125

plained to Mama that none of us would have anything to do with her, Mama replied, "That's right, they won't. And I don't blame them. We've all petted you, and you're spoiled."

As she gained strength that spring, Wanda played with newly hatched chicks in the brooder house and new born kittens in the sheds and barn. After latching on to one particular gray kitten, she carried it around everywhere she went, stroking and caressing it as if it were a doll or a baby until it languished and died.

Despite Dad's repeated warnings to all of us against going anywhere near an old sow or boar, Wanda sometimes slipped out into the woods west of the barn where she liked to sidle up close to a sow nursing her pigs and rub her back, side, and belly with a corncob while the sow lay still, grunting with pleasure. One time when she was rubbing the contented sow, she gave in to her impulse to pick up one of the sucking pigs, the little pig squealed, and the sow chased her through the woods toward the barn lot where I stood. I thought Wanda was a goner when the woof-woof-woofing sow snapping her huge jaws threatened to overtake her, but instead of slowing down, Wanda dropped the squealing pig in midstride and sailed over the tall wooden gate sideways like a seasoned high jumper.

"Are you hurt?" I asked her, as she lay still on the ground.

"I don't think so," she whispered, "but I got the breath knocked out of me. Don't tell Dad. He'll whip me if he finds out what I've been doin'."

"I won't tell," I said.

Wanda's bad luck continued in the spring when she went to bed with a high fever and severe stomachache that Mama's double dose of castor oil and Epsom Salts only made worse. After Wanda's bowels finally stopped moving, Mama dropped to her knees at the side of the bed and prayed hard while Dad hitched Old Bird to the buggy and drove three miles to Madry where he bought a twenty-five pound block of ice. Mama had just finished promising Jesus she'd start going to church again if He'd heal Wanda, when we heard the sound of ice breaking as Dad pounded a tow sack with the flat side of his ax.

"How's she feelin'?" he asked Mama when he came inside with the ice.

"I've been prayin', but I don't think she's any better," Mama said. "I'm afraid the Lord's gonna take her to teach us a lesson."

"Teach us a lesson my hindend!" Dad yelled, glaring at her. "Get off your knees and start doin' somethin'!"

"Fred," he said, "go get a fresh bucket of water and bring in the tub. Run!"

"Joyce, build up the fire in the cookstove and make sure the teakettle's full."

"And Geneva, you take off Wanda's clothes and be ready to hold her in the tub. If cold water and ice don't bring her relief, we'll switch to hot water. And if neither one works, I'll ride to town and get the doctor. I don't have any money, but I bet he'll come when I tell him I'll sell a cow if I have to."

As strange as it was to see Dad take charge in the house, what was more remarkable was how the strong prohibitions against seeing anyone naked were forgotten as Mama undressed Wanda in front of us all. Is that all there is to it? I wondered, as I looked at her. Her flat little titties were no more interesting than my own, and her smooth slit and narrow butt were equally disappointing. While all the rest of us kids watched from the back of the room, Dad helped Mama hold Wanda in the icy water until she shook uncontrollably and cried harder, prompting them to take her out of the tub and dry her off before placing hot towels on her tender belly. The hot towels calmed her and, to everyone's surprise and relief, she soon closed her eyes and slept.

When Mama murmured "Thank you, Jesus, thank you," Dad scowled, then turned and motioned Fred and Jay and me outside with a quick jerk of his head. We did our nightly chores by lantern light.

Wanda's temperature was near normal by morning, and she told Mama her belly felt better. Nothing more was said about Dad going for the doctor.

* * *

Not long after Wanda's sick spell, Fred and I were awakened in the middle of the night by sounds of Jay sobbing. "What's the matter?" Fred asked him.

"I've got a terrible toothache," he said. "Go get Mama."

Mama, already awake, soon climbed the stairs carrying a lamp. "What are you cryin' about?" she asked him.

"My tooth hurts real bad," he said, "and I can't go to sleep."

"Your jaw's swollen," Mama said. "Maybe somethin' hot will help. I'll be back in a minute." When she returned, she carried one of the sad irons she kept on the back of the cookstove. "Here, try this," she said. "Hold on to the handle and try not to untie the dish rag so you won't burn yourself."

"Okay," Jay said, but the heat against his jaw failed to lessen his pain, and he started crying again. Jay's moans and Mama's impassioned prayers rose and fell after she dropped to her knees, raised her shaking outspread hands in the air, looked upward, and first demanded then begged for help. "Oh Lord, heal this boy," she pleaded in the quavering voice she reserved for the worst situations. "Strike down right now, Lord. Take away this child's pain. You can do it, Lord. I know you can do it. Not my will but thine be done. In Jesus' name." A sudden hubbub outside in the nearby hen house momentarily broke Mama's concentration, and when she resumed praying, Jay's cries and her words were joined and overridden by prolonged cackling and squawking sounds much louder than the isolated noises a doomed hen made before being killed and eaten by a marauding possum or skunk. After the outside noises stopped, the back door banged, and Mama stood up and called down through the vent at the foot of the bed, "Is that you, Clay?"

"Yeah, why?"

"What was all that racket out in the hen house?"

"That was me stuffin' old hens in tow sacks."

"What for?"

"I'm takin' that boy to the dentist as soon as it comes daylight," he said. "I can surely get enough money out of a dozen hens to pay for havin' a tooth pulled."

Jay was dressed and ready to go when Mama shook me. "Your dad wants you to go along to keep Jay company," she said. "I'll help Fred with the chores." She handed Jay and me a biscuit and sausage and bundled us up in a heavy wool comforter on a tomato crate in the back of the wagon before we headed for town. I ate my sandwich fast, while it was still good and hot, before Jay started in on his. "You better eat that before it gets cold," I said.

"I can't eat it. Here, you go ahead," he said, and handed it to me.

Dad drove the team at a fast walk, their usual pace on the road, and the sun was high by the time we pulled up at the hitching rack in back of the Farmers' Exchange. "I'll be back as soon as I can sell these old hens," he said. When he returned, he reached in the wagon and lifted Jay down. "We'll leave the horses tied here." I had a hard time keeping up with Dad as he carried Jay a short block and a half down main street and climbed the stairs at the dentist's office.

"What's the problem?" a kind looking man in a white coat asked as he beckoned us into the empty waiting room.

"This boy," Dad said, pointing at Jay, "needs to have a jaw tooth pulled."

"Jump up here in this big chair so I can take a look," the friendly dentist with a heavy southern accent said. "Now just relax and open your mouth wide. I promise I won't hu'tcha. It's gonna have to come out, all right," he said after examining the tooth. "You'll feel a little pin prick, but that's all. Remember, I won't hu'tcha."

Although Jay flinched, he didn't cry when Dr. Larson stuck a needle in his gum, but he bugged out his eyes when the dentist pulled a shiny, long handled pair of stout pliers out of a drawer. "Let me make sure you can't feel anything," he said, as he tested Jay's gum with his thumbnail.

"Hold him tight," he told Dad, and he grasped the pliers in both hands and pried and twisted until a sharp pop followed by a grating sound signaled his success. Jay didn't cry out loud, but tears were running down his cheeks when the ordeal ended and the dentist handed him the bloody tooth. "Here you go, son," he said. "Put this under your pillow tonight, and when you wake up in the mornin' the tooth fairy will have left you a dime." When Jay mumbled a reply, the dentist turned to me, "What'd he say?"

"He said tooth fairies don't come to our house."

Jay with all his teeth

"Oh. Well, let me tell you boys about somethin' even better than a tooth fairy. If you won't stick your tongue in the hole where an old tooth's been, the new tooth will grow in solid gold. "

"A gold tooth would be worth a lot of money, wouldn't it?" I asked.

"Speakin' of money," Dad said, butting in, "how much do we owe you, Doc?"

"Is a dollar too much?"

"We can afford that," Dad said, and he counted out a dollar in change from the hen money and placed it on top of a fancy cabinet by the door.

It would be a long time before I had any idea how much pain Jay suffered after having his tooth pulled. "When it broke loose it felt like a bomb explodin' in my mouth," he told me. "And ever' time I put my tongue in the hole, somethin' sharp stuck me."

"What was it?"

"It was a piece of tooth Dr. Larson missed."

"Why didn't you tell the folks?"

"I was scared they'd take me back and the dentist would hurt me again."

"How long did you put up with it?"

"I'm not sure," he said, "but a long time. A year and half, maybe two years later, after we'd moved to our second place in Wichita, I was workin' the piece back and forth with my tongue and somehow it worked loose."

"What'd you do with it?"

"I did what I'd made up my mind to do a long time before. I hunted on the slope west of the house until I found a flat rock; then I took Dad's ballpeen hammer out of his toolbox, and I put the piece of tooth on the rock and I smashed it to smithereens."

THIRTEEN
WAR AND WICHITA

As the war continued the folks talked more and more about setting a date for our farm sale. We'd move to Wichita where, according to neighbors who took the local paper, both men and women could find high paying jobs in airplane factories.

In the fall talk turned into action. Dad bought a gallon of bright reddish orange paint which he daubed on his rusty old tools and the metal parts of his machinery. The slow drying paint was still tacky the morning of the sale, as Chesty Earnhart pointed out, and the tools and equipment went for a song. But the two well broke teams brought good prices, especially Old Dick and Dock, the young dappled, iron gray matched geldings out of Oral Hilton's Percheron stud horse and the best working mare we ever owned, Old Bess. It hurt to watch the horses sell. I also hated to see Old Tuffy go, but Bob Reavis got him with the high bid of ten dollars, a fair price. Anyway, I felt confident the seven Reavis boys would hunt Old Tuffy and give him a good home.

The ten or twelve cows also brought good prices when Otho Black, our milk hauler, bid up and bought most of them. Otho knew how well the Jersey-Guernsey crosses produced, while keeping up their butterfat for the cheese plant in Nixa. The cowbell went with Old Jo, leader and boss of the herd. We knew she'd have been unhappy without it.

The sale brought right at seventeen hundred dollars. That's also close to the figure Jay remembers Everett Ray said he wanted for his sixty acre farm west of White Oak. The folks discussed buying Everett's place – Dad said they could pay cash – but they decided it would be better if the entire family moved to Wichita. A farm of our own in Missouri would have to wait.

All of us kids were opposed to leaving the Brechbuhler Place – I wondered why Dad didn't buy it – but as the time to leave grew near we speculated at length about what living in a big city would be like. We knew we'd be living in a new suburb, Planeview, in barracks like housing built to accommodate an influx of workers attracted to Wichita's airplane industry.

Our house would not only be new; it would be like everyone else's house. The houses, units as they were called in the brochures we read, were heated with coal which was furnished free in big bins on the street. Maybe it wasn't totally free, but the coal was included in the thirty dollars a month rent. We wondered if everything might be furnished in the new house, including dishes and silverware. We thought when we arrived we might simply throw away our backless chairs and other shabby belongings. Maybe there'd be poor people in Wichita who'd need our cast-off plunder.

Fred, who had been cutting sprouts for Efton and Carrie Robbins after graduating from the eighth grade at White Oak, went ahead on the train with Dad. They stayed with Dad's folks while looking for work. Before leaving, Dad made arrangements with Martin, his youngest brother, who was living on Grandpa and Grandma's place on Honey Creek with a farm deferment. Martin would haul the rest of us, with our belongings, in a one ton truck Dad rented from Buck Reavis.

It was a cold, late November evening before we got under way. Martin and Mama rode in front with Lottie Jean in the middle. The four of us in the back hollowed out soft places where we huddled under thin covers. Martin filled up with gas east of Aurora at a station across from the Cockatoo, the infamous roadhouse we'd all heard stories about. Mama's flashing eyes zeroing in on sinful couples outside the Cockatoo showed her fears that we were on the road to hell. I didn't care if we were. I was sick and tired of my drab life on the farm.

A couple of hours after we left Aurora, a loud bang and a lurch announced a blowout in the truck's right front tire. Martin located a jack under the front seat, but no spare could be found, so we settled in for a long, cold wait until morning. A false dawn, a dim light in the east early in the morning, was our first sign of hope as the five of us kids sat around the bonfire by the edge of the highway while Martin and Mama slept as far away as possible from one another in opposite corners on the truck's cramped seat. An early passing motorist offered Martin and Mama a ride to Lamar, where Mama's loud nervous words of desperation persuaded a filling station owner to not only sell her a new tire, but mount and deliver it as well.

It was nearly noon before we reached Nevada and highway 54, which we would follow west into Wichita. There, in our first eating out experience, Mama treated us to a late breakfast of thick pancakes slathered with butter and syrup. "Where's the milk?" Wanda timidly inquired.

"Milk costs extry," Mama said. "Wash your pancakes down with water." But upon seeing our reactions to the foul smelling alkaki water, she relented and ordered five small glasses of milk. She drank no milk herself, but then Mama was already getting in the habit of drinking nothing more than an occasional glass of warm water with her meals. Martin ordered coffee, but after doctoring it with lots of cream and sugar, he still couldn't drink it. The water was that bad.

134

Before we settled in for the long stretch toward the Flint Hills, Martin swung through downtown Nevada. From my perch high in the back of the truck, I saw on the sidewalk below something I'd heard about but never before seen. "Looky, looky," I hissed to the other kids. While we stared, open-mouthed, a dark complected young man coolly looked us over before casually walking away. At a roadside rest stop in Kansas, I asked Mama if she'd seen what we saw in Nevada.

"Yes, I did," Mama said, pulling her mouth down at the corners. "And you'll see worse sights. Why, out here in Kansas nigras and white people go to school side by side."

Farther west, I was intrigued with the far away lonesome look of the sparsely settled Flint Hills, but the hills all too soon flattened into monotonous checkerboard squares outlined with closely set hedge trees meant to soften the landscape and provide windbreaks and fencing for livestock.

Martin drove straight to Planeview. And he found McFarland Street even though there was fresh snow and no landmarks to go by. While he eased the truck between two bulging coal bins, the four of us in the back jumped out and ran to an open door where Dad and Fred stood waiting. When we dashed into the small kitchen, we saw a sink and cabinet, a four burner gas cookstove, and an icebox, all new and gleaming white. A narrow door led to a closet filled with a water heater and furnace. The good sized living room beyond was bare except for the stairs.

The bathroom was located at the head of the stairway. We'd never had running water or electricity before, so we were ignorant of certain amenities. "How much toilet paper should we use at one time?" Joyce asked.

"Three squares should do it," Mama said, "Unless you have the runs."

"How much water can each one of us have on Saturday nights?"

"Not too much. Two or three inches. Save enough for the rest of us."

135

We were disappointed to see that the three upstairs bedrooms were empty, but after we'd set up our three chipped and rusty iron bedsteads with their familiar wool comforters, the rooms looked more like home. The kitchen table looked all right, even with our odd looking wooden box which served as a bench. But the backless chairs and the bare wooden floor were an embarrassment. Since we didn't have a stick of furniture for the living room, Joyce and I decided when someone came to the front door we'd pretend the empty room was our oversized entry to the kitchen. Although we admired the furnace in its tiny cubicle, we soon realized that not having a warm stove to gather around in the kitchen was a big drawback. Oh, well. From the outside our place looked just fine.

While Jay and I were busy carrying tomato crates filled with jars of canned vegetables, fruit, and potatoes, I saw a kid about my age hanging around. "Howdy," he finally said. "I see you got a Missouri license. Whereabouts in Missouri are you'uns from?"

"Osie, west of Crane. Where are you from?"

"We're from Missouri too, out in the country, not far from Avie."

"Well, pleased to meetcha. My name's Wayne."

"Dewey's my name."

I could tell Dewey was ignorant the minute he opened his mouth. He not only said you'uns for you all; he said hain't for ain't, hit for it, yander for yonder, years for ears, and many more country words as well. His folks must have forgotten to tell him he'd be laughed at in a big city such as Wichita for talking like a hick. But he was friendly and, although he'd been in Planeview only a few days, he seemed to know the ropes.

After Jay and I had finished carrying all the rest of our odds and ends into the house, Mama told me to ask someone the way to the store while she made a list. Dewey would know. I knocked on his door in the adjoining unit and asked his mother if he could show us to the grocery store.

"Sure," she said, "Just as long as he don't git into no trouble."

When Dewey and I went back to get Jay, Mama handed me money and a list. The last item surprised me. "Why coffee?" I asked.

"We've decided we can afford coffee, now that your Dad has a good paying job. Now go on."

We had fun pulling the little wagon on the sidewalk. When we stepped off the sidewalk to make way for people coming and going, no bumpy rocks slowed us down. Downtown in a cluster of buildings Dewey showed us a doctor's office, a Walgreen's drugstore, a cleaners, a wickedly inviting picture show and bowling alley, a barbershop with six chairs and, down an incline, a grocery store as big as a barn.

"Gittin' here didn't take long." Dewey said. "You wanta see where me and you'll be goin' to school?"

"If it's not too far."

"Here, it's thisaway," he gestured. In a few minutes he pointed out a long wooden building. "There it is. Some school, huh?"

"Yeah, it's big all right."

While we admired the building, three boys drifted by. "How about a snowball fight?" one asked us.

"Whatta ya think?" Dewey whispered. "Can we take 'em?"

Remembering all the fun we'd had in snowball fights back home, I said, "Sure, why not?" and the battle was on. Dewey, Jay and I had good throwing arms, and we soon had the other boys on the run.

About the time it was clear we'd won, three more boys, boys our opponents seemed to know, rounded the corner of the schoolhouse. "We need help!" one of the first group yelled.

In an instant, just as I saw that the new boys weren't the ordinary run of the mill boys I expected, Dewey yelled out a slur we'd all used freely back home. As he started to repeat the short rhyming jingle, he'd barely got "Two on one's nigger fun," out of his mouth when our original opponents took off and the newcomers quickly brandished open bladed knives which they used to motion us against the schoolhouse wall. There, while two of them held their menacing weapons against Jay and me, the third heavy set boy methodically and brutally beat Dewey's pale face to a bleeding pulp.

"That's enough," the tallest boy finally announced.

"But I'm not done with him."

"That's enough, I said." The beating stopped and the knives disappeared.

"Where are you guys from?" the tall spokesman asked Dewey.

Leaking blood, snot, and tears, Dewey was in no condition to respond.

"We're from Missouri," I meekly replied.

"Oh. We might've known. Hillbillies," he said, and they turned and left us standing in the bloody, trampled snow.

"I better git home." Dewey said. Jay and I retrieved our little red wagon from a snowbank and hurried to the store.

* * *

I missed Missouri. I missed the isolation of the Brechbuhler Place, the routine of farm chores, and the sounds and smells of the animals. I even missed hearing the raucous cries of our half wild guineas. And most of all, I missed the musical sounds of hounds running a fox around and around in the dark as I drifted off to sleep. At first I was awed by the sights and sounds of town, especially when the huge B-17's came in low for a landing at Boeing a mile away. But soon even the loudest planes were no more than a momentary distraction.

Despite all my fantasies about sinning in Wichita, my opportunities failed to materialize the way I'd imagined they would. With no allowance, I had to depend upon infrequent odd jobs such as shoveling coal and snow because much of the sinning I aspired to wasn't free. Mama warned me to stay away from such degenerate places as pool halls, bowling alleys, and picture shows, but because I'd made a pact with myself to sin until I was sixteen, I felt free to disregard her warnings.

After learning that one of the living units nearby was being renovated for use as a teen town, Mama was upset when I said I planned on hanging out there. She allowed that one of the planned activities, Ping-Pong, might only be idle mischief; but she was sure dancing to a juke box was every bit as sinful as dancing to a fiddle. I tried Ping-Pong, but my coordination was so poor I never won. When I finally succumbed to one girl's urging and stumbled out on the dance floor, I quickly realized I had no aptitude for dancing. Worse, the instant I held her in my arms I became all hot and worked up, as the girl could feel and everyone watching could plainly see. Mama was right about dancing.

When I had money in my pocket, I sometimes slipped off alone to the picture show on Saturday afternoon. Once, a young woman sitting next to me in the dark lightly but deliberately touched me. Sensing I was immediately receptive, she slowly and adroitly had her way with me while I sat as still as possible in the dim room. Afterward, ignorant of the young woman's needs, I rushed to a stall in the restroom to clean up, then hurried outside and headed for the creek where I stayed until the incriminating stain had mostly disappeared before I went home. Later, after hearing Mama's dire warnings about loose women, it occurred to me that maybe I'd been molested at the show. But someone that tender couldn't have been bad. Regrettably, as much as I longed for a repeat of the episode, I never saw or felt the young woman again.

Meanwhile things gradually picked up at church. Back in Missouri the number of churchgoers had been small, enabling a parent with a glaring eye to shape up a restless kid in a hurry, but in the big church in Wichita a youngster could often escape a parent's surveillance. With help from an older acquaintance, I soon learned to sneak out between Sunday school and church and go to a nearby drugstore where we avidly read comic books and pocketed candy bars while the busy druggist waited

139

on paying customers. By keeping our eyes peeled, we were able to make it back to the church steps just ahead of the dismissed congregation. On Sunday nights the drugstore was closed, and because there was only one church service, I was stuck for at least an hour with the same old hymns and sermons I'd heard many times before. While I read and listened to the words of the hymns, and sometimes joined in, I wondered why there was such a discrepancy between the hymns of joy and their sad sounding tunes.

* * *

The preachers in Wichita were slicker than those I'd heard in Missouri. Itinerant strangers brought in for revivals often related riveting stories of their earlier sin filled days. The scarier and more vivid his story, the better the preacher. When the story of Cain and Abel came up in Sunday school, I got crossways with the teacher: she couldn't explain why Cain's offering wasn't as satisfactory as Abel's. I decided Abel was the Heavenly Father's favorite; He understandably preferred the cowboy to the farmer.

At the Fitinella C... in Planeview

A GROUP OF TEEN-AGERS gathers around the bar of the new club which was set up by the high school students themselves as their own solution to the present-day problem of finding wholesome entertainment and recreation. Here they pause for a soft drink or sandwich between

The Wicked Fifinella Club
Wayne Holmes (top row 4th from right)

Why, I silently wondered, given Mama and Grandma's faith and fervor, did their goiters keep growing instead of disappearing after they'd been prayed for and rubbed at healing services? I also couldn't understand what was going on when a young man who

140

regularly walked with crutches threw the crutches down and smilingly walked up the aisle, wobbly but unassisted, after his healing at a revival, but then a week later looked downcast and ashamed as he hobbled about on his crutches again.

Also baffling was one revivalist's impassioned statement that Jesus was returning soon, and the preacher was certain that he, like Elijah of old, would cheat death and be lifted into heaven where he'd join the Lord. As I tried to envision the miracle, I thought it would take a mighty strong wind, maybe a tornado, to lift and carry the heavy set old preacher that far. Such were my troubled thoughts, but I kept quiet. Had I spoken up, I almost certainly would have been branded an infidel, then shunned both at church and at home.

Several of us in the neighborhood, including John Benn, Warren Benn, Keith Garland and I, skipped school as often as once a week. We'd take a bus downtown to Douglas and Main where we'd play pool. Under the watchful eye of the proprie-

In a house like everybody else's

tor, we basked in the sinful atmosphere of the big, smoke-filled room. John and I weren't smoking yet, but the others copied Humphrey Bogart's studied nonchalance while calculating their careful shots. After playing pool for two or three hours, we'd head a couple of blocks southeast to a small Mexican eating place we'd discovered. For a quarter, each of us bought two big chili dogs and a twelve ounce bottle of Pepsi. The wonderfully piquant smells and tastes of the jacked up food, the mystifying sounds of the owners' rapid fire speech, and the mixed pride and fear in their eyes as they pointed out the three service flags in their bay window, along with pictures of their handsome sons underneath: All this added to the mystique of our exotic, forbidden hideaway.

After lunch we'd saunter back to Douglas and head east where we'd check out what was playing at the two cheap picture shows. For a dime at one place and twelve cents at the other, we had a tough choice. When we were short on money we chose the cheaper one, even though we could hear, see, and sometimes feel rats as they scurried about. But we generally opted for the more expensive show, without the rats, where we could count on seeing the enigmatic Charlie Chan. By the time the show was over and we'd ridden the bus home to Planeview, it was roughly time for school to be out, not that our parents paid much attention to what we were doing.

If my folks had known what I was up to they would have insisted that I quit school altogether and get a job the same way Fred and Joyce had done after they'd finished the eighth grade. Although I hadn't finished the eighth grade yet, the folks would have assumed I could read and figure well enough to get by on.

* * *

After the weather moderated in February, instead of going downtown, my friends and I sometimes walked south along the Arkansas River. One balmy afternoon we stripped off and swam in a sand pit next to the river. It was invigorating and fun, but shortly afterward I came down with a high fever. The folks weren't alarmed at first, but when the fever persisted, they bundled me up and took me on the bus downtown to Wesley Hospital where, after tests, the doctor admitted me for rheumatic fever. At first I was weak and indifferent, but when I began to recuperate I greatly enjoyed being petted and made over by the nurses. During visiting hours I wondered why the folks didn't come see me the way other patients' folks did, but I knew it was a long trip on the bus. When Mama finally came to take me home, my favorite nurse whispered to me when we said goodbye that she was glad I wasn't an orphan, after all.

For the remainder of the school year, I went by the nurse's station every Monday morning where the nurse took my temperature and then sent me home until the following Monday. Slowly walking home in my malaise, I'd detour by the public library where I'd pick out five books—all I was allowed—and then return home for bed rest, following the nurse's instructions. There in bed, alone with my Zane Grey and Jack London books, I'd read and sleep. Best of all, on Sunday mornings when everybody else had to go to church, I got to stay in bed and read.

But Dad didn't like it. On the infrequent occasions when he looked in on me, he was out of sorts, red faced and frowning. One time he threw a conniption fit when he discovered I was reading my five books simultaneously. He was certain I couldn't keep the various story lines straight.

After he'd finished chastising me, he went on to say that, whatever I did, I should never read the end of a book before coming to it in its natural sequence. "If you ever do that, and I catch you at it, I'll whip you," he growled. I couldn't imagine what made him think I was so lacking in character that I would even think of doing such a dishonorable thing.

About the time the school year was over my chronic low grade temperature ended, and I was able to be up and about. Naturally, I had to start attending Sunday school and church again. That was bad enough, but then Mama enrolled me, along with the three youngest kids, in vacation Bible school. The Bible school teacher might have put up with my deliberately disruptive nit-picking questions, but after I'd chased and caught some of the squealing and laughing bigger girls behind the drapes, the alarmed woman told me I was no longer welcome at vacation Bible school. When Wanda told Mama about the incident that evening, I expected her to whip me, but she didn't. Instead, she insisted that Dad go to the pay phone a block away and call his brother Martin in Missouri to see if he had summer work for me on the farm. When Dad returned, he said Martin had plenty of work, but he couldn't afford to pay me more than five dollars a week.

"That's not much," Mama said, "but maybe he'll stay out of trouble on the farm. Let's call Martin back and tell him we'll have him on the train as soon as we can."

FOURTEEN

HONEY CREEK

Martin was considerably smaller than his dad or his two brothers and he looked and acted as if he'd been rooted out long before by his two sisters as well as his brothers. Even his nickname, Nit, was belittling. But I liked Martin. When we were cultivating corn—I drove while he plowed—he never yelled at me when the big, black Percheron horses stepped on the corn stalks with their oversized hooves as we turned around at the ends of the rows. Martin, like Dad before him, didn't have wire muzzles which would have kept the horses from snatching tops out of the corn stalks, but at least he had checkreins on the bridles which helped keep the horses' heads up. But the most important difference between the men was that, unlike Dad, Martin smiled and laughed while we worked. No doubt he was sometimes annoyed, but he never once yelled or threatened to whip me.

Martin's wife, Ernestine, was serious, solemn even, and she was polite. Instead of the bossy adult commands I was used to:

145

"Go get the hammer! Now run!" she prefaced her soft-spoken requests with "Would you mind?" or "Would you please...?" causing me to respond with ready good will to tasks I ordinarily despised. The youngest of four daughters, and her parents' favorite, Ernestine had taken music lessons for many years and had become an accomplished pianist. Now married and with two young children, the frustrated prodigy longed to be at her solicitous mother's side. After church on Sundays, she and the kids regularly ate dinner with her folks, then stayed all afternoon and went to church again before returning to Honey Creek. Martin didn't mind because he disliked attending church. When Ernestine succeeded in talking him into going to church with her, it was understood that I would go too. But when he balked, I got to stay with him. It was almost worth attending church services just to hear Ernestine play the piano. Instead of the inept playing I was used to, her highly skilled performance made me tremble with envy and excitement as her long white fingers flew effortlessly over the keys, bringing passionate life to the old hymns.

To my delight, Martin often made taunting remarks aimed at Christianity in general, and fundamentalists in particular. I never tired of hearing him retell an account of a testimonial service in northern Kansas when a member of the congregation had stood and related how, on the previous Sunday night while driving his family home after church in a wagon, a threatening bank of thunderheads had formed in the southwest. "Lord God Almighty," the man had prayed, "If it's thy will, spare me and mine from this storm." In the words of the staunch believer, "The storm clouds slowed, and the rain fell in the back of our wagon all the way home."

"How about that?" Martin laughed. "Wasn't that amazing?"

Never content until he'd poked fun at Ernestine's Holy Roller church, Martin's next question seemed directed at me, but it was for her benefit. "What do you suppose is goin' on between Brother Baker and his sissy songleader?" he'd ask. I'd noticed that the stout preacher preferred his prissy young assistant's company to that of his heavily corseted wife, but until Martin asked his leering question, I'd thought little about it.

"Martin," Ernestine warned, "That's enough. Just shut up."

Martin winked at me, suggesting I knew what he was getting at, but although I could tell it must have been something vile, for the life of me I couldn't decide what. Of course, I couldn't admit I didn't understand, so I simply smiled and wondered.

When Ernestine's cousin, Hilda, perhaps twenty years old, whose husband was in the army, came for an indefinite stay with two toddlers in tow, I noticed that Hilda and Martin's easy banter made Ernestine nervous. Not only that. When Hilda and I were in close quarters she'd often look straight at me in a way that made me blush and squirm.

One night when I had to get up and take a leak, as I passed the open bedroom door where Hilda slept, I saw that she was awake. On my return I stopped when I heard her low "Psst. Come get in bed with me. Everyone's asleep. Come on. There's plenty of room." Instantly excited, I ached to join her, but the sight of the babies at her side quickly dampened my ardor. Wordless, I scurried to my room where I finally slept.

Neither of us let on the next morning, but it was hard for me to meet Hilda's bold gaze, and I was relieved when she and the kids left shortly afterward. Still, my feelings of cowardice and frustration lingered for the rest of the summer. Many a time I lay stiff as a board on my cot berating myself for not taking advantage of that middle of the night opportunity. While I couldn't understand what was going on between the preacher and his song leader, I could well imagine what might have transpired between a woman and a young man—if only that young man had had more backbone.

Mama and I ordinarily exchanged weekly one page letters, but one week, just two days after I'd received her routine letter, I received a second one with the bad news that Lottie Jean was in Wesley Hospital in Wichita with polio. That news was sobering and bad enough, but Mama went on to make the most disturbing request I could imagine. She wrote that she wanted me to pray for Lottie Jean's recovery. Knowing as she did that I had never been saved, I wondered how she had the nerve to ask me to commit such blasphemy. Although she didn't go so far as to say that my prayer should be exactly the same as hers, I could tell that's what she wanted. "My prayer," she wrote, "is that Lottie Jean will recover completely, or die." When I read that last line, I thought of Mama's response back on the Snuffer

Lottie Jean

Place after I'd showed her my two headed chicken: "Mothers know what to do when somethin's wrong with their babies." Despite Ernestine's pleas, I refused to answer Mama's outrageous letter. Instead, I made a wish that Lottie Jean would totally recover, but with no mention of hoping she'd die if her recovery wasn't complete. I wondered why Mama couldn't remember that one of our best mares had limped every step she took. She'd been blemished, no doubt about that, but she was still a good mare.

* * *

After Martin and I had filled the barn with timothy and lespedeza hay and we'd cultivated the corn twice, he decided to go to wheat harvest in western Kansas. He wanted me to help Ernestine milk the dozen or so fresh cows while he was gone, and if I thought I could handle it by myself, cultivate the corn one last time before laying it by.

As it turned out, Ernestine was deathly afraid of staying overnight on the farm at Honey Creek without Martin, and she and the kids spent most nights two miles away with her folks. She was reluctant for me to stay alone at night by myself, but after I convincingly lied that I wasn't afraid, she kept me supplied with food so I didn't have to totally batch it. Sometimes Ernestine helped with the milking at night, sometimes not, but I didn't mind milking. When everything went right I'd finish the actual milking in about an hour and a half. Of course there was the extra time spent going after the cows, but with Old Shep's help, that was fun. Additional easy chores included pumping fresh water into the half barrels before stirring and cooling the warm milk, and securing wet tow sacks around the milk cans to cool the milk so it didn't turn blinky overnight.

Although I had most of my growth at five foot eight that summer I was thirteen, the mismatched Percheron geldings were hard to harness. The taller one, Old Tom, easily sixteen hands, had been half the team Pap and Lottie, along with Martin and Xerpha and Vincel and their baby Ben had ridden behind when they journeyed to Missouri in the spring of 1933, at the same time we travelled to western Oklahoma in two wagons before coming to Missouri. Unlike Dad, who'd shod his two teams before heading out, Pap didn't shoe his horses. After travelling the sharp gravelly roads north of Joplin, his two horses went lame, and Pap had to hire a truck to transport everything to Barry County where Grandma had lived as a girl.

Martin had warned me that Old Prince sometimes ran away and that Old Tom, old and gentle as he was, might run too. If they start running, Martin said, I should sink the cultivator shovels as deep as I could into the loamy bottom soil, then keep pressing down until the winded horses stopped. Sure enough, while cultivating corn one morning, the prancing shorter horse suddenly lunged, Old Tom quickly followed, and we careened wildly across the cornfield knocking down and plowing up the half grown winter feed for fifty or more yards before the panting horses stopped.

When I told Ernestine about the exciting episode at noon, she told me to unharness the horses and turn them out. Martin could cultivate the corn when he came back if he wished, but she wasn't about to send me back to the field where I might be killed by a runaway team. I felt guilty about giving up on cultivating the remaining corn, but Ernestine was the boss while Martin was gone, and from then until he returned my duties were restricted to milking the cows and doing the rest of the daily chores.

One cool, rainy Sunday evening, I was milking earlier than usual when I heard a loud cackling and general commotion from the chickens on the east side of the barn. When I looked out through a crack, the first coyote I'd ever seen chased and caught a half grown rooster. My first inclination was to rush out and scare the coyote off, but then I remembered that Grandpa's twenty-two rifle was on the back porch, and I could likely run to the house and back, using the barn as a shield, without being detected.

By the time I'd returned the coyote had killed the rooster and carried it a couple of hundred yards east of the barn. Although the coyote was out of range, I fired two shots at it before it loped off, carrying the dead chicken. It went east almost a half mile and then turned south where I lost sight of it after it jumped through a brushy fence line. Maybe the coyote had stopped on the other side of the fence to finish its meal. Calling on all of my skills, real and imagined, including trying my best to walk as quietly as Lew Wetzel had in Zane Grey's early frontier books, I was nearing the place where I'd last seen the coyote when just across the fence, no more than forty feet away, he stood eating the rooster.

I was a good shot at close range with a stationary object, but I had a hard time deciding whether I should risk my preferred head shot, since the coyote kept moving his head up and down while alternately eating and looking around, or go for a chest shot like I'd read about and seen illustrated in *Sports Afield*.

I ever so slowly and carefully lifted the cocked gun to my shoulder, took careful aim at the invisible heart, squeezed off the shot, and, man, oh man, the coyote jumped high in the air and fell flat on the ground. I cleared the fence and was half way to the downed animal, all the while anticipating how carefully I'd skin him out and show off his hide to Martin, when he suddenly jumped up and ran off. It hadn't crossed my mind to pump another quick shot into his head. In fact, I hadn't even ejected the spent cartridge from the barrel, much less pumped in another bullet. By the time I'd regained my wits the coyote was out of range, not that I'd have likely hit him at any range because I was such a poor shot on a moving target. I carried what little was left of the chicken back to the house to show Ernestine when she returned home the next day.

After I'd finished milking, I walked a mile south to Charley Howard's and told him about the coyote. Because Charley had running dogs, and he often hunted coyotes, I thought he'd want to put his dogs on the trail where I'd last seen him. Charley was a loud, hearty kind of guy, but after I told him I'd shot the coyote, he wasn't the least bit friendly. Wordless, I trudged back to the barn and finished my remaining chores in the dark. Late in the night while I worried and wondered why Charley Howard seemed mad at me, it occurred to me that the coyote hunters, wolf hunters as they called themselves, might be much like Arthur Jay and the other fox hunters had been around White Oak. Maybe they also were in it for the joy of the race, not the kill, and I had unknowingly violated their code. Now I better understood why Pap had been so secretive and close-mouthed about shooting hungry stray hounds that sometimes raided his chicken house. Besides being quiet, Pap was always in a hurry to get rid of the evidence with a fire in a big, well tended brush pile.

* * *

After Martin returned from wheat harvest, I told him right off about the runaway, and how Ernestine wouldn't let me finish plowing the corn for fear I'd get hurt. Unlike Dad, who would have pitched a shit fit in a similar situation, Martin laughed and said, "Don't worry about it." When we went after the cows that evening, we were near the red hill when I pointed out the long, crooked trail the cultivator had made before I'd finally stopped the running team. Martin surveyed the ruined corn, then exclaimed, "You cut quite a cat's ass, didn't you? Come on, let's go milk." When we'd finished milking and turned the cows out into the lot, he said, "The cows have fallen off a little in their milk, but they're doin' fine for this late in the summer."

Wednesday morning, Ernestine started in on Martin about going to prayer meeting that evening. "Everybody'll be glad to see you," she wheedled.

"Ernestine, you know I can't stand prayer meetings," Martin answered. "Besides, Wayne needs to fill me in on what he did while I was gone. Maybe I'll go to church on Sunday. We'll see."

Ernestine turned away, her deep frown firmly in place. Before she and the kids left in time to eat supper and visit with her folks, she said, "There's a pan of cornbread warming in the oven." Martin was irked at the prospect of eating nothing more than cornbread and milk for supper. Though I said nothing, it seemed to me that the general opinion in the family that Lottie had spoiled Pap and her boys was correct. Plenty of thick, crusty cornbread and fresh warm milk was good enough for anybody's supper.

We'd eaten and I was well into my story about shooting the coyote when Martin grew increasingly distracted, finally butting in: "I just thought of somethin'. I need to make a phone call." The door into the living room from the screened in porch where we were sitting was open, but the phone was on the north wall of the narrow dining room beyond, preventing me from hearing Martin's words.

Even so, I could make out an animated quality in his voice, a sound strikingly similar to Dad's voice when he turned on his charm as he talked to women and girls out of Mama's sight and hearing. Martin explained nothing when he returned to the porch. When I tried to pick up the thread of my interrupted account, I saw I'd have to finish it later.

After we'd finished chores the next morning, Martin announced he was going to Mt. Vernon, the county seat. "You're welcome to come along," he told me, "but after we go to the exchange, I've got to go see a man about a dog." Knowing that when someone said he had to go see a man about a dog meant he had private business to attend to, I was instantly intrigued. What private business could Martin have in Mt. Vernon?

Pap's 1934 black Chevrolet coupe settled a little when a man at the feed store threw two sacks of shorts and one sack of cottonseed meal into the trunk. Martin drove up the incline to the square past the forbidding jail with its massive chunks of limestone and sandstone on the corner, around the handsome courthouse, then a short distance south where he stopped across from a dingy beer joint. "Stay here in the vicinity," he said. "I'll be back after while." It was a mighty long while, I thought, as I passed the time in and out of the car for longer and longer intervals, finally circling the square and entering the courthouse where a toilet in the basement provided relief. Later, dozing in the car, I was awakened by the sound of a door opening. Martin, smelling of stale beer and cigarettes, started the engine and we headed home.

Now taciturn instead of his usual talkative self, Martin drove to the dirt road turning off the highway where he stopped. "It's time you learned how to drive, young man," he said. There he patiently coached me from neutral through low, second, and high and back to a steady stop, over and over, until I finally got the hang of it. As we neared the jog in the road near the slough south of Cyrus Cox's place, Martin told me to slow down and proceed across Honey Creek and up the steep red hill in second. I did as he directed, but then, over confident, I shifted into high and was going too fast at the turn in a quarter of a mile away.

Martin tried to grab the steering wheel but he was too late; I snubbed the left rear fender on a stout hedge corner post Pap had set when he'd grazed sheep in the yard. The unyielding post ripped a tear across the top of the fender before I could stop the car.

"Well, you almost made it," Martin laughed. "All you need now is a little practice. Pull her on down to the barn and unload the feed. Easy does it."

A few days later in Aurora, Martin pulled into the back of the John Deere dealership on the square to see about getting the fender fixed. Jack Eubanks, maybe twenty, married to Eva, that beautiful black headed Allman girl, brazed the torn metal with as pretty a seam as I ever saw. When he'd finished, Martin asked, "How much?"

"Six bits, I reckon," Jack said.

I started to pay, but Martin beat me to it. "It was my idea for you to drive," he said. Nothing more was said about the accident or the trip to Mt. Vernon, at least not for a long time.

Forty years later, after Ernestine was dead and Martin dragged his oxygen tank to church every time the doors were open, I quizzed him about that long ago unexplained episode. "Who was that man you went to see in the beer joint in Mt. Vernon the summer of 1943?" I teasingly asked.

"Man? Who said it was a man?"

"You did. You told me you had to go see a man about a dog."

"Well, I might have said that," he laughed, "but you know that's just a sayin'."

"I know that now, but I didn't know it then," I lied. "Do you mean to say you weren't talkin' to a man that day?"

"Maybe I shoulda said I had to go see a woman about a pussy cat."

"Who was it?"

"Don't you know?"

"Maybe. Was it Hilda?"

"Yes. How'd you know?"

"Call it a good guess."

There was a time when Martin would have lied in a pinch, but not since he'd found the Lord. I pressed on, "Did you ever get a little from her?"

Pausing for an extra whiff from his lifeline, the red eyed old man stared me down. "None of your business. You get outta here and leave me alone."

FIFTEEN

WHEAT HARVEST

Back in Wichita that fall, I enrolled in school again. I was in the ninth grade except in math and English. As the year progressed, I managed to keep my mouth shut long enough to pass math by the skin of my teeth. But because I still refused to diagram sentences, I failed eighth grade English for the second time.

Near the end of the school year I spotted an ad in the *Beacon*: "Young man needed in wheat harvest." Awkward on a telephone, I waited until dark before calling from the corner pay phone. "Do you still need a hired hand?" I stammered. "I'm calling from Wichita."

"I sure do," a man replied. "Have you ever worked on a farm?"

"Yes, all my life."

"Do you know how to drive?"

"I've driven a car," I bluffed, thinking of my single ill-fated attempt at driving Martin's car in Missouri.

"When can you go to work?"

"Right away, whenever you need me."

"All right. Give me directions so my daughter can pick you up. She'll be there around eight o'clock in the morning."

"3412 East McFarland in Planeview."

"My name's John Farley. What's your's?"

"Wayne Holmes. One thing I forgot to ask, mister. What's the pay?"

"Three dollars a day, plus room and board. Will that suit you?"

"That'll be fine. Well, 'bye."

The wheat farmer's daughter picked me up the next morning and drove me south past Clearwater where I was immediately put to work swinging a mattock, chopping down head high burdock and rank jimsonweeds in what had once been a pig pen. Mr. Farley looked dubious when he saw how young I was, and the weed patch appeared to be a test. Soon I had broken blisters on my tender hands, but I didn't complain. Mr. Farley didn't say anything that evening, but he seemed satisfied with the showing I'd made on the weeds.

After our skimpy supper, Mr. Farley took me outside, where he told me it would be better if I didn't tell the other hired hand how much I was making. Slow to catch on, I agreed before I learned that the good-natured, red faced old man with a drooping white mustache was a ward of the county poor farm. For the past several years he'd worked during the summer driving a tractor for the Farleys. I never knew how much the old man made, but since Mr. Farley didn't want him to know my wages, I guessed he was paid very little, maybe no more than a dollar a day.

With the steady old man at the tractor's controls and Mr. Farley on the combine, my job was to wait until the combine bin was full and then pull alongside close enough—but not too close – in order for the cascading wheat to fill the bed of the pickup before I drove to the elevator a few miles away. Sometimes Mr. Farley jumped down and swung the pickup in place.

Although he'd repeatedly told me to set the emergency brake anytime I stopped, in my anxiety I often forgot to release it. I drove off three different times only to realize too late that the smoking brake pads were ruined. After Mr. Farley had worked late into the night on his third brake job, I was on the way to the elevator the next day when I met a truck on a small bridge. Nervous, I oversteered beyond the bridge and the pickup gently turned on its side, spilling its load into a marshy tangle below. The driver of the other vehicle stopped to make sure I wasn't hurt, then drove over to tell Mr. Farley about my accident. Mr. Farley soon arrived on his tractor, and he quickly hooked a log chain to the pickup and pulled it upright and out of the ditch. The two of us scooped up most of the soggy and dirty wheat into the truck, and I drove to the farm and scooped it into an empty bin because the elevator wouldn't take wet wheat.

I expected to be fired, but Mr. Farley only said, "You need more practice drivin'. Maybe drivin' the old '28 John Deere will help." The farmer's chubby daughter drove the pickup for the remainder of wheat harvest, and I started plowing. But first I was shown where all the grease zerks were located. "Keep an eye on the oil gauge," Mr. Farley warned. "If it ever drops, shut her down." Chastened, I gradually became proficient driving the cumbersome tractor on steel wheels with its distinctive putt-putt. Rank wheat straw and weeds sometimes clogged the three bottom turning plow, causing long stops when my only recourse was to punch and dig with a long, narrow sharpshooter shovel until I was free. Occasional bogs, old buffalo wallows according to the Farleys, caused me a lot of misery. The heavy steel lugs on the back wheels of the tractor afforded tremendous traction, but the overtaxed engine sometimes coughed and died. Wiry and slight at no more than a hundred and thirty-five pounds, I lacked the necessary heft to spin the fly wheel with enough authority to start the hot engine. Mrs. Farley, noticing my delay from her kitchen window, sooner or later drove out to help. With a single mighty heave, she expertly started the tractor. Once I got the hang of driving the John Deere and learned how to avoid clogging the plow, my job became monotonous, making me yearn for the constant interaction with the horses I'd enjoyed while plowing in Missouri.

I wanted to go to town on Saturday nights, but because no one in the family went and it was too far to walk I whiled away my weekend nights upstairs listening to the old hired hand reminisce about cowboying in Arizona as a young man. While the old man's nostalgic accounts droned on, I tried to eavesdrop on what was going on below in the parlor where the Farley girl was courted by a tall hayseed while the two sat close together on a severe, horsehair Victorian sofa. I couldn't make out what the young couple said, but as the evening wore on, sharp slapping sounds punctuated the old man's words. Feigning thirst, I crept downstairs and looked into the parlor where the two, locked in a tight embrace, swayed to the accompaniment of the young woman's encouraging blows to her suitor's back.

On Sunday mornings the old man went with the family to a nearby country church, but I begged off. A midmorning nap alone in the still, cool upstairs room beat going to church anytime.

When the plowing was finished, Mr. Farley took me to the bank in town where he asked me how I wanted to be paid.

"How much do you owe me?"

"A little over a hundred dollars."

"I'd like to have a hundred dollar bill. The rest doesn't matter."

With my extra money I bought a bus ticket to Wichita and a pale blue shirt I'd been admiring in the window of the local dry goods store. When I unfolded the shirt to put it on, I saw that most of it was dark blue, unlike the pale front square long exposed to the sun's rays. Oh, well.

The first thing I did after arriving home was to run over to John and Warren Benn's house to show off my callused hands and my hundred dollar bill. They acted unimpressed, but I knew better.

* * *

Football practice was underway when I returned from wheat harvest. "Why don't you try out for the team?" Warren asked me.

"My folks won't let me."

"Why not?"

"I don't know. They just won't." But I did know. That evening, trying a new approach, I asked Mama, "Why can't I just practice with the team?"

"It's too dangerous."

"No it's not. Everyone wears protective equipment."

"I said no."

"I'll bring some equipment home and you can see how safe it is. OK?" I thought it was a good sign when she quit responding to my badgering. Next day I asked Coach Hunter if I could borrow a helmet and pads to show the folks.

"Go ahead," he said.

My plan worked. When I trotted out on the field in my armor the following day, the team was busy scrimmaging. Rex Childs, halfback, followed his blockers time and again as he swept around left end and down the field against the timid defense. The burly line coach, a fireman who had once played for a professional team, encouraged one player after another before he yelled at me: "Get in there at outside linebacker and see if you can stop those end sweeps."

Rex made another of his many long runs before I got set. Then, by anticipating the flow and warding off blockers, time after time I tackled him before he could round the corner and shift into high gear. This was the most exciting thing I'd ever done, including heading cattle on foot and on horseback back in Missouri. The line coach walked alongside me as we headed inside. "Good job," he said, "You'll be starting at linebacker Friday night."

The coaches tried me out at fullback where, slow runner that I was, I usually made good yardage by running directly at tacklers and jarring them loose with a hard, smashing forearm. But come game time, even with the basic plays drawn upside down across my thigh pads, I couldn't remember my assignments. And I fumbled two out of the three times I carried the ball. "You better stick with defense," Coach Hunter said at a time out. That suited me. The rest of the game, worry free, I ran wild at middle linebacker, taking much needed breathers when we had the ball. We lost the game but, unlike my teammates, I didn't mind. Running into opponents full tilt and busting up plays fed my youthful egotism, especially when coaches and players on the side lines yelled encouragement. Not to mention all the girls who suddenly took notice of me.

After practice on Monday, Mama told me she'd received a card from Fred, who was working in broomcorn harvest in western Kansas. "Fred says they're real short on workers." I cringed at what followed: "He says you can get on at the same pay he's gittin', four dollars a day plus room and board. That's good money." She continued: "Your dad and I have talked it over. Since you're havin' to take some of your classes over again, and you wasn't wild about going to school this year anyway, we think you ought to quit school and go to work with Fred in the broomcorn."

"But I like school this year."

"What you like is playin' football. Your dad thinks you might amount to something if you worked as hard at a job as you do playin' football." No job is as exciting as football, I thought, while she continued: "You bought clothes and a bicycle with some of your wheat harvest money, which was good, but we've decided you need to send half of what you make in your next job back home for us."

Dad said nothing, and he wouldn't meet my gaze, but I could tell he wasn't going to argue with Mama and I was a goner. Before we'd played our third football game, I'd quit school without telling anyone why. Saturday, carrying a small cardboard box with a change of clothes, I was on a bus headed west. In Dodge City I transferred to a long car where I was the lone passenger all the way to Hugoton, a dirty little town with hardly a tree in sight. Mama had written Fred, telling him when I'd arrive, and he was waiting to meet me when the limousine pulled up.

Ironically, Fred's earlier job had played out, but we were soon approached by a man on the street who needed two workers. "I live by myself way out on the Colorado line," he said, "and the accommodations ain't the best. But I'll feed you the best I know how, and I'll pay you the goin' rate, four dollars a day."

Fred did the talking: "We'll take the jobs, mister. When do we leave?"

Motioning toward his rusty old pickup parked in front of a tavern, the man told us to throw our belongings in the back, and to hang around in the vicinity because he'd be finished with his business shortly. We'd gone down the single main street about a block when another man asked us if we were looking for work. "Not exactly," Fred said. "We agreed to take a job just a few minutes ago."

"For how much?"

"The goin' rate, four dollars a day and room and board."

"Listen up. Somebody's tryin' to cheat you boys. The goin' rate is six dollars plus room and board. I'm lookin' for two more men to round out my crew."

"How are your accommodations?" I ventured.

"Good," he replied. "My wife and daughter do the cookin'. Besides breakfast and supper at our house next to the bunkhouse here in town, you'll eat your noon meal out in the field and have two breaks, one at mid mornin' and the other in the afternoon, when you'll have sandwiches, soup, and coffee brought to the field. Besides all that, I keep all the watermelons you can eat bedded down in straw under the cots in the bunkhouse."

162

"This sounds a whole lot better than the other place," Fred said. "If we can find our clothes, we'll go with you." Fred and I hurried up the street where the old pickup still sat in front of the tavern. Quickly, furtively, we retrieved our belongings and ran back. "Sign us up," Fred said.

We were assigned the last two cots in the bunkhouse, Fred's on the far side and mine on the near side next to the door where everyone came and went. The bottom halves of the up-turned wooden orange crates at the heads of the cots provided plenty of room for our change of clothes, and the top halves made handy places for our personal items, including our cigarettes and ashtrays.

A raucous poker game in the middle of the room kept me awake for a long time that first night, and after I fell asleep I was awakened twice by drunken revelry and loud swearing, the likes of which I'd never heard or imagined. Most of us slept in Sunday morning, skipping breakfast, and then after a big dinner we lounged around in the bunkhouse, smoking and getting acquainted. The poker game resumed while the bulk of the crew lazily whiled away the afternoon and evening catnapping, eating watermelon, and marking time.

Early Monday morning, well before daylight, Ed Ozbun, our boss, banged open the door near my head, and yelled: "Hit the deck and wash up! Breakfast'll be ready in ten minutes!" The eighteen of us took turns as we halfheartedly pumped cold water from the pump in the yard and washed our hands and faces, ran our fingers through our hair, then filed into the living room where old wooden doors on sawhorses served as tables. We ate big bowls of oats and generous amounts of bacon, sausage and cured ham, with as many eggs and fresh biscuits and gravy, and as much milk and coffee as we wanted.

It was still dark outside in the cool September dawn when we climbed into Ed's tarp covered truck fitted with benches. Driving north and west, Ed proceeded several miles before he stopped and we all piled out. "Ever'body check to make sure he's got his knife and whetrock. I'll show you the way to cut broomcorn," he said, placing the stubby knife in his palm with the sharp wide blade facing out between his two middle fingers. "It'll seem awkward at first if you're new at it, but you'll soon get the hang of it. We've built racks ever' so often where you can stack the heads. Stack 'em neat, all in the same direction. One more thing," he warned, "Try not to step on any rattlesnakes."

We all stayed pretty well bunched together as we walked briskly along bending the broomcorn stalks horizontally in that first of many mile long rows, but after we'd turned around and started cutting and stacking it became clear that some workers were considerably better than others. More precisely, what became apparent was that while most of the workers maintained a fast, uniform pace, no matter how hard I tried, I steadily fell farther and farther behind. The row boss frowned at me occasionally, but he didn't yell. Maybe he held off because at fourteen I was four years younger than the two next youngest workers in the crew, Fred and a good looking guy from Arkansas nicknamed Arky.

By the time Ed returned with sandwiches for our mid morning break, everyone knew I was hopelessly slow and inept, and Fred was the best and fastest worker in the crew. Ed, Fred, and the row boss spoke briefly, privately, causing me to suspect I'd be fired, but when work resumed Fred and I were assigned adjoining rows. Soon Fred steadily pulled ahead of the other workers while I again fell behind. Saying nothing, he moved from his row to mine where he worked for a long stretch, catching me up. I never knew whether it was because of his unfailing generosity, his attempt to keep me from being fired, or his desperate need to show off, but from then on Fred unbegrudgingly worked his frenzied pace seesawing back and forth across the seemingly endless rows.

Six days a week, all through the long fall season, we worked from dawn to dusky dark, with little to interrupt the tedium. Occasionally the mind numbing drudgery was broken by the sight of a rattlesnake, but with no handy rocks in the sandy soil, most of the snakes got away. Only Fred and Arky were foolish enough to grab a fleeing snake by the tail and pop off its head in the direction of whoever seemed most fearful of snakes. The occasional startling whir of pheasants suddenly skyrocketing ahead of us, highlighted by the brilliant, gaudy plumage of the cocks, also briefly broke the monotony of our work.

But for excitement, snakes and birds couldn't hold a candle to the German prisoners of war who worked in adjoining fields. From a distance, I imagined the swaggering Nazi storm troopers would likely make a run for it, and I'd get to see the shotgun toting American guards mow them all down. But when the dreaded Germans came close by, to my surprise and disappointment, they shrank to ordinary looking individuals not unlike some of our German neighbors back in Missouri such as the Brechbuhlers and the Seitzes.

As it turned out, three of my fellow workers scared me even worse than the POWs did. Both the row boss and another man almost a dead ringer for him had red and weepy left eye sockets as a result—according to rumors—of earlier fierce no-holds-barred fights when eye gouging and biting off ears and noses was practiced. Although we never knew for sure how the two men lost their eyes, when an infrequent fight threatened to break out in the bunkhouse, someone invariably called out: "Fight fair! Fight fair!" no doubt because of the grisly looking one eyed men in our midst.

Blackie, the dark complected gambler who played poker every night, was even ghastlier looking than the one eyed men. By his own admission, Blackie had once welshed on a bet, after which his two opponents had overpowered him, cut the corners of his mouth back to his jaw hinges, and then sewed him up with a curved horse needle in rough wide stitches.

Many a night I watched from my cot while Blackie and his drunken red faced partner raked in their winnings. When I dozed off I sometimes confused Blackie and his perpetual grimace with pictures I'd seen of P-38 fighter planes painted to resemble sharks. I'd almost quit walking in my sleep by this time, but I sometimes had nightmares in which I confused the leering gambler with the scary caricatures of the Japanese I'd seen in newspapers, magazines, and graffiti. Not that Blackie was menacing in the daylight. Not at all. The bandy-legged little man merely looked maimed. But in the low, flickering coal oil lantern light of the bunkhouse, and later in my darker dreams, his hideous and grotesque visage made me shudder.

Fred and I went our separate ways on our short weekends, he with his friends from Missouri, the Brechbuhlers and Clarence Watkins, and I with Arky.

Despite his countrified nickname, Arky was more sophisticated than the others in our crew, and he parlayed that sophistication into considerable success with young women in Hugoton, especially with a pretty waitress at the cafe who, in his words, was stacked like a brick shithouse. Arky encouraged the waitress to fix me up with a seventeen year old blonde she knew. With no transportation and with nothing going on in the small town after the cafe, the drug store, and the picture show closed, the four of us often took long walks in the country, followed by a return to a small vacant park at the edge of town. Arky and his girl slipped off to their private business, while the small, plain girl and I talked and kissed hour after hour. Late one night, she turned to me, "I like you. You're not like all the other boys I know."

"How's that?" I asked.

"They're all interested in just one thing. But you're different." I was flattered by the young woman's words, but, young and green though I was, I recognized a put-down when I heard it.

Put-down or not, running around with an older woman was more fun than hanging out in the bunkhouse. While broomcorn harvest steadily wound down, Arky and I continued meeting the two girls at the cafe after closing time. The park was our favorite hangout, but with colder and wetter weather setting in, we needed to find shelter. We learned that a hard

166

jerk on a back door at the high school provided access, but I was afraid we'd be discovered and arrested there. After walking up and down the few streets a time or two, more often than not we ended up in an old abandoned sedan in the alley behind where the waitress lived with her parents.

I mostly deduced what was going on between Arky and the waitress in the park, but the smells and sounds in the car, especially when the lovers got down to the short rows, both embarrassed and aroused me. The two of us in the front seat never let on. My girl was very likely experienced, but if she knew the ropes she wasn't bold enough to take me in hand and teach me, and I was a slow learner on my own.

An argument erupted in the back seat of the rusty car one Saturday night when the waitress confronted Arky: "A guy at the cafe said you have a wife back in Arkansas."

"Well, I don't."

"The man who told me said he's your father-in-law."

"That's a lie. Ask Wayne."

"This is the first I've heard of it," I said.

"Arky," she said, "Why would someone tell me somethin' like that right out of the blue?"

"He was just spreadin' lies, makin' trouble," Arky said. "I was married for a little while, but I'm not now. We're separated." Maybe because the word separated often meant divorced, the waitress seemed convinced and the sounds of the squabble were soon replaced by the muffled grunts and groans the two of us in the front had grown accustomed to hearing.

A few days later, in one of his rare late evening visits to the bunkhouse, Ed made the announcement everyone was expecting: "Listen up, boys. We're done with the broomcorn. I'll need two hands for a couple of more weeks, but I'll settle up with the rest of you in the mornin'. You've been a good crew."

Both girls sniffled a little when Arky and I said our goodbyes and my girl asked for my address in Wichita. Although it seemed unlikely she'd ever look me up, I couldn't risk it. "1707

South Roosevelt," I lied, as I wondered who I'd be most ashamed of if she showed up, her or the folks.

No one was surprised the next morning when Ed asked the two best workers, Fred and the row boss, to stay on when he paid the rest of us. Fred was pleased at being picked to stay, and I looked forward to returning home alone. I'd have plenty of time to daydream and catnap on the long, desolate stretch between Hugoton and Wichita, and maybe enough time to decide what to do about school.

I've forgotten the actual trip home, but I distinctly remember stepping in the back door and seeing the transformation of the two downstairs rooms. The wooden pine floor in the kitchen was covered with a shiny new eight by ten gray linoleum. I recognized the round table and the long box with its smooth worn lid the three youngest kids sat on, but the stools—broken backed chairs—had been discarded and replaced with four sturdy secondhand, but whole, kitchen chairs.

Even more dramatic was the change in the living room. Entirely bare when I left ten weeks earlier, the floor was covered with a gaudy maroon linoleum with an endless twisting border. The furniture consisted of a fairly decent looking but worn dull green davenport and matching chair, along with twin naugahyde covered battleship gray chairs with skinny pickled oak legs. Oh, and a tall, wobbly, three-legged end table.

"Where'd all the furniture come from?" I whispered to Joyce.

"Mama bought it from Uncle Steve, who was goin' back to Arkansas."

"Where'd she get the money?" I asked.

"She used the money she made you send home. Isn't everything pretty?"

"No," I glowered, "It's ugly. I hate it." And I stomped upstairs to see Jay.

SIXTEEN

GEORGE MOUNTS

As much as I disliked having my money used to help furnish the downstairs rooms while I was gone, I now felt comfortable about inviting my friends over after school before Dad and Mama got home from work. Anytime we went to John and Warren's house, there'd be something tasty for us in their cupboard or icebox, but not at our house. The best I could come up with when someone asked "What'cha got to eat?" was a box of raisins or rolled oats. "Raisins? Oats?" they'd snort. But eating natural foods at my house eventually became a good-natured joke.

Going to school beat working in the broomcorn fields by a long shot. I especially liked going to school early and walking from one end of the long building to the other while checking out all the pretty girls. Most of the classes were boring, especially eighth grade English, which I was now taking for the third time. I might have mastered diagramming sentences, but it seemed nonsensical and I refused to do it. Oddly, I liked Miss

Bond and I never spouted off at her as I sometimes did to other teachers, especially the math teacher who'd go on and on with her foolish stories about her darling baby until I'd raise my hand and ask: "But what does your kid have to do with math?"

I admired Coach Jay Hunter. A full-blooded Indian, Coach Hunter didn't take guff off anyone. Never one to play favorites, Coach liked me, I thought, until one day I began to have doubts when he placed the entire gym class in two opposing lines and told us to count off. Boys with matching numbers would be opponents in boxing matches for the next couple of weeks.

Near the end of one line, I confidently barked off my number. George Mounts, well known bully and the only white boy in school I was afraid of, was far down on the opposite line, and he wasn't likely to have my same number. But he did. While the boxing matches proceeded, I searched out boys in my line who might not know George's reputation. "I'll give anyone a dollar to boot if he'll trade numbers with me."

"No way, Holmes. You're dead meat," one said, "What did you do to piss off Coach Hunter? Ever'body but you knows he set you up. Dummy!"

"Whatta ya mean, set me up?"

"Just what I said. Didn't you see how careful he was when he put you and George opposite one another that first day?"

"I thought it was an accident."

"Accident?" he laughed. "He rigged it so all of us would get to see George whip your ass."

Devastated by the possibility that Coach Hunter set me up to be publicly humiliated, and further galled by my own naivete, I sullenly awaited my fate.

On Friday Keith Garland tied on my gloves. The instant the gong sounded, before George had time to get out of his corner and put his dukes up, I bolted across the canvas and began hitting him in the head with both fists as hard and fast as I could. Badly dazed by my sudden barrage, George stood upright, stupefied, while I battered him until the bell signalled the end of the round.

In the second and final round, George vainly tried to protect his face from my fierce and desperate onslaught. During the last thirty seconds or so while I repeatedly hammered him in my vain attempt to knock him down and out, my surprised classmates cheered. At the clang of the bell, I glanced over at Coach Hunter. Expressionless, he gave me a sly wink.

I was walking down the hall between classes, basking in my tardy realization of who had been tricked, when Victor Wright, sophomore class president, stopped me. "I heard you beat the shit out of George Mounts."

"Yes," I said, "I did."

Everything started falling into place after that. Many boys I barely knew, some of them upper classmen, nodded or spoke when we met in the hall or out on the street. Better yet, increasing numbers of girls flirted with me and made me believe they'd go out with me if I could only work up the nerve to ask them.

Rosemary Mounts, George's volatile little sister, was young, maybe too young at thirteen to fool around with, but the bouncy blonde was fun to be around and we hit it off, so why not? Her folks wouldn't let her date, but we'd meet after school, then slowly walk along afterward toward her house, flirting away. One afternoon, impatient with our juvenile antics and banter, I told her I longed to touch her.

"You better not."

"I'm goin' to."

"You do and I'm through with you."

"We'll see about that," I said, and I reached over and playfully pinched her hard, round butt.

She didn't slap me, but she might as well have. "That's it," she said, pointing down Sayles Street toward my house. "This is where you get off, Buster."

Warren Benn soon told me about Beverly Nelson, a hot number in his study hall who had expressed interest in me.

171

Later, when I was in the back seat with her while Warren drove his dad's car, he complained about not having a date.

"Do you know Rosie Mounts?" I asked him.

"Barely," he said.

"I think she's old enough to date now. Why don't you ask her out?"

"Maybe I will. Let's go see if she's at teen town."

She was there and, yes, she'd like to go for a ride. We parked south of Boeing where Warren and Rosie quickly got acquainted, causing Beverly to acidly whisper, "She's a shy little thing, isn't she?"

* * *

Although I'd smoked my allotted pack of cigarettes a day in broomcorn harvest the same as all the other men, I quit smoking once I was back in Wichita. The folks wouldn't have let me smoke around the house, and I knew Coach Hunter disapproved. Besides, I wasn't sure I could afford cigarettes.

I never let on that I'd been paid six dollars a day the entire broomcorn season instead of the four dollars Fred had originally said we'd make, and the folks didn't know I'd pocketed the difference. Lying about my money rested easy on my mind. The only worry was that Mama would discover my stash of money in a nest in the old mattress Jay and I slept on and she'd make me cough up what she thought I owed. To make sure my hidden money lasted, I told Mama one Friday evening that the quarter a week allowance the four of us kids got for doing the dishes might do for the three youngest, but since I went to the drug store and teen town, and sometimes the picture show, a quarter wasn't enough for me.

"Don't you still have some of your broomcorn money?"

"A little," I admitted. "But I don't want it to run out. I need a dollar a week."

"Well, I'll talk to your Dad about it after supper. He's in a better mood after he eats."

Although Mama worked long hours gluing and tacking canvas in a glider factory, she wasn't free to give me money.

Predictably, Dad blew up. "No!"

"I think he needs it."

"I don't care what you think! I'm not givin' him any more money!"

Back and forth they argued, until Mama said: "We took half of his broomcorn money to pay for furniture. As a matter of fact, we bought that very chair you're sittin' in with his money." Beat, Dad sullenly took a dollar bill out of his billfold and placed it on the table. Mama handed it to me in the kitchen where I'd been listening. Wordless, I scooted out the back door. From then on Dad and Mama held their same battle every Friday night. Mama always won, but never before Dad drew blood.

Fifteen and back in school.

Having extra money improved my status, especially after I started dating Doralee Ricketts. Auburn haired, freckle faced and filled out, the well dressed only child could have dated anyone, but she chose me. On our first date we went to school and signed annuals. As I walked her home, I longed to try out my newly learned western Kansas kissing technique, but her swollen face and lips from a bad case of poison ivy caused me to hold off.

On our second date I walked her to the outdoor picture show Boeing provided for its employees. Dad didn't own a car, but our next door neighbors, the Scotts, sometimes invited the folks to go to the grocery store with them. As Doralee and I walked along, holding hands, the Scotts' 1936 black Chevrolet sedan, packed to the gills with three Scotts and six Holmeses, slowly pulled alongside us. I tried to look away, but the jam-packed vehicle with its load of gawking, grinning and waving occupants couldn't be ignored. Jay even had the gall to stick his head out the window.

"Who in the world was that?" Doralee gasped as the car gradually pulled away.

"I have no idea."

One night, instead of going to the show, we walked past Boeing to a secluded place John Benn and I had found while we were hunting jackrabbits. There we talked and necked ever so long—longer than if we'd gone to the show. On Monday morning Doralee hiked up her pretty pleated dress and showed me angry red welts where her mom had whipped her with a belt, making me better understand why Mrs. Ricketts always hid when I picked up Doralee. She was even more suspicious than Mama.

Planeview's population was highly mobile, so it was no surprise when Doralee told me she was moving to Hutchinson, some sixty miles away. Her dad promised she could visit her friends in Planeview, and when she returned we could get together. Sure enough, over Christmas vacation I ran into her at the drugstore. "I'm stayin' all night with Marcia," she said. "Can you meet me at her house?"

"Sure. What time?"

"Anytime. The sooner the better. Marcia's folks are out of town."

Dad and Mama were also gone, visiting Mama's folks in Oklahoma; Fred was in the army and Joyce, sixteen, left in charge, would be no problem.

Marcia's date was Paul Jay, an eighteen year old sophomore Indian, the star running back of the football team. His and Marcia's easy familiarity, first on the couch and then in the bedroom, made getting reacquainted awkward for Doralee and me as we shared an overstuffed chair. Sometime before midnight, Paul and Marcia sauntered out of the bedroom. "We're goin' downtown," Marcia said. "We'll be back later. Don't wait up."

174

Soon, bolder than I remembered her, Doralee said, "Let's go in the bedroom. Come on."

"I will if we don't have to get under the covers."

"What are you scared of?"

"Nothin'," I blustered, as she led me to the bed.

Try as she might, she couldn't persuade me to join her under the comforter. Finally, our passion cooled by my fears and the encroaching cold, we huddled on the narrow bed until we heard Marcia's cry, "Get up, you sleepyheads! It's our turn."

Doralee and I staggered out in the early morning dark and climbed into someone's truck parked next to a coal bin. There we briefly hugged and kissed. "It's cold, I better go," I said. "See ya later. Have fun with your new boyfriend."

"Don't worry, I will," Doralee said. "He knows how to warm me up, and he can do more in fifteen minutes than you did fumbling around all night long."

Joyce had been up since midnight and she was crying when I entered the front door. More relieved than angry, she never breathed a word to the folks.

* * *

When Fred came strutting home on leave after completing his basic training in Texas, it was clear he thought he could whip me. Sullen, arrogant, and smart mouthed as I was, a sound whipping might have done me good, but the way he went about it was all wrong. First, he bought a new pair of boxing gloves and insisted on settling some old scores in the backyard next to the coal bin. He didn't know that I'd beat the shit out of the school bully a few weeks earlier, and I was confident he'd wilt under my fierce attack even more quickly than George had. I was right. After I worked him over, he took Jay aside and told him he guessed the gloves were a bad idea. I hoped he might back off after that. But no, he kept right on circling.

Dad and Mom put little stock in Christmas, but on Christmas day, instead of her usual refurbished toys, Grandma

175

Holmes brought brand new gifts meant to suit each one of us. My flashy yellow celluloid vanity set, complete with mirror, comb, and brush, fit me just right.

Fred grew restless after dinner. "I'm gonna change into my dress uniform and go downtown and find me some action." Not content with the bright sheen on his spit shined boots, the first shoes of any kind he'd ever polished, he looked around, grabbed my new hairbrush, and delivered a couple of smart licks.

"Fred," I said, "That's a hairbrush, not a shoe brush."

"It don't make no difference," he replied, and buffed the boots twice more.

"It does to me, and it's mine." With that my temper flared and I hit him full in the face, sending him down.

But he didn't stay down. Part boxing and part wrestling match, our vicious fight raged upstairs where first one and then the other seemed to win. Flimsy drywall caved in where our hard flailing fists and shoving shoulders crashed. I was on top of him for good, I thought, punching his face and banging his head on the floor, when Mama bounded up the stairs, broom in hand, screaming, "Shame on you for fighting your soldier brother!" while she struck me repeatedly over the head and shoulders. I got up, retrieved my brush, and went downstairs and outside.

My soldier brother with Lottie Jean in the background

SEVENTEEN
WAR'S END

We didn't have a radio, but Dad kept up with the war by reading the *Beacon*. Late in the war, after Fred was in Japan, Mama hung a star in the kitchen window next to the placard that showed how many pounds of ice we needed each week.

I was surprised at how many teachers and students cried during the somber hastily called assembly when President Roosevelt's death was announced. One teacher's response: "This is the worst day for mankind since the death of Jesus Christ," shocked me because most of the adults I knew opposed FDR and his radical policies. I felt proud when President Truman ordered the bombings of Hiroshima and Nagasaki, but when the Japanese surrendered, I felt cheated out of my dream of joining the marines. My encounters with German prisoners of war in western Kansas had modified my blanket condemnation of the Nazis, but nothing had changed my hatred of the Japanese. I'd swallowed hook, line, and sinker the propaganda that all of the Nips deserved extermination.

The black headlines announcing the Allies' victory in Europe and the war's end meant huge cutbacks in the airplane industry, and Dad was one of the first to lose his job at Boeing. He soon landed a job in a feed mill, but he'd gained weight on the Boeing assembly line, and he wasn't prepared for the heavy all day lifting required in his new job. "I'm ready to go back to Missouri," he declared one evening at supper.

"Where?" Mama asked.

"Lottie says Martin's tired of farming on Honey Creek," Dad said. "And since she and Pap have no intention of going back, what do you all think of us movin' to Honey Creek?"

Mama nodded in approval, while Joyce and the younger kids clamored excitedly. "When can we leave?" Lottie Jean shouted.

"Right away, as soon as I can locate someone to move us," Dad said. "And this time nobody'll have to ride in a wagon or in the back of a truck. I'll ride along with the truck driver, and the rest of you can go on the train, the same way other folks do."

The prospect of riding the train brought another outburst from the kids, but I felt terrible. I didn't want to leave Plane-view and Wichita. The thought of returning to Missouri made me sick. Dad, seeing my forlorn look, suddenly turned solicitous. "What's wrong with you? I thought you liked Honey Creek."

"I liked it when I was little," I answered, "But not now."

"I'll tell you what," Dad said. "If you've still got some of your broomcorn or wheat harvest money stashed away, as your mother thinks you do, you can help me and we'll go together fifty-fifty on a car."

"But I'm not old enough to drive," I said.

"You'll be legal in a little over a year. In the meantime, you can practice driving on the back roads. Whatta ya think?"

When I perked up he pushed his advantage, "And since you like to hunt, maybe you ought to be thinkin' about gittin' yourself a dog."

Next day after school I rode my bike out to the pound where I spotted an extra good looking, long eared black and tan hound pup. "I want that pup," I told the caretaker, "but I'll have to bring my dad out to okay him."

"That's fine, but a good-looking pup like that will go fast. You better take him now," the man said.

Dad and I rode the bus downtown Saturday morning, then transferred to a second bus which took us to the pound. The prize pup was gone. "Look around," Dad said. "What about that spotted pup over there? A feist often makes a good squirrel dog." The black and white terrier cross wasn't what I had in mind, but I paid the five dollar fee and carried him home on the bus. "You better decide what you want to call him," Dad advised. "A dog needs a name."

"How about Tippy?" I asked.

"Tippy's a good name for a pup," he said. "When he's grown he'll be Old Tip."

Dad quit his job at the feed mill and made arrangements to have our belongings hauled to Missouri.

When I checked out of school, officially this time, Miss Bond frowned as she looked at my English scores: "You're flunking for the third time," she said. "But if you'll promise to do better in Missouri, I'll give you a D- instead of an F."

"I promise," I said.

The hardest part was saying goodbye to Coach Hunter. He was outside his office, between classes, when I told him I had to leave. "Don't get into too many fistfights," he said, and winked.

"I'll try," I said, and shook hands with him as hard as I could.

"Ouch, you're hurting me. Well, good luck."

"'Bye," I said.

Telling the guys so long at teen town that evening was a lot easier. "Maybe you all can hitchhike to Missouri this summer," I said. "We've got a good swimmin' hole at our place on Honey Creek."

179

"Maybe we will," Warren said. "Stock up on raisins and oats."

"Okay, see you guys later."

"See ya," they called.

Beverly had left teen town before I could tell her good-bye. On the off chance I'd be able to catch up with her, I headed over the bridge towards her house. She and her friend Charlotte were lying on a pallet in her back yard when I arrived. Bev was pleased I'd made a special effort to see her.

"Let's write," I urged her, and I grabbed her and kissed her hard, almost as hard as I'd shaken Coach Hunter's hand.

"Well, 'bye," I said. "I'll be back," and I quickly turned and ran, Missouri bound.

*　*　*

The best part of the trip back to Missouri was hearing the black conductor call out the names of the approaching towns to the rhythmic clickety-clack of the lurching train. The man's practiced chant made towns such as Neodesha and Fredonia sound exotic.

The worst part was having to sit in close quarters with Mama while she buttonholed anyone who'd meet her gaze with loud, personal details of our family's history and aspirations. "We're headin' back to Missouri," she'd begin, quickly gathering a full head of steam until only the rudest traveller could stop her.

"You may have heard of Honey Creek in Lawrence County? That's where we're goin'. The kids' dad has gone on ahead in a truck with our stuff. He's gonna meet us in Aurora. Maybe you know where that is?" Naturally, no one had heard of Honey Creek or Aurora, but that didn't stop Mama.

When we finally pulled into the station at Aurora, Dad was standing next to a 1946 Ford ton truck. For a minute I thought he had bought the new green vehicle, but then I recognized Jeffie Pannell, a neighbor, standing nearby. I was disappointed that the slick new truck wasn't ours, but a truck wasn't what I

180

had in mind for when I'd be driving and dating soon. As I rode in the back of Jeffie's truck with the other kids on our way to Honey Creek, it occurred to me that Dad might have bought Pap's '34 Chevrolet coupe at Martin's sale, but when we pulled up in the yard, it was nowhere in sight.

After a quick romp with Tippy, I asked Dad: "What are we gonna do about a car?"

"I was gittin' ready to tell you," he said. "Jeffie has a '28 Hupmobile he'll sell us for a hundred dollars. It's a good car with a soft leather seat."

"Seat?" I asked. "You mean seats?"

"No, I'm afraid not. It's a coupe."

"But all of us can't ride in a coupe," I protested.

"Yes, we can," Dad said. "You'll see. Do you have fifty dollars to put in for your half, as we agreed?"

"Yes," I weakly answered.

"Well, run get your money. I'll walk to Jeffie's and tell him we'll take the Hupmobile."

When I first saw the low-slung, powerfully built car slowly coming down the road, I marveled at its heavy oversized chrome headlights, its extra long hood covering a powerful sounding motor, and its heavy but elegant wooden spokes. Above the windshield a nifty cowl stuck out like the bill on a baby's bonnet. As Dad turned into the driveway, my admiration for the car nose-dived when I saw the crude, ugly, ill fitting, rough sawn oak pickup bed Jeffie had installed in place of the original luxurious leather covered rumble seat. The bed was approximately four feet wide by five feet long and had four feet high racks that made the handy vehicle ideal for transporting a few hundred pounds of feed home from the exchange, for hauling three or four good sized calves to the sale barn, or several hogs to market. And, yes, Dad was right: It was plenty big enough to haul seven of us to town or church, with three sitting in front and four standing in the back.

I knew right away I was in a bind. Since the car was half mine, by rights I should have been able to ride in the front with the folks, but I couldn't tolerate riding in the middle, and I knew Mama wouldn't scoot across and sit close to Dad.

At fifteen I was way too old and sophisticated to ride in the back, but Joyce, seventeen and desperately shy, couldn't be expected to suffer the gibes and jeers the town kids were likely to hurl at us as we slowly circled the square. But since Joyce, who often acted as buffer between Dad and Mama, wouldn't mind sitting between them in the front seat, the only thing for me to do was crawl in the back with Wanda, thirteen, Jay, eleven, and Lottie Jean, nine. After a couple of miserable trips to Aurora, I decided I'd rather go squirrel hunting or looking for arrowheads than be a laughingstock. The folks didn't seem to mind when I quit going to town. In fact, they appeared relieved that they didn't have to put up with my surly behavior on Saturday afternoons.

But Sunday was different. There was no way I could get out of going to church. Nobody saw us on the two mile trip on the dirt road to Rocky Comfort, but when Dad pulled up in the churchyard, a large group of young people looked us over as we crawled down from our odd looking car. No one spoke, but then nobody snickered, either. Actually, we were soon made to feel welcome, not only at Rocky Comfort but in the larger community as well.

Mama was too self-conscious and sanctimonious to take part in a shivaree we were invited to, but Dad took us older kids. We all had a good time banging pots and pans, ringing bells, and joining in the raucous off-colored yelling and general merriment aimed at embarrassing while congratulating the surprised, recently married couple. Mama would have had a hissy fit if she'd known what all went on at the shivaree, but nobody told her. The grinning groom was about to be placed in a wheelbarrow and rolled to a pond, but at the last minute he produced candy for the women and kids and cigars for the men and big boys, averting a dunking.

* * *

Even more fun than the shivaree was the play party Joyce and I attended. I was too clumsy and self-conscious to fully enjoy the dancing, but I cavorted around in the moonlight, briefly and lightly touching my partners' hands. Anything more than a slight touch was strictly taboo because our chaperones were convinced that regular square dancing to the Devil's instrument, the fiddle, along with swinging and embracing our partners, would inflame our passions beyond repair.

I'm not sure how the final game of the evening, Spin the Bottle, managed to sneak in past the vigilant adults. Maybe they'd gone to the house. Although I was initially dubious of the country girls, I quickly learned that out in the dark they were as eager and accomplished at kissing as any of the girls I remembered in Wichita. Well, any but Betty Baumchen.

The Marionville school bus stopped at our driveway, almost at our front door. Shy and reserved, I'm sure I also exhibited more than a touch of arrogance at the prospect of mixing with all the hicks I'd soon encounter. As I walked toward the back of the bus on the lookout for an empty seat, a ruggedly handsome yet almost homely boy about my age scooted over, nodded, and said, "Howdy. I'm Hosie Gold. Glad to meetcha."

Hi," I said. "I'm Wayne Holmes. Much obliged for the seat."

Hosie took me in tow when we arrived at school. "First, you'll need to see the secretary." The mild mannered secretary told Hosie to take me to the principal, Mr. Williams.

"Welcome, young man," Mr. Williams said. "What grade are you in?"

"Well," I began, "It's hard to say."

"Hard to say? You're in a grade, aren't you?"

"Not exactly. I'm in three different grades."

"Whatta ya mean?"

"I'm in the eighth, ninth, and tenth grades," I said.

"Oh, you've flunked courses, some of them three times," Mr. Williams surmised.

183

"Yes," I admitted, "but only one course three times. Eighth grade English has been hard for me."

After frowning at my transcript, Mr. Williams brightened. "To simplify matters, how'd you like to be a freshman?"

"Fine," I said, and he signed me up.

My main interest was girls. I saw that most of the Marionville girls dressed simply and used little makeup, and as a result they were often plainer looking than the girls I'd known in Planeview. But I also noticed that a number of the girls, and not just the older ones, often looked at me in a direct way I found exciting and disturbing. On the other hand, some of the girls, girls I was often attracted to, were lacking in social skills. Betty Williams, for example, two or three classes ahead of me but about my age, was smart and beautiful, but painfully shy. She and I often spoke and looked longingly at one another, but nothing more developed. I wanted to ask her out when I turned sixteen and got my driver's license, but I couldn't risk showing up in my automobile. Later, as I recalled the green sweater which highlighted her soft curves, the lone sweater I remember her wearing, I wondered if Betty's family was as hard up as we were. She might have been glad to ride in my transformed Hupmobile.

Flora Jean Taylor was another shy girl who piqued my interest. She rode our bus, but if Flora Jean ever looked at me, much less smiled at me, I never caught her at it. But since she rarely looked at any boy, I thought I might have a chance. That chance came in February when I learned there was going to be a party in the study hall during the last hour on Friday after Valentine's Day. Doyle Norris went with me downtown to the dimestore where I paid two dollars for a big box of wrapped chocolates, and a nickel for a card that said, "Be My Valentine." I printed "To Flora Jean Taylor" inside the card and placed it, along with the heavy box, on the study hall table. Mrs. King, who kept study hall, read the names aloud and handed out the cards while she tried to keep some semblance of order. Having saved the single box of chocolates for last, she finally called out

"Flora Jean Taylor," and the prim beauty, her normally milk white complexion now blazing, walked demurely forward and retrieved the candy while the hall erupted in rude whistles and catcalls.

Later, I was seated on the bus, watching, as Flora Jean climbed on with the box of candy clasped against her full bosom. When she sat down, halfway back, I turned and tried to catch her eye, but there wasn't a glimmer of recognition. I pretty much gave up after that. For one thing, word got around that the Taylors were strict Campbellites. I never knew whether the rumor was true, but if it was, that might have explained why Flora Jean never wore a sweater. Her stern looking mother apparently didn't want to take any chances with her precious daughter.

Actually, I didn't totally give up on Flora Jean. A couple of years later, when I was a senior at Aurora, and was driving a slightly more presentable car, Dad's oil burning '36 Ford sedan, I got up enough nerve to call her from a pay phone. "Hi, Flora Jean?"

"Yes, who's this?"

"Wayne, Wayne Holmes. How ya doin'?"

"Fine."

"Listen," I stammered, "How would you like to go out with me?"

"Mm, I'm not sure," she hedged.

"There's a good movie playin' at the Princess in Aurora. I think you'd like it."

"I don't know. I'm not sure," she repeated.

"You ought to go out with me if only to make up for how you treated me after the Valentine party that time," I said.

"What do you mean, for how I treated you after a Valentine party? I don't know what you're talking about."

"Remember gettin' a box of chocolates?" I reminded her.

"Well, yes."

"I gave you that candy."

"You did not," she said.

"I most certainly did," I asserted.

"Oh," she said and laughed. "And all this time I thought it was Thomas Hadley."

"Thomas Hadley? What made you think it was Thomas Hadley?"

"He was always real polite. For some reason I thought he gave it to me."

"Well, now you know," I said. "How about a date next Saturday night?"

"Maybe," Flora Jean said. "Call me Friday night and I'll tell you for sure. Okay?"

"Okay. I'll talk to you Friday. 'Bye."

Flora Jean didn't beat around the bush on Friday. "I can't go with you," she said, "I've found out you have a bad reputation."

"Whatta you mean, bad reputation? I have a good reputation."

"That's not what I heard. I can't go with you. 'Bye."

"Well, 'bye," I said, and hung up.

Who was spreading lies about my reputation? Not a single girl I'd dated could say I'd taken advantage of her. Maybe Flora Jean had heard about a couple of fights I'd had, fights I couldn't honorably avoid, or maybe skipping school had sullied my reputation. Worse, maybe she'd hoped the candy came from timid Thomas all along. Whatever the reason, I never knew what I did to muff my chances.

* * *

In some ways I liked school at Marionville better than school in Planeview. I liked the kids with their rude camaraderie; the friendly secretary, Bessie Webb; the janitor, Mr. Rapp, with his ready smile and foxhunting stories he shared with me after school; and Mrs. Rapp and the other women in the basement of the home economics building who fed us lunch with hearty good will.

The curriculum was narrow, causing me to take courses I would have normally avoided, including business education and Future Farmers of America. As it turned out, both of these courses would have helped me considerably later on had I applied myself, but I was scornful of the prospect of becoming anything so mundane as a businessman or a farmer.

I liked the business teachers, first Mrs. Jones and then Mrs. Dent, and tried to get along in their classes while doing as little work as possible. Similarly, first with the well-dressed Mr. Hillhouse, and then with the gruff but good-natured Mr. Muhleman in FFA, I coasted through. The single project I completed in shop was cutting out and soldering a small funnel. More interested in language than shop, I was struck by how many of the boys said sorder for solder.

But it was Mr. Shelton who turned my life around at school. At first the high strung little man with his ill fitting clothes and active Adam's apple under his obligatory tie seemed too ludicrous looking to take seriously. However, it was soon clear that Mr. Shelton took everything seriously, including all of the subjects he taught, as well as the initially indifferent and unruly students who showed up for his classes. I don't exactly know how he managed to hold our interest. For one thing, when we discussed our assigned readings in English, it was evident that Mr. Shelton expected us to not only have read the assigned material, we were expected to be ready to say something pertinent about it. Mr. Shelton's own perceptive comments and anecdotes nudged our discussions right along.

Mr. Shelton had more nerve than most teachers. Once, after mentioning Joe Christmas and his brutal treatment at the hands of his adoptive father in William Faulkner's *Light in August*, Mr. Shelton went on to speak heatedly about an unnamed abusive father. Although he didn't spell it out, all of us in class that day assumed that his father was the abuser and Mr. Shelton had been abused as a child.

Another time when we were discussing something we'd read concerning divine retribution, perhaps in one of Emily

Dickinson's poems, he announced: "Some people think I'll go to hell. But I don't believe it for a minute. I haven't sinned enough for a good and just God to punish me eternally."

The surprised class clammed up completely, but I felt like jumping up and yelling: "Yea, Mr. Shelton!"

I felt a decided tug-of-war between going to school and playing hooky. There wasn't anything even close to the excitement of Wichita available while skipping school at Marionville, but I still thought a guy ought to be able to spend one day a week as he pleased. After lunch when the weather was right, Doyle Norris and I liked to go by the dime store and buy a sack apiece of stale Spanish peanuts and then head out toward Polk Spring and beyond where we'd laze away the afternoon. We never bothered to fish or swim or do anything in particular except amble alongside Honey Creek while we talked and ate our peanuts, living the life of Riley. Neither of us had a watch, but we tried to gauge it so we could be back in time for me to catch the bus and Doyle could walk home shortly after school let out. On the days we'd gone too far or loitered too long, we'd split up and Doyle returned to Marionville while I followed Honey Creek the three miles or so on out to our place. When I showed up late with my lie about missing the bus, the folks didn't seem to mind as long as I was there in time to do my share of the chores.

Dad fishing at the sycamore on Honey Creek

188

* * *

Strictly speaking, I did more than my share. Both Dad and Jay were sorry milkers. Dad was slow because he strip milked and Jay was forever gazing off into space, milking slower and slower as he daydreamed. Mama was as fast as I was, maybe faster, but since she was busy in the kitchen and the three girls never learned to milk, Dad and Jay and I did most of the milking.

Although I enjoyed milking, I was always uneasy because Dad was forever on edge, ready to explode when one of his nervous cows started moving around. When a cow stepped into or kicked over his milk bucket he didn't cuss—he never cussed—but he'd grab the milkstool, chain kickers, wire whip, whatever was nearest at hand, and he'd beat the offending animal until she stood still, trembling but quiet. Jay and I learned that the only thing for us to do when one of these violent outbursts occurred was to go outside and wait until the awful commotion had ended.

Once, after I'd finished milking my cow, Dad told me to turn his next cow, the red cow, into a stanchion. After I did as he said he jumped up from his stool and yelled, "Didn't you hear what I said? I told you to turn in my white cow!"

"Yes, I heard you," I said. "You told me to turn in the red cow. And that's what I did."

"Don't you dispute my word, young man!" Dad screamed in my face. "I'll slap the shit right outta you."

Staring him down, I defiantly held my ground, then quietly changed the two cows. That was the last time Dad threatened me. He must have figured out I wouldn't take that kind of abuse anymore. Not that a fifteen year old boy would have been any match for a grown man: leaving home would have been my only recourse. After the blowup over the red and white cows, Dad treated me considerably better, but his cruel treatment of the cows continued, and he didn't let up on Jay. At eleven, Jay couldn't possibly stand up to him.

I learned to look forward to brisk Saturday mornings when Dad drove the team to the field where he and I shucked out a shock of corn, providing enough grain the following week for the pigs, chickens and horses. While we shucked, Dad repeated the stories he'd told many times before about coon and coyote hunting in northern Kansas when he was a young man and, later, when he'd cowboyed and trapped on the Cimarron in Oklahoma. His accounts of coon hunting with Old Lead, his prize black and tan hound, made me yearn for the fine looking hound pup I'd missed getting at the dog pound in Wichita, especially since Old Tip wouldn't tree anything, not even a possum or squirrel.

Once I asked, "Whatever happened to Old Lead?"

"I sold him," Dad said.

"How much did you get for him?"

"Five dollars."

"You sold your prize coon hound for five dollars?" I asked. "Why did you do that?"

"I needed the money," Dad said. "Times were hard back then."

Later, while scanning the want ads in the Springfield paper, I ran across just what I thought I needed: "Good tree dog, $10, 809 North Robberson." When I showed the paper to Dad, he said, "Nobody'll sell a good tree dog for ten dollars."

"Can I drive to Springfield tomorrow and find out about it?" I asked.

"You don't have a driver's license."

"No," I said, "but I've been driving on the back roads and you said yourself I'm a good driver. I'll be careful."

"Well, make sure you are," he said, to my surprise.

Next morning, instead of catching the bus, I drove to school. Before books took up, I asked Doyle and Hosie if they'd like to go to Springfield with me. "I'll have you back before the end of the last period," I promised.

"Sure, why not?" Doyle said, and Hosie grinned and grabbed his coat.

190

I'd only been to Springfield once, but by asking directions we found North Robberson and the right house. "Do you still have that dog you advertised in the paper?" I asked the man who came to the door.

"Yes," he said. "But not here. You'll have to follow me."

We drove to a big open lot in northwest Springfield, in a part of town I'd later know as Little Italy. In a kennel a big bunch of dogs, all hounds, commenced baying when we drove up.

"Shut up!" the man yelled and the din subsided. The man pursed his lips and made the half whistling, half kissing sound commonly used to summon dogs. "Here, Bell," he said, and a small intelligent looking gyp with a heavy tail, medium sized ears, and brown and red ticked coat immediately went to him.

"She's an extra good July bitch, and she'll tree squirrels all day and possums and coons all night as long as you stay in the woods with her."

"Will she lie?" I asked.

"No. I'll guarantee you she won't lie."

"My dad says there's bound to be somethin' wrong with a dog you're tryin' to sell for ten dollars."

"Your dad's right," the man laughed. "On the Niangua, where I sometimes hunt, she strikes an occasional deer."

"We don't have deer in Lawrence County," I said. "I like her looks. I'll take her."

"She's as good as she looks, son."

"Here's your money, mister," I said. I loaded Old Bell in the front with us, since it was too cold for her to ride in the back. Not surprisingly, with the heater going full blast, she started drooling, and between Republic and Billings, before I could pull over, she'd puked a gob of undigested food as big as a man's fist on the floorboard. Doyle gingerly kicked the wet ball out of the car, and we continued on to Marionville.

By the time I got home that afternoon, the weather had warmed up enough to try out my new dog. Jay and I were headed out to the west forty when, to our surprise, Dad joined

191

us. We hadn't reached the woods when, ranging ahead, Old Bell jumped up on the trunk of a tree and began treeing solid in a pretty chop.

"Sounds like she's treed a squirrel," I said.

"She's pro'bly lyin'," Dad said.

But when we circled the tree, a red squirrel moved on the bare upper trunk.

"Here," Dad said, as he handed me the twenty-two. "Maybe you've got yourself a good squirrel dog after all."

A few nights later, as the weather continued to moderate, Jay and I took a lantern and flashlight, a tow sack, the twenty-two, and Old Bell and headed south toward Charley Howard's old place and beyond to a tangle of woods we thought looked promising. There, before midnight, Old Bell treed one possum after another, until the tow sack bulged. Finally, after the tenth possum, I pulled a piece of binder twine out of my hip pocket and tied the sack with a slick miller's knot Dad had recently taught me.

"Let's go home," I told Jay. "And we may as well walk down the road. We can't carry any more possums." Halfway home, next to a strip of woods, Old Bell treed yet another possum up a small slanting oak a few feet from the road. After Jay shot it, he carried the dead possum, the lantern, the flashlight and the twenty-two, while I shouldered the loaded tow sack.

Too bad the folks were asleep and missed our triumphant return. We dumped the eleven dead possums next to the door on the screened in porch so Dad would be sure to see them in the morning as he headed for the barn. Wouldn't he be surprised?

Shortly after I got my new hound, a fine looking but worthless stray fox terrier showed up, most likely as a result of having been dropped off at the bottom of the hill near the creek. Dad didn't say much about the dog I named Pedro but, knowing him, I knew Pedro's chances for a long life were slim. Sure enough, one afternoon when we got off the bus the handsome stray was nowhere around. After Jay and I repeatedly whistled

and called, "Hyow, Hyow," we realized Old Tip was also missing. We had a good idea what had happened to the dogs, but
because big boys didn't cry and we couldn't have discussed it
with one another without crying, we said nothing. I considered
confronting Dad, but it seemed better to hope the dogs had run
away than to know their fates for sure.

EIGHTEEN
THE RUNAWAY

A short while after the dogs disappeared, I told Dad Mr. Shelton had announced in class that he had a good team of geldings for sale. "Are they well broke? How big are they? Do they have any bad habits? What does he want for them?" Dad asked.

"He didn't say much, except that they're a good well matched team," I said, "And he'll sell them for a reasonable price."

"Ask him more about them, and tell him your dad might be interested in looking at them Saturday afternoon."

Mr. Shelton looked different in his khaki work clothes and somehow shorter than usual as he and Dad, six feet tall, walked ahead of me to the horse pasture. On the way, I overheard Mr. Shelton remark: "Wayne's a good English student. I'd like to have a roomful like him." Surprised and embarrassed, Dad quickly changed the subject to the horses up ahead.

"They're well matched except for their colors," he said, while critically examining the solid black and white animals. "Let's take 'em to the barn where I can see how they drive. Their feet need trimmin' and they oughta be shod," Dad said at the barn. "But they don't look like they've ever been foundered."

"They haven't been foundered since I've had them," Mr. Shelton said, then grunted and stretched as he threw the heavy harness on the tall team. After a few figure eights in the barn lot under Dad's expert handling, the team stopped at his whoa and backed smoothly at his command.

"They're broke to gee and haw," Mr. Shelton said.

"That's all right," Dad answered. "I mainly depend on the lines. What's your low dollar on your horses, Mr. Shelton?"

"I want a hundred dollars apiece, and I don't want to separate them."

"They're soft and big bellied, but they appear to be sound. I'll tell you what. Throw in that old set of harness and I'll give you your price."

Mr. Shelton hesitated, then said, "Since I'm planning on staying out of the horse business, I'm going to take you up on your offer, Mr. Holmes. You've got yourself a good team."

Dad paid Mr. Shelton, they shook hands to seal the deal, and Dad drove the team home while I followed slowly behind in the Hupmobile. From the first there was never any trouble with either horse. In fact, after he'd worked them into shape, Dad said they were as good a team as he ever owned.

That winter and spring Dad and Jeffie Pannell logged off the old Clayton Place nearby. During the week, they felled the white oak trees with axes and a crosscut saw, leaving me with the job on Saturday of snaking out the logs with the new team to a central place where Dad and Jeffie later cut the logs into stave bolt lengths meant for whiskey barrels. While Mama made it clear that she didn't approve of having anything to do with the whiskey making industry, the need for extra money outweighed her scruples.

Holding the heavy doubletree and singletrees up with one hand while driving with the other took considerable strength and dexterity, but recalling what Mr. Shelton had said about the team being broken to gee and haw, I learned to nudge them right and left between the many stumps with voice commands. Another recurring problem was keeping the horses still while I rolled the logs over enough to secure the chain, and then keep them from lunging and hitting the ends of their tugs too hard as they initially set the logs in motion.

I thoroughly enjoyed the rough job of driving the powerful team up hill and down while they dragged the logs to a flat area where a truck would later come to load and transport the shorter bolts. After a particularly long or heavy haul, I'd stop and give the horses a breather. I didn't want to be responsible for breaking their wind and ruining them.

When we'd finished logging and before the spring rains started, Dad agreed, as a favor, for us to clean out Jeffie's dry pond. With Dad handling the lines, it was my gut-wrenching assignment to load and unload the wide and cumbersome two handled slip. Only after many frustrating and botched attempts was I able to gauge the angle correctly and press down or lift up on the handles of the equipment in such a way as to ensure that the right amount of the gray gumbo filled the sliding open-ended metal box. Dad was surprisingly patient, perhaps because the extreme exertion of my job might have overtaxed his damaged heart had we switched places. Virtually always somber while working, Dad busted out laughing once when I misjudged the slip's angle and, as a result, went flying through the air onto the offside horse's hindend. In time, judging the right angle for the slip's sharp edge came easy, much like using a drawknife, and the dreaded heavy work turned satisfying.

* * *

One Saturday morning a strange truck pulled in our driveway. It was old friends, Buck and Thelma Reavis and their seven sons from the Osie community west of Crane near where we lived before we went to Wichita. Dad immediately put on his best company smile and manner: "Howdy, ever'body. Git out and come in," he said.

"Howdy," they exclaimed.

"Whatta ya know?" Dad asked.

"Not much," Buck said. "We're on our way to Chesapeake, and I thought you needed to know that Charles Gaydou wants to trade his team of young horses."

Cutting cane with the Shelton team

"What's wrong with 'em?" Dad asked.

Buck laughed at Dad's suspicions. "Nothin' that I know of, but they've got their bluff in on him, and he's ready to trade for a well broke team."

"My team is as good as there is around here," Dad said.

"I've heard they're good," Buck said. "But I thought you might be interested in tradin' if you got enough boot. Besides, you may be the only person I know who can handle Gaydou's team."

197

Dad grinned. "Well, I might or might not be able to handle 'em. Tell Gaydou I'm not in any hurry to get rid of my horses, but I never had anything I wouldn't trade or sell if the price was right."

"I'll tell him," Buck said, "We better go."

"Tell Mis Holmes 'bye," Thelma said, and the seven Reavis boys clambered into the back of the truck.

Dad and Gaydou got together a few days later. I missed out on the haggling, but they finally traded teams, with Dad drawing two hundred dollars to boot. I hated to see the good team go, but when Dad asked me if I'd help him with Gaydou's snorty dappled grays, memories of Mr. Shelton's well broke horses quickly faded.

Dad said there was no need of inviting trouble, so we hooked the more sensible new horse, Old Ben, to Old Tom, the eighteen year old Percheron gelding Pap had driven from Kansas in 1933. After a few outings, Old Ben gentled right down. Even before we hitched up the other horse, Old Jim, I was afraid there'd be trouble. For one thing, he was wall-eyed and Roman nosed, both bad signs, as anyone who knew horses could tell. Too, his neck was heavy and curved, suggesting he might have been cut proud. Any gelding that looked and acted like a stud horse was suspect. While I held him still but trembling with the twitch, Dad harnessed him, then snubbed him close to Old Tom and ran a lariat through a ring in his left hame and tied one end securely to both rings in a fierce bicycle bit.

"Old Tom's too old to run," Dad assured me, "but just in case, brace your legs against the front of the wagon bed and be ready to pull. Are you ready?"

"Yeah, I'm ready," I said.

"Ease up on that rope," Dad said, "so I can start 'em."

With a couple of quick clicks and a slight loosening and popping of his lines on the horses' hindends, the standard signal for a team to move, Old Jim lunged up and forward, jumping instantly from a standstill to a dead run. With me flat on my back pulling with all my might on the rope, and Dad standing upright seesawing the lines, the runaway horse pulled the reluctant old horse and the careening wagon for a half mile before we slowed down and stopped at the end of the pasture. Both horses needed to blow, but Dad wouldn't have it. "Back, back," he commanded, turning them around and heading toward the barn. Old Jim still showed plenty of fire, but with the exhausted old horse at his side as brake, and with my tight lariat and Dad's know-how, we made it back without further event.

The rest of that early spring we worked Old Jim alongside the old horse as often as we could after school and on Saturday mornings. Dad hoped to work the team of grays together during spring plowing and give Old Tom a rest.

One Saturday morning, we finally hitched the grays and headed across the west forty to shuck corn when Old Jim started prancing and rearing.

"Remember what I've told you," Dad warned. "There's a time to jump."

"How will I know when that time comes?" I asked.

"I'll tell you," he said, and the team headed full tilt toward the woods ahead.

"Remember, roll up in a ball and try to protect your head!" Dad yelled. "And roll out the back of the wagon! NOW!" Scared to act, but even more afraid of staying in the bouncing wagon, I hit the ground hard. I was still rolling when Dad jumped sideways and rolled.

The team veered sharply left, dislodging the bed from the running gears. As they raced toward the gate, they hit a big bump, causing the tongue to drop from the neck yoke and plunge into the ground. The horses' momentum against the suddenly stopped wagon broke the linchpin holding the doubletree, and the horses were free of everything except their harness, the neckyoke, and the wildly bouncing doubletree and singletrees at their heels. They took a hard left at the road in front of the house and went in a dead run down the red hill out of sight.

Mr. McCarty, hearing the commotion, waved the tired team down in front of his house a half mile away, then drove the sweat drenched horses home. "Anybody hurt?" he yelled.

"I guess not," Dad said. "Much obliged. Wayne, go unharness them outlaws and turn 'em out. They better enjoy themselves while they can, 'cause they're Joplin bound."

"Joplin?" Mr. McCarty asked. "What's at Joplin?"

"A pretty fair horse market," Dad said, matter-of-factly.

"The horses'll be butchered?"

"Yeah," Dad said, "some go for dog food and some for humans. I hear the French will eat anything."

Dad with three of his Joplin bound horses

While he was at it Dad loaded up Old Red, Old Prince and Old Tom and sent them along with the big grays to the Joplin meat market. Old Red was a good horse, but he'd developed a fistula. For a while it looked as though the blue vitriol Dad packed in the running sore would dry it up but, sooner or later, it always broke and ran again. Old Prince was a headstrong rascal who'd run away with an inexperienced driver. Dad could handle him, but he thought the recurring limp in Old Prince's right front foot came from malingering instead of an old injury. Eighteen years of hard work had caught up with

Old Tom. I thought the faithful old horse should have been turned out to pasture and allowed to die naturally, but Dad crowded him into the back of Buck's truck with the culls and the outlaws.

NINETEEN
FRED'S HOME

After school was out in the spring, I called Mr. Farley in Kansas to see if he needed help in wheat harvest. "Mr. Farley, this is Wayne Holmes. Do you need me in harvest again?"

"Yes, I do. I need you to drive the pickup. Have you been practicin' your drivin'?"

"I sure have!"

"Well, be here by the end of the first week in June," Mr. Farley said. "Pay's up to five dollars a day and room and board. Okay?"

"Okay," I said. "I'll be there. 'Bye."

While studying Missouri and Kansas road maps, I asked Dad, "What would be wrong with me hitchhikin' to Clearwater?"

"Nothin' except the long wait between rides," Dad said. "It's a cheap way to travel."

"What about hoppin' a freight train, like you used to do?"

"Absolutely not," Dad said. "Your Uncle Bobby had to go to the hospital after he lost his grip when we was ridin' the rails in Colorado. You better stick to hitchhikin'."

"Okay," I said.

"Let me give you a few tips," he said. "Always stand, no matter how tired you are. And when someone pulls over, run to the car. And somethin' else," he said, "don't clam up or sleep. People who stop for hitchhikers want company."

Dad took me over to Mt. Vernon early the next day and let me out north of the sanitarium. "Take care of yourself," he said.

"I will," I said, "'Bye."

It was an all day trip from highway 39 to 96 and then west through Carthage and beyond where I jogged over and picked up 160 which roughly paralleled the Kansas-Oklahoma line all the way to Arkansas City before I travelled northwest to Clearwater. When I arrived it was dark and I was hungry. The leftovers Mrs. Farley offered were skimpy, but I was glad to sit down and eat whatever she placed before me. Mr. Farley was brusque, much as I remembered him from the previous summer.

"Where's the old cowboy who was here last year?" I asked, looking around.

"He's at the county farm, unable to work anymore. I've hired three young men from Arkansas. They're upstairs. By the way," Mr. Farley said. "You won't be drivin' the pickup after all. One of the men can't drive a tractor, so I'm puttin' you on the '28 John Deere again. Hope you don't mind." I did mind, but Mr. Farley was the boss, and from all appearances I was low man on the totem pole.

"Looks like you're gettin' along all right," Mr. Farley said one evening.

"Yeah," I said, "Except at the corners. What're the chances of gettin' a spinner knob?"

"I've never needed one," Mr. Farley said, "but if you want one I'll get it for you."

"Thanks," I said, "I think it'll help." It did help, but Saturday night when we got paid, I said, "Accordin' to my figures, you've shorted me a dollar and a half."

"That knob of yours cost a dollar and a half," Mr. Farley said.

"Oh," I said. "I didn't know it was mine."

"I told you I didn't need it, remember?"

"Yes, now that you mention it."

It rained on Monday, so the four of us spent most of the day napping. After supper, when everyone was downstairs, Mr. Farley motioned me to follow him upstairs. Something was wrong. "One of the boys is missin' his thirty dollars. He thinks you took it."

"Well, I didn't."

"I've talked to them, and all three think you did," Mr. Farley said.

"I don't care what they think: I didn't take it," I repeated.

"I hate to say it," Mr. Farley continued, "but I'm afraid they're right. You're the most likely suspect."

"You listen to me, Mr. Farley," I said. "I may be a lot of things, but I'm not a common thief. And as far as I'm concerned, you're the most likely suspect!" I thought Mr. Farley was going to hit me, but instead he stormed downstairs and out of the house.

Next morning all of us settled uneasily into our routines. At dinnertime, instead of joining us at the table, Mr. Farley was out at the road intercepting the mailman. Upon his return, he motioned the men from Arkansas upstairs. When they came down I noticed the youngest one held back. "The mailman cleared up the question of the missing money," Mr. Farley announced. "Bill here sent a sixty dollar money order to his wife. Since he's admitted taking the money and agrees to pay it back as soon as he can, ever'thing's all right now. Okay?"

Mr. Farley hadn't looked my way, but I could tell his final word was directed at me.

"No, it's not okay," I said, standing. "You accused me to my face of stealin' that money. Pay me the two-fifty you owe me. I'm goin' back to Missouri where a man's word means somethin'."

Since it was past noon when I quit my job, I knew better than to take a chance on being caught out on the road hitchhiking after dark. The best thing to do was to catch a ride into Wichita, stay all night at Pap and Lottie's, then start early the next morning for Missouri. Before leaving I called John Benn in Planeview: "Have you guys thought any more about visiting me in Missouri, like we planned?"

"Yeah, we were just talkin' about it."

"Good, why not try to make it in the next few days? All of us need some time off before school starts."

"We'll see about it," John said. "Do you have telephones in Missouri?"

"A few," I said, "But I don't remember our number. It's listed under J.P. Holmes out of Aurora. Got it?"

"Yeah, I'll call you."

"Okay, see you later. 'Bye."

"'Bye," John said.

I rode a city bus early the next day east past Beech and the city limits, where I caught my first ride. The land was flat and dull past Eureka, but the terrain gradually changed to the high lonesome Flint Hills prairie, with hardly a tree in sight. Sometimes I got to see the individual brands and ear notches marking nearby cattle, reminding me of Dad's accounts of cowboying in Kansas and Oklahoma in earlier times. All too soon I was out of the Flint Hills and on flat land again. Nothing changed much before I saw the familiar hills of Missouri.

The folks were surprised to see me back so soon, but they expressed little interest in the details of why I'd quit my job. They were mainly concerned that I hadn't made much money, nothing even close to the haul I'd made the previous summer and fall.

"You've still got time," Dad said. "Cyrus Cox always needs an extra hand."

"I'm not sure I want to work for Cyrus," I said.

"Why not? Cyrus is all right."

"Yeah, he's all right," I agreed, "but I've heard he pushes his hired hands pretty hard."

"I hadn't heard that," Dad said, "but come to think of it, ever'body moves at a pretty fast clip over there."

Mom chimed in, "You don't have much choice, young man. You better hightail it over there first thing in the mornin'."

Cyrus seemed glad to see me. "Yes, one of my men quit and I need someone to help Jim Moody shock wheat."

"It's not easy for two men to keep up with a binder," he said, "but they oughta be able to do it."

"I need the work and I'll do the best I can," I said. "When do we start?"

"Be here in the mornin' at seven sharp." Cyrus said. "Bessie'll fix dinner."

Tall, long armed, long legged, and graceful, Jim was a natural at shocking wheat. Short coupled, awkward, and new at the job, I had to scramble to keep up. Cyrus tripped the bundles close together, but Jim and I gradually dropped farther and farther behind the tireless machinery. We expected a break when James stopped the tractor at his dad's yell, but Cyrus waved us over and said, "You boys are gonna have to pick up the pace. Anytime you're empty-handed, you need to run."

We followed his instructions briefly, then slowed, first to a trot and eventually to a tired shuffle. Bessie's big dinner helped—especially her coconut cream pie—but all too soon we were back in our hopeless race with the binder.

When I dragged home late that evening, Mom was in a dark mood. "John Benn called from Wichita and said he and Warren and Keith are comin' on the bus tomorrow."

"Tomorrow?"

"Yes, tomorrow," she said. "You know how I feel about company. Call him up and tell him one of them can come for a few days, but that's all."

"But I invited all three of them."

"I don't care," she said, "Only one can come. Call him."

I was embarrassed to tell John the bad news. "I'm not surprised," he said. "Your mother was always nervous with a bunch of us around. I'll still come if you're sure it's all right." "It's all right," I assured him, "but I have to warn you, I'm working for a neighbor and won't be able to run around with you much."

"What'll there be for me to do?" he asked.

"You and Jay can go to the creek and swim and fish and mess around during the day. I'll be home at night."

"Okay," John said. "See ya later."

John was already there when I got home the next evening. Dad had picked him up at the station. Mom thought the two of us ought to sleep on the bed in the washhouse that night so we wouldn't keep the rest of them up with our talking.

"Don't stay up too late," she warned me. "You've got a hard day ahead of you."

"Okay," I said, but we stayed up past midnight while John caught me up on everything I'd missed. Jay kept John entertained the best he could during the days, and although the bluegill they caught were small, Mom fried everything they caught and cleaned, including two good sized turtles, a snapper and a leathery softshell. Easy to be around, John spent part of his time with Mom and the girls. Mom ordinarily resented having anyone extra around to cook and do for, but John won her over. He bragged on her hearty breakfasts and the generous portions she dished out, and he said her daily homemade rolls and light bread, old hat to the rest of us, was the best bread he'd ever eaten. Mom improvised special desserts for supper a couple of times that week. Her sharply piquant, one of a kind, green grape sauce on hot rolls was a big

207

hit all around. But no matter what John said to the contrary, the vinegar pie was a flop.

One night Jay wasn't paying attention, and he started to take more than his share of the canned purple plums Mom had opened. "Take two," she hissed, and he, red faced, started in on the exact portion all seven of us took – two plums each.

* * *

Following his tour of duty in Japan, Fred was mustered out of the Army and came home to Honey Creek. Before he arrived, I grew antsy as I recollected the last time he was home, over two years before, when we'd had our knock-down-drag-out fight on Christmas day, and the only thing that had saved his hide was Mama's help when she knocked me off him with a broom. I hoped his rough edges would be smoothed out by his worldwide travels and experiences, but I feared we'd have trouble.

Fred must have been rich; instead of calling for Dad to pick him up at the train station, he hired a cab. Upon his arrival, he and Dad awkwardly shook hands in the yard, Mama hugged his skinny neck, and the rest of us grinned and checked him out. He was taller, right at Dad's six feet, but I doubted he weighed much more than my 140 pounds. His rumpled uniform improved his looks, but when he opened his mouth he still sounded suspiciously like a hick. After Mama warmed up a big bait of brown beans and cornbread for him, Fred smacked his lips and said, "This is awful good, awful good." He was the same old Fred.

"You must be tired," Dad said to him later in the evening. "I don't suppose you're used to sleepin' double, much less triple the way you boys used to sleep, but for now why don't you try sleepin' in the back bedroom with Wayne and Jay."

"Don't worry, I'll make out just fine," Fred said, and after he'd smoked a cigarette in the bathroom, we went to bed. Jay fell asleep immediately and I, spooned between him and Fred, soon followed suit. I had an awful nightmare: I dreamed someone was after me, about to hurt me, someone, it seemed like it was Fred, who'd taunted me and chased me and caught me and bent my little fingers all the way back until I'd finally mustered the strength and courage to hold him in a desperate headlock until he'd hollered "Calf Rope."

Shaky and groggy, but finally sure I was awake, my first inclination was to give Fred the benefit of the doubt. He was probably dreaming and no one should be held accountable for his dreams. But he wasn't dreaming. He was wide awake and on the prod, intent on conquering me once and for all.

"Get away from me and turn over," I growled.

"No, not yet," he said. "This won't take long," and he snuggled up tight against my hindend with his hard-on.

"Yes, right now. I don't care what you did in the army, you're not gonna cornhole me," I said, backing him off with a hard blow to his dick. Fiercely, but as quietly as possible so as not to wake Jay, I twisted and squirmed while delivering vicious, well aimed rabbit punches until he gave up and turned over.

"I'm sleepin' somewhere else," I hissed, and grabbed a cover on my way to the daybed on the porch. It took a long time for me to relax enough to go to sleep, and I was awake early the next morning when Mama came out for kindling on her way to the kitchen.

"What are you doin' out here?" she asked.

"I couldn't sleep back there in the bedroom," I said. "It was too crowded."

Fred and I didn't have much use for one another for a long time after that. He went his way; I went mine.

* * *

After buying a hot '36 Ford, Fred tried to date some of the younger girls at Rocky Comfort, but they were put off by his rowdy behavior and fast driving. He was struck on Nadine, the sixteen year old middle Simpson girl, and she dated him a few times, but everyone except Fred knew she was just being kind and marking time for when she'd find someone more suitable. One Sunday Nadine and her older sister, Irene, invited Fred and me home with them for Sunday dinner. Their folks were friendly and Mrs. Simpson, an outstanding cook, outdid herself with the table piled high with fried chicken, mashed potatoes and gravy, fresh green beans from the garden, homemade light bread with plenty of butter and jelly, and corn on the cob in the cramped dining room.

"Everything's awful good," Fred said, while taking big second helpings.

"Save room for dessert," Mr. Simpson warned. "Her lemon meringue pie will melt in your mouth."

"I cain't wait," Fred grinned, prompting Mrs. Simpson to pass the pie before he expected it, and as he juggled it, the whole thing capsized upside down in his lap.

"Don't worry about it," Mrs. Simpson kept saying as she scraped the yellow and white mess off his lap and legs. The spilled pie episode may have further cooled Nadine's feelings for Fred, because she quit him and took up with an older guy she soon married.

Fred bought a fierce German Shepherd, English Bulldog cross, ordered a fine set of heavy harness with brass fittings from Sears and Roebuck, and he talked at length about farming for a living, but before he got around to buying a team, he'd decided to go to California.

According to Fred, the Aurora police had it in for him. They'd pulled him over more than once and lectured him, harassed him, he said, for the way he drove. One night, after he'd talked me into going into town with him to see a movie, he was cutting dangerous didoes next to the shoe factory, a trick meant to scare whoever was with him, when we heard an approaching siren. "I can outrun him," Fred said, and he swiftly accelerated east to the stop sign, crossed the rough railroad tracks and headed north, hell bent for leather. "Once we git out of town we're home free. City police ain't got no jurisdiction in the country." We outran the cop, but at the city limits sign he kept right on coming.

"You better pull over," I told Fred.

"Maybe so," Fred finally conceded.

"Get out and put up your hands!" the policeman yelled.

"You cain't arrest me," Fred said. "We're out in the country."

"Just watch me," the policeman said as he handcuffed Fred and shoved him into the back of his patrol car. Turning to me, he asked, "Can you drive?"

"Yes sir," I said.

"Then turn around and follow me to city hall."

"Yes sir."

Fred was meek at the police station, but he heated up on our way home. "That's the last straw!" he yelled. "No tellin' how much my fine'll be. If I could afford a good lawyer, I bet I could get off scot free with a big settlement for false arrest."

"You better just pay your fine," I said.

"You're prob'ly right," he said, "And as soon as I do I'm outta here." After paying his fine, he gave his new set of harness to Dad and made preparations to leave. "I've about decided against takin' Old Spot. He'd be more trouble than he's worth. I'll take ten dollars for him, Wayne. You want him?"

"I wouldn't mind havin' him," I said, "but you're way too high."

"What's he worth?"

"I'll give you what you've got in him."

"You don't know what I paid for him."

"Yes, I do. Five dollars."

"Okay, okay. Pay me," Fred said. He crawled in the car, waved great big, and said, "Bye, ever'body, see you in the funny papers," and peeled out, burning rubber.

* * *

Since Old Tip's disappearance, I'd missed having a dog at my side when I explored the surrounding countryside. Old Bell was fine when I wanted to go hunting, but for a companion the new dog I'd bought off Fred turned out just right. The short haired white dog with occasional black and brown spots was of mixed ancestry, but I couldn't decide whether he was part German Shepherd, part English Bulldog, as Fred thought, or some kind of duke's mixture. Not that it mattered. Old Spot wasn't exactly belligerent, but his fearless and alert look, along with his upright ears and wide head and chest, made lots of people leery of him. And he wasn't a bit afraid. When two or more dogs jumped him he'd fight them by charging into them, knocking first one and then the other off his feet and slashing away. But when there was only one dog to fight, Old Spot changed his tactics. After knocking his opponent down, he quickly got what was meant to be a death grip on his opponent's throat.

The first time I saw Old Spot fight a single dog, he had Mr. McCarty's shepherd in what appeared to be his death throes before I managed to pry his powerful jaws apart. After Mr. McCarty and his defeated dog left, Dad gave me some advice: "You'd better put a heavy loose leather collar on that white dog of yours so you can choke him off a little sooner next time. If you don't, he'll kill somebody's dog and you'll be in a world of trouble."

"That's a good idea," I said.

After our hogs started getting out, we learned that Old Spot could hold the biggest and meanest hog on the place by the ear while we inserted sharp copper rings in its tender nose. I also learned that if I was careful and easy with him, Old Spot would do a fair job of working cattle. Unfortunately, one day Dad threw one of his shit fits and sicced Old Spot on a breechy cow. Before we knew it, the eager dog had bitten the cow's tail entirely off about halfway up.

"If that dog ever does that again, he's outta here," Dad warned. I wanted to tell Dad that if he didn't yell and get Old Spot excited, he wouldn't get out of hand, but I didn't dare say anything.

212

After word got out that I had a hog dog, Cyrus Cox asked me to move a big bunch of his hogs across Honey Creek. Although he paid me only a dollar, considerably less than I expected, I didn't care. The experience and prestige of moving the hard to manage animals more than made up for the sorry pay.

One day a man in a big truck with stock racks pulled up in our driveway.

"Git out," Dad said.

"I'm lookin' for a hog dog, and a man at the stockyards told me you had one," the stranger said.

"I don't have one, but my boy here does," Dad said, pointing to me. "And that's the hog dog, right over there."

"He looks stout, but he's not as big as I expected. What'll he weigh, forty pounds?"

"Maybe, but no more than that. What are you lookin' for in a dog?"

"I'm lookin' for a good dog to replace my old Catahoula I used to hunt wild hogs on the Buffalo River in Arkansas."

"Do you wanta see my boy's dog work?" Dad asked.

"Yes, I do," the man said.

Old Spot, quivering with anticipation, stayed next to my side as we walked to the pigpen. "Which one do you want him to catch?" I asked.

"That big boar'll do," he said, and I pointed Spot towards the big hog and whispered, "Git him, boy." Spot caught the bounding woof-woofing boar high on the left ear and hung on, causing the animal to come to a squealing halt.

"He made that look easy," the man said, nodding in approval. "What'll you take for him?"

"He's not for sale."

"Not for sale? I wouldn't have driven all this way if I'd known he wasn't for sale. You'd price him, wouldn't you?"

"No," I said. "I won't."

Dad butted in: "You'll drive a long ways before you'll run across a hog dog as good as this one. What's he worth to you? What'll you give for him?"

"I'll give a hundred dollars, and I won't back out."

"Whatta ya think, Wayne?" Dad said. "He's your dog, but that's a lot of money."

"I appreciate your offer, mister," I said. "But I won't sell him at any price."

The man smiled and said, "I'm disappointed, but I can't say that I blame you, son. I wouldn't sell him if he was mine, either."

A couple of weeks after my hundred dollar offer, a newly freshened cow came into the barnlot trailing a newborn calf. My heart sank when I saw the cow's switch was missing and blood dripped from her shortened tail. "What in the world do you suppose happened to that cow's tail?" I asked Dad.

"I know exactly what happened," Dad said. "That white dog of yours has had a hold of her. I told you what'd happen if another cow lost a tail around here. Tie that dog up right now, and I want him off the place within twenty-four hours."

"But I don't think Spot did it. He won't attack anything unless somebody sics him on it."

"I don't care what you think!" Dad yelled. "You git rid of him or I'll git rid of him for you! You should've sold him when you had a chance."

Since I had no way of finding the man from Arkansas, my only hope was Pete Woods, who had once said he'd like to have a dog like Spot. Pete and his family lived a couple of miles south in a two room unpainted house surrounded by junk, and he didn't have a phone, so the day after the cow lost her switch, I walked south, with Old Spot at my side.

"Are you still interested in ownin' a good hog dog?" I asked Pete.

"Yeah, but I'm short on money. How would you swap him for that Walker gyp over there?"

"Is she any good?"

"I don't know, I haven't tried her," Pete said. "I'll tell you what. If you're in the notion of gittin' rid of your dog, I'll trade you that gyp and throw in a pretty redbone pup to boot. How about it?"

"I'll trade with you," I said. "His name's Old Spot. Be good to him, and try not to get too loud when you work him. Oh, and don't sic him on anything unless you're serious. He'll take hold of and hang onto anything you put him on."

"Another thing," I said. "Be sure to keep him tied until he's had time to forget me. If he follows me home, Dad'll kill him."

"I understand," Pete said. "I'll keep him tied, like you said."

A couple of days later, when Jay and I were going after the cows, we came up on a mashed down place on the edge of the woods where we could tell a cow had recently had a calf. As we looked around, Jay spotted the switch of a cow's tail in the crotch of a hickory sapling close by. The blood on the bone was dry and dark.

TWENTY
THEM WELDYS

With two summers of wheat harvest under my belt and ten weeks of broomcorn harvest one fall, at sixteen I thought I was a man. When school let out for the summer, this time, instead of working in Kansas, I was headed for Freedom in western Oklahoma where Fred had worked the previous summer before going on to California.

Dad had some advice for me before I left: "Whatever you do, stay away from them Weldys around Freedom. They're dangerous. When I was a young man livin' out there, two of the Weldy boys was fixin' fence on their ranch with a couple of hired hands when a fight broke out. The Weldys ended up knockin' one of the men in the head with their saddle pliers. Accordin' to the one who got away, they trussed up the other one and dragged him with their horses down a canyon outta sight. Nobody ever knew for sure what happened to the body, but most people who knew the Weldys thought they prob'ly stashed it in one of the hundreds of caves in them rough gyp hills out there. The man who got away hightailed it plumb out of the country. The law never did much investigatin', and ever'body else knew better than to cross the Weldys. It wouldn't do to go snoopin' around out there back then, and I bet it wouldn't now, either. Remember what I said, them Weldys are a dangerous bunch. Stay away from them."

Nodding to assure Dad I'd heard him, but dismissing his exaggerated warning, I boarded a Greyhound bus for my ten hour trip west. Lacking anything to read concerning sex, violence, or religion, or anything else to feed my fantasies, my ride was uneventful, boring.

Walt Blevins stood waiting in the dusky evening light in front of the drugstore on the single main street of Freedom. Tall, thin, and courtly in his pale Levis and subdued cowboy shirt and hat, he was what I imagined Dad might have looked like had he stayed in Oklahoma and prospered. Mary, Walt's wife, stood beside him clutching the picture of me Mama had sent ahead.

"You have to be Wayne, Fred's brother," Walt said, shaking my hand and grinning. "You're better lookin' than Fred, but you'll have to hump to match the way he worked."

"I never could keep up with him workin'," I replied. "But I'll do my best to make you a good hand."

"That's all anyone can expect," Mary said. "Come on, Walt, let's go home, Wayne's had a long day and I'll bet he's hungry."

My job, like Fred's the year before, was to drive the pickup out in the fields next to the combine just long enough to catch the wheat, then ease the load into a converted barn, and with an eighteen inch wide aluminum scoop furiously lift and throw shovelful after shovelful until all was gone. Again and again, all day long, the interminable work continued. Many times those first three days, I thought: "I can't go on." But by the end of the first week the ten minute rest between each run sufficed: I could and did go on. And by the end of the second week, I relished shoveling nonstop with no more respite than a slight pause as I shifted the wide shovel from one hand to the other.

Unable to keep up with the fields of dead ripe wheat with his single outfit, Walt hired someone with another set of machinery along with two more men to round out his new crew. Friendly Pie Cavett, thirty-five, the town drunk, but dried out and working for the Lord just then, could drive a truck or tractor, but hard work often aggravated a severe rupture in his scrotum. The second new hand, Ed Weldy, eighteen years old, a dead ringer for Steinbeck's Lennie, had never learned how to drive, but he could scoop wheat all day without raising a sweat.

Back home I'd fervently wished for rainy days—a sinner dared not pray – but with few books and no squirrels to tempt me in western Oklahoma when promising clouds gathered, I welcomed other work. Besides, each working day's six dollars helped provide gas, clothes, and money for the following school year. One wet morning after breakfast, I gladly ran with Ed and Pie through driving rain past several full wheat bins toward old corn cribs in need of repair for the continuing bumper harvest. We'd worked steadily a couple of hours, driving galvanized nails into narrow laths covering gaps in the cribs, when Pie paused and said, "Time for a break."

After Pie and Ed had finished smoking and we'd rested a few minutes sitting in the breezeway, Ed's coarse face brightened as he nodded in my direction and said to Pie, "Let's throw him down and take off his pants and spit on it." Pie, quick to laugh, snickered when I stood up. Ed crouched slightly and slowly moved toward me, loose lipped and ugly, while I turned my hammer handle a half turn. Glad that the claws stuck straight out instead of curving, I marked his pulsing temple where I aimed to sink my deadly weapon. Ed stopped short, just out of hammer's reach, while I, with killing in my heart, stared him down.

"We better git back to work, boys," Pie said. Ed swallowed hard and walked away.

I never told Dad.

TWENTY-ONE
ROCKY COMFORT

A two week revival got underway in late August at the Rocky Comfort Baptist Church. Instead of our regular old ho-hum preacher, a hotshot from Springfield was brought in. Auctioneer turned evangelist, the swag bellied man with his coal black pompadour electrified the crowd with his whizbang performance that first night.

At the opening words of the hymn for the altar call:

> *Why do you wait, dear brother?*
> *Why do you tarry so long?*

Irene Simpson left my side and marched forward and knelt at a low bench. Before the last stanza ended, she turned to the congregation and testified to her newly saved condition as tears of joy streamed down her bright and shining freckled face. Not to be outdone, her younger sister Nadine quickly followed suit.

Night after night the practiced chant of the preacher proved persuasive, thinning the rows of sinners on the back pews, but I hardened my heart and withstood Irene's tearful entreaties and her strong sweaty hands. As the second week of the revival wore on, I was holding up pretty well, I thought, when it occurred to me that I was in a bad way: now that all my new friends were saved, I wouldn't have anyone left to sin with. Even Gene Emlet caved in. On the next to last night, he walked forward as the congregation sang:

Bringing in the sheaves,
Bringing in the sheaves,
We shall come rejoicing,
Bringing in the sheaves.

In record time he was back on his feet, blubbering and testifying away, leaving me alone as the last holdout.

The next day, Saturday afternoon, under heavy conviction, I slowly made my way down the narrow path through the woods next to Honey Creek. Maybe I'd pushed my luck too far at eight when Fay Hilton had begged me to be saved and I'd gotten off the hook by reminding myself that Jesus had waited until He was twelve to begin His father's work. Or maybe I'd committed sacrilege, or blasphemy, whichever was worse, when I broke my promise at twelve after puberty, galloping, galloping, overtook me behind the smoke house and I had deliberately put off becoming a Christian for four more wonderful sin filled years in wicked Wichita. Now at the end of my second grace period, and in my prime, at sixteen, just when I hoped my experiences might catch up with my fantasies, here I was surrounded by God-fearing Christians. I thought and thought about it, then made up my mind.

The one room cobblestone church was packed the last night of the revival. As the preacher tugged at his suspenders and warmed to his task I, impassive as always, sat in my seat next to the aisle on the back pew. At the conclusion of the preacher's by now familiar harangue, Betty Mitchell had started playing "Softly and Tenderly" when I, without Irene's prompting, stood and strode forward and knelt. Two older men, deacons, dropped to their knees on either side of me. There, following many earlier examples, I prayed the prayer of a sinner while one brother poured instructions in my right ear and the other struck me hard in the middle of the back to the measured beat of the music.

It took longer than I expected to confess my sinful past, longer by far than any of the others who'd confessed their sins. I related the long ago time when, at seven, I'd lied about taking a dump in Dad's tool shed rather than go to the woods as I was supposed to do; I admitted to stealing and hiding a bucket of eggs at the Snuffer place, and then lying about finding them; and I confessed to a number of vague sexual sins which I quickly glossed over when I thought the preacher showed undue interest. I even admitted to being in on stealing that '28 Plymouth coupe with the rumble seat some of us boys took turns hiding for several weeks when we were going back and forth with three foxy girls to frolic in the sand pits next to the Arkansas River south of Wichita. Hardest of all, I said out loud that I was guilty of dishonoring my father and mother many times, black sins which I feared merited my damnation.

The congregation remained standing as they sang the four stanzas of the same song over and over again. When I finally paused, the man hitting me stopped and the other one shifted his weight and hoarsely whispered, "I believe you're saved. Let's get up."

"No, I don't think so," I said. "I don't feel good."

"Did you tell everything?" he asked.

"Well, almost everything," I admitted.

"You better start over," he said. "And this time make sure you don't leave anything out."

I whispered as I described the most shameful sins I'd left out the first time around. First, I admitted that as an eleven year old, the winter Dad was bedridden, I'd sometimes dis-

221

obeyed Mama and lingered behind in the milk barn where I had impure thoughts as I petted my favorite cow.

After shifting my elbows on the rough oak bench where I knelt, I confessed that I hadn't been able to resist pinching Rosemary Mounts' tight little bottom one time as I walked her home from school in Wichita, even if I did know that she would never have anything to do with me again. And I went on to tell about another incident when an older girl sitting next to me at the picture show touched me, then began rubbing the inside of my thigh. Before I'd finished describing this wicked experience, the impatient preacher stood over me. He'll hear me, I thought, but I've got to tell everything. And I quickly murmured that I'd helped the girl unbutton my pants so she could more easily have her way with me.

Before I'd finished the second time around, the music from the played out congregation and tinny piano sounded like a scratchy old phonograph that needed rewinding. When I stopped speaking, the man coaching me said, "Get up. You're saved for sure this time."

"No," I replied. "I don't think so. I still don't feel good. I'm gonna get up and go back and sit down." Confused and humiliated, I headed for the back bench.

The shaken preacher seemed to think he owed the tired congregation an explanation: "Brothers and sisters, here's something we've all heard about but few of us have actually seen. This young man has committed the ultimate sin, the sin for which there is no forgiveness, the sin against the Holy Ghost."

"Shit fire," I thought.

Instead of ending the revival with the familiar and joyful "In the Sweet By and By," the stern faced evangelist led the congregation in singing a hymn ordinarily reserved for the most hard-bitten and unrepentant sinners. As the song wound down, I slipped outside in the dark where I faintly heard the last lines:

Almost persuaded,
Almost, but lost.

Next day, Sunday morning, I was too embarrassed to go to church, and the folks didn't say anything when I headed out the door for the creek instead of getting ready. But that night I jumped in the back of the Hupmobile with the other kids as Dad pulled out toward Rocky Comfort. A quarter of a mile west of the church, where the road made a sharp turn to the right, I dropped off when Dad slowed down, then took my good sweet time walking the rest of the way.

I stayed outside, waiting to intercept Gene Emlet after church. Gene was a straight shooter who'd tell me the truth if I could get him off by himself. "I want to know somethin'," I finally said to him in the half light. "Last night, when you got saved, what happened?"

"Whatta you mean?"

"Just what I said. What happened?"

"Nothin' happened," he said. "Why do you wanta know?"

"From all of your grinnin' and crying' and carryin' on, I thought somethin' important happened," I said.

"Naw, nothin' happened. I let on like that so I could hurry up and get it over with."

"Oh," I said. "Well, 'bye. See ya later."

Some of the young people at Rocky Comfort attended school at Mt. Vernon, and some at Aurora, but since most of them went to Marionville, I was afraid they'd talk and I'd be shunned.

One thing that may have helped divert attention from me was the big ruckus in study hall one day when E.E. Street, the cranky school superintendent, came in looking for someone to make an example of. "I want to see every last one of you busy in here," he growled. While many of us opened our books and made halfhearted attempts at looking busy, Mr. Street— Mortimer Snerd as he was referred to in witty bathroom

223

graffiti—spotted Joe Steele on the back row repeatedly opening and closing his legs, a comforting nervous habit Joe had.

As everyone except Mr. Street knew, Joe was likable and good-natured, but he was the last person in school anyone ought to mess with. Joe had a strong sense of right and wrong, and though he hadn't grabbed a book and pretended he was studying, he took offense when Mr. Street grabbed his arm and yelled: "I said I want to see everybody studying, young man, and that includes you!"

Maybe Mr. Street slapped Joe, I'm not sure since everything happened so fast, but I remember hearing Joe say, "You better turn loose of my arm," and when Mr. Street refused, seeing three short powerful blows to the big man's red nose and the blood gushing out onto the front of his blue suit and white shirt.

When Mr. Street took him home, Joe said his dad told him, "Go ahead and whip him if you want to," but the superintendent declined. In fact, Joe was back in school the next day. Unlike other boys who might have turned sullen or cocky in similar circumstances, Joe Steele remained the same person he'd been all along.

Another thing that may have helped me get past my trouble at Rocky Comfort was the poetry contest Mr. Shelton organized soon after school started. If the assignment had been from anyone else I would have ignored it, but because I liked Mr. Shelton and wanted to please him, I tried hard to write something acceptable, something better than the Dick and Jane drivel that filled my head.

As the deadline for the assignment neared, I searched through the skimpy library for something obscure which I might pass off as my own. Since the evangelist had officially declared that I was going to hell for sure anyway, I didn't think stealing a poem would make any difference. Finding nothing suitable in the library, I racked my brain for something, anything, that might do. Then, almost at the last minute, I remembered the words of a short poem I'd read, but to save my life I couldn't recall the poem's catchy title. Undeterred, I supplied the poem with my own mundane title, and turned it in just under the wire. Imagine my surprise when my stolen poem received first place in Mr. Shelton's poetry contest. There it was, in print at the bottom of the front page of the school paper:

SHORTY
This poem 'orter
Be two lines shorter.

By Wayne Holmes

Because I played football I had an in with the jocks already, but my success in the poetry writing contest may have made me acceptable to the Marionville literary crowd and helped with beating out Max McBride for class president. News of the results of the voting was barely out when I was summoned to Mr. Williams' office.

"I hear you've been elected president of your class," he said.

"That's what I hear too."

"I'm concerned about one thing," Mr. Williams said.

"What's that?" I asked, fearing the worst.

"You're a poor example for your classmates."

"What do you mean, a poor example? I haven't been in any trouble, have I?"

"Not here at school," he said, as I braced myself for his version of my trouble at Rocky Comfort. "But if you think I'm unaware of how many times you've skipped school, you've got another think coming. There's no way I can keep you in school, but I do have the authority to block your election as class president if you don't qualify."

"You mean skipping school once in a while disqualifies me?"

"You've got it. I'll give you the rest of the week to make up your mind. Either come to school every day, or step down from your new office. It's one or the other."

"Okay," I said. "But I won't need any extra time to think it over. I'll be here."

"Good," Mr. Williams said.

* * *

My main duty as class president wasn't presiding over meetings, as I feared. Instead, it was my job to make sure the vending machine was kept filled and running, and the steady trickle of nickels and dimes was counted and turned into Mr. Williams' office for the day when the proceeds would eventually help pay for our senior trip.

With no facilities of any kind at our improvised football playing field at the edge of Baldy's orchard, and with more players than onlookers, it wouldn't have paid to set up a stand at the afternoon home games. A bottle of pop would have been refreshing for us as we rested under nearby apple trees at half time, but we were restricted to warm sips of water before resuming what passed for football, crunching affairs kept partly in check by the whistles, yells, and instructions of the two officials, Shelby Rainey and Jim Ewing.

Following football season, I planned on helping man the stand at our home basketball games. But the new coach, Mr. Allen, a seedy looking tattooed former carney and boxer, stopped me after watching an especially spirited pick up game—more like a free-for-all—some of us played in the gym after lunch one day.

"I like the way you mix it up on defense," Mr. Allen said, popping his knuckles and flexing and hunching his arms and shoulders in his oddly menacing way. "How about trying out for the team after school today?"

"Sure," I said, "but I'll have to tell my brother I won't be ridin' the bus."

After warming us up with a few exercises, Mr. Allen started a scrimmage.

"Here, Holmes, guard this man. Whatever you do, don't let him score. Got it?"

226

"Yeah, I think so."

My long legged assigned man had dribbled the length of the gym and was going up for what looked to be a sure layup when I managed to overtake him, jump high, grab him around the neck, and slam him to the floor. Coach Allen's sharp whistle preceded his guttural yell: "You better stick with football!" as he waved me off the floor toward the lockers. Hosie was sympathetic as we walked home after practice, but I could tell he agreed with Mr. Allen.

One Friday night in December when Doyle Norris and I were running the class stand, we decided we could save time and keep the pop plenty cold by stacking several cases outside the south door of the gym. Following a flurry of activity at the half, I stepped outside to replenish our supplies when I saw that an entire case of Coke was missing.

"Are you sure you counted right?" Doyle asked.

"Yes, I'm sure. And I've got a good idea who might have done it. Remember the four guys who kept coming around but never bought anything?"

"Yeah," Doyle said.

"They haven't been around for some time now. I bet they took our pop."

"I wouldn't doubt it," Doyle agreed. "Whatta ya think we oughta do?"

"I'm not sure," I said, "but let's get someone to watch the stand while we go outside and look around." Finding no one near the school, we crossed the street and entered Bill Burgess's store. "Bill," I asked, "Have you seen four suspicious looking guys hangin' around here?"

"Maybe, maybe not," he said. "What did they look like?"

"Nothin' out of the ordinary, all of 'em but one was about our size, and he was tall and heavyset."

"Yeah, they've been in here a couple a times," Bill said.

I'd taken a big bite out of a Milky Way I'd just bought when the ringleader and his three friends entered the store. The big kid turned belligerent when I glared at him: "What's wrong with you? You got a problem?"

"Yeah, I do," I said. "Someone stole a case of our pop outside the gym."

"Are you accusin' us of stealin'?" he asked.

"Not exactly, but I saw you guys hangin' around over there in back of the schoolhouse, and I think you're likely suspects."

"I have a notion to take you outside and beat the shit outta you," he blustered.

"Come on," I invited him. "Let's get with it." Excited, and not knowing what to do with my candy bar, I stuffed the last half in my mouth. All that chocolate and sugar, mixed with a rush of adrenaline, made me gag as if I'd puke, but I kept it down while Doyle and the other onlookers made a circle. There in the light of Bill's store window, I methodically ringed both eyes of the overgrown kid with angry raised welts while evading his clumsy blows.

"Stop! Stop!" he finally cried. "We'll pay for the pop we took."

"Okay," I said, breathing hard, "But you'll have to settle up with Mr. Williams."

I didn't get a chance to see the kid's face later, but Doyle's dad said both eyes were black and blue and so swollen his friends had to lead him around for a couple of days. Doyle's dad may have exaggerated, but I don't think so.

I was giving the horses a breather Saturday morning while dragging logs when Dad noticed my red and puffy knuckles. "What happened to you?" he asked.

When I told him about the fight Dad's eyes shone the same way they had many times before when Fred and I had fought. His unconvincing "now you boys quit that," along with his furtive looks and smiles, showed how much he'd enjoyed our fierce battles, and I could tell that he wished he'd witnessed my latest scrap.

228

TWENTY-TWO
THE MODEL A

While I was in wheat harvest in Oklahoma the second time, Dad traded our Hupmobile to Roy and Washie Madewell for a Model A Ford sedan. Since I owned half interest in the Hupmobile, I thought Dad should have asked my permission before he traded, but his name was on the title and he could do what he pleased. Actually, although the Hupmobile was classier, the Model A was a better family car than the Hupmobile had ever been; now all seven of us could ride inside. Although it was a step up from being seen in downtown Aurora in the ridiculous makeshift bed of the Hupmobile, it was still humiliating to be stared at while five of us, some of us almost grown, were packed like sardines into the back seat of the black Ford.

Following my miserable failure at being saved at Rocky Comfort, it was my choice to attend church, or not, according to how I felt, and I generally declined.

229

Dad drove Mama and Joyce and the three younger kids to church on Sunday mornings and evenings, but he often balked at Wednesday night prayer meetings. Mama was too nervous to drive, and Joyce, eighteen, hadn't learned how, which put the monkey on my back. One evening, after I'd agreed to take Mama and the kids to prayer meeting, Windy Grider headed north, driving fast, as was his custom, in his old coupe without headlights.

Later, almost home from church, I crossed Honey Creek and shifted into second and sharply accelerated to be sure I could make it up the steep narrow hill. Three-quarters of the way up, we saw Windy's car in the Model A's weak headlights, careening backward down the hill toward us. I'd shifted into reverse and we'd almost made it to the bottom when a heavy, crunching blow knocked us into a deep ditch where good sized saplings cushioned our fall. I rolled down my window and climbed out before giving the kids in the back a hand. Mama may have been dazed, I'm not sure, but she was heavy, and instead of placing her feet on the metal, she stepped on the back door glass and fell through, cutting a long, deep gash in her leg.

Joyce ran home and called Jeffie Pannell, who helped Dad take Mama to the hospital. While he was waiting for the doctor, Dad called the law and a highway patrolman was sent to the crash scene where Windy and I waited. Windy mostly stayed down the road where his vehicle had come to rest, but once he came up where I waited beside the overturned Model A. "I bet you don't have a driver's license," he said.

"I bet I do," I replied, and Old Spot, who had come down from our house nearby, growled at the heavyset man, backing him off.

The highway patrolman briefly checked my driver's license before examining Windy's vehicle with its broken axle and no lights of any kind. Windy had no insurance, but he agreed to replace our two broken back windows. I don't know whether Dad ever dunned him, I know I never did, but Windy never replaced or paid for the broken glass. He may have thought losing his driver's license for a year was penalty enough. With winter approaching, Dad cut out two pieces of plywood and replaced the broken glass. At first I thought the plywood looked tacky, but eventually I liked it because I couldn't be seen in the back seat when we went to town.

Jay and I heard Dad and Mama late at night discussing the possibility of moving again. I never knew how much rent they paid for the 120 acre place on Honey Creek, but they would have kept on paying the modest amount indefinitely if Pap and Lottie hadn't decided to sell. Although Dad and Mama rarely saw eye to eye, they agreed that the sixty-five hundred dollar asking price for Pap and Lottie's farm was out of their reach.

"Let's get out of here," Mama blurted out to Dad one evening. "Why don't you go see if you can rent us a place down around Osie where we used to live. We still have friends down there."

"All right," Dad said. "I'll go first thing in the mornin'." When he returned late the next day, he looked pleased.

"I've rented the Parvin Place," he said. "I got it for a hundred and twenty-five dollars cash for a year's rent. We can git possession now."

"Good," Mama said. "How big's the house?"

"It has a good sized front room and two small bedrooms, plus an average sized kitchen."

"That's big enough. The girls can sleep in one bedroom, the boys in the other, and me and you can sleep on the rollaway bed in the kitchen."

Although I hated leaving Honey Creek, and I liked going to school at Marionville—even every day—I still felt uneasy in the community over having been exposed as a hopeless sinner. Maybe I'd be better off someplace far away from Rocky Comfort where I could get a fresh start.

All of us were busy clearing out the house when Dad and Mama got in a yelling match after Mama pried the medicine cabinet in the bathroom off the wall with a claw hammer.

"What are you up to?" Dad demanded.

"Can't you see?" Mama replied.

"Anything that's nailed down is supposed to stay," Dad raged.

"It's not nailed down now," she said.

"What'll you do with it? There's no bathroom at the Parvin Place!"

"We'll still need something over the washstand in the kitchen."

Dad ordinarily won when he and Mama argued, but not this time. She slipped a pillow case over the cabinet and carried it to the truck where she packed it in the long wooden box where she kept the few things she treasured most, her ever dwindling stash of Indian head pennies and her porcelain doll head.

* * *

The hardest part of the actual move from Honey Creek to the Parvin Place for Jay and me was moving the cattle. "Right at fifteen miles will take most of the day," Dad told us. " We shouldn't have much trouble once we get lined out."

We loaded the haywagon with a double shovel, a turning plow, the pond slip, a spring toothed harrow and various other odds and ends, including Mama's two wash tubs, leaving room for a mound of loose hay on the back to feed and help control the cattle.

It was mid March, and the fresh young grass and wild onions on the road right of way caused the hungry cattle to scatter, but with Dad driving the team ahead at a steady pace, and our occasional yells and well aimed rocks from behind, the procession southward was largely uneventful.

Dad picked up the pace a few miles down the road in order for him to have time to stop and pitch hay on the railroad tracks to lessen the chance of the cattle spooking as they crossed over, and he did the same thing a couple of hundred yards farther on at the scary railroad overpass on Highway 60, where we jogged west briefly before going south on the dirt road again.

With the danger of the railroad tracks and overpass behind us, the trip turned into drudgery as we trudged past increasingly familiar landmarks, including a 640 acre piece of land known as the Section, where many local men and boys often cut wood and hunted squirrels and possums. At the south edge of the Section, where Lawrence County ended and Barry County began, I wanted to stop at the Sage Hill store, but Dad kept right on going, and Jay and I didn't have the nerve to dodge in for a quick bottle of pop.

As we went by the first house on the right past the county line, I thought of the buxom black headed young woman with her two blond headed boys who had stayed there with her in-laws for a time during the depression while her husband was away, supposedly in Jefferson City, for a six month stay after being found guilty of stealing a half dozen tow sacks from the back of the Farmers' Exchange at Aurora.

At the next house on the left, I shuddered as I recalled how the news spread in the area once when a young woman who lived there killed herself with a 12 gauge shotgun while her husband celebrated the Fourth of July in town.

When we waved at a man busy working on a car in the next yard, I saw it was the same man who had spent eighteen months in the pen for the midnight requisition of a neighbor's two hens. I'd admired this soft-spoken man years before when I'd heard how he refused to name his two faster running companions after he was caught. And from the looks of his place now, he seemed to be doing all right as a shade tree mechanic and livestock trader. I took my eyes off our straggling cattle long enough to imagine I saw the man's beautiful curly headed daughter—Fredalene Ethylene Maureen Hutchinson—in the doorway, but it had been four years since I'd seen her, and I couldn't be sure how she looked now.

Half a mile away, at White Oak, Dad circled the schoolhouse before he stopped and threw the remaining hay to the gaunt and increasingly tenderfooted cows while Jay and I pumped water into first one and then the other galvanized tub. We rested briefly while the cows cleaned up the sparse hay and browsed in the yard, then headed east on the last part of our trip. Wilma Wilkin, one of Mama's few friends, who lived with her family at the first house on the right, yelled a friendly greeting as we passed. We went by the Watermelon Charley Smith place where Dad and Fred and I used to stop and get a drink at the spring before listening to one of the bawdy old man's fascinating stories while his two kids, Stell and Eddie the Little Booger, stood quietly in the background.

Beyond the Bood Williams' Place, where I vainly tried to spot signs of the huge log barn I once played in, we eased the cattle around the corner and forded Crane Creek between Oxford Cope's house and Dick Wiley's deteriorating old canning factory nearby. I hoped to catch a glimpse of Mona Lou Cope to see if she was still as fetching as she'd been in the eighth grade, but I didn't see even so much as a curtain move in the front window.

When we turned back east at Iry Wilson's, I remembered an earlier time when Dad and Fred and I, from our vantage point in the tomato patch high on the hill, watched Iry's son hightailing it across the bottom toward the ditch and safety on the initial leg of his flight to California. The young man apparently thought running was better than facing the irate father of a girl he'd knocked up.

The long, steep hill going up to the Bowers Place where we'd laboriously dug a cistern with the aid of a windlass was the most tiring part of our all-day trek, making the remaining gradual uphill half mile climb to our new place seem easy. When we topped that last hill, we could see Dad standing beyond an open wire gate, waiting to block the road while Jay and I shooed the played out cattle into the barn lot. After cutting the dry stock out, we enticed each milk cow into her strange new stanchion with a pound coffee can full of bran shorts covered with a sprinkling of cottonseed meal. The cows

234

gave little milk that first night, but soon they were back to their usual production.

As time passed, Jay and I forgot just how humdrum and tiring trailing cows really was. With no one left to dispute us, we fired our imaginations with our rousing embroidered stories of the last big cattle drive in the southwest.

TWENTY-THREE

COLD SPRING HOLLER AND THE SWARTZFEGER RANCH

After milking and finishing my regular Sunday morning chores, while everyone else scurried around getting ready for church, I slapped together a sandwich or two out of leftover breakfast biscuits and cured ham, sausage, or sowbelly—whatever was left over—then grabbed an apple and a big handful of unshelled peanuts and went out the back door.

At the edge of the yard I unsnapped James from his chain while ignoring George's frenzied lunging and bawling. As unfair as it was to take only one hound, I'd learned the hard way that one dog would stay with me and be good company, but two of them would go wherever a scent or a notion took them, sometimes for days on end.

I sometimes walked a mile or more north, but Crane Creek was small and tame and made me feel homesick for Honey Creek. A spring bubbling up below a big white oak tree near

236

the site of the old Sycamore School and a nearby slough filled with beautiful clamoring red-winged blackbirds briefly held my interest. More exciting was walking southwest into the heavily wooded Hartin Ranch, where Parker Cave with its easy access and south facing opening had long before been used as cold storage for apples.

After following a trail through the old Bassett Place and on to Parker Cave, before I'd leaned over to drink from a pipe I was startled to see a buzzard fly out of the cave's opening. Looking inside, I found a large mottled egg on the ground inside the cave, a replica of the buzzard egg Fred had found in the same place several years before. It reminded me of a story a woman told. When a child she'd asked an old granny woman, "Where did I come from, Aunt Mary?"

"A buzzard puked you out on a hot rock."

I also wondered how the story got started that the big black birds with their long red necks and shiny, bald heads somehow knew who was guilty of incest in a community, and marked depraved people by puking on their heads. We put little stock in such outlandish ideas at our house, but I was hunting rabbits with Fred once when a circling buzzard dropped more than a smattering of puke on his head. I also wondered if the buzzard Jack Walker helped catch and bell in the twenties when he worked on Willow Branch still returned every year on March 15th, as Jack said it continued doing in the thirties. Probably not. Buzzards surely didn't live that long.

When I had plenty of time and the inclination, I crossed the Hartin Ranch catty-cornered to the southwest, then drank from a small horseshoe shaped spring called Jay Rickey beyond an old homestead where Marion Robbins and his wife had raised their family of nine children. I followed the narrow bumpy road, little more than a trail, where it twisted and turned through gnarly outcroppings of limestone, then straightened beyond a low water crossing. Past the next house, where James always bristled and sniffed at barking hounds, I walked south into less familiar territory. At a tee in the road I jogged east

237

past Liberty School and then headed southeast cross-country to the Swartzfeger Ranch in the direction of the solid log house down in the draw with its two big downstairs rooms separated by a dogtrot. Thirsty again, I kneeled a few yards west of the house at a clear, small spring before sitting on the floor of the open dogtrot and eating my lunch.

I carefully looked the house over, inside and out, wondering all the while why such a good and handsome house in this excellent setting was empty. The two 16 by 16 foot square rooms on either side of the 8 by 16 foot dogtrot were bigger than any of the rooms at the Parvin Place, or any other rooms in the several houses we'd lived in, and one long sleeping room upstairs, accessible by ladder, was plenty big enough for three or four beds. But the most remarkable and compelling feature of this house was its fireplace. It was the first of a number of houses, both log and clapboard, with what I came to recognize as the handiwork of the McCubbin family stonemasons with their carefully cut and faced limestone expertly laid into uncommonly handsome and straight as a die fireplaces.

Although the house was empty, the packed down grass and weeds in the yard made plausible the rumor that cockfighters sometimes gathered here in the late afternoon to fight their matched roosters on the dogtrot. While I saw no actual evidence of these clandestine activities, it was a likely looking place for such a gathering. Dad may have gone there himself when he occasionally picked a rooster out of a cock walk, put it on the back floorboard of the car under a weighted tomato crate, and headed out. His standard evasive reply when asked where he was going, "I'm goin' to see a man about a dog," was all we ever got out of him.

Jay and I were strictly forbidden to go any place where gambling or drinking might go on, but when Dad returned, the rooster he left with was often bloody and boogered up. And sometimes he returned empty handed. I was always afraid to look under the lining in his right shoe to see if the five dollar bill he liked to keep hidden there for an emergency was still there. Several times I thought I could smell tobacco smoke on him, but he would have bit our heads off if any of us, including Mama, had suggested anything of the sort.

* * *

Because the school year was almost over when we moved to the Parvin Place, I didn't get much of a feel for school at Aurora before it was time for wheat harvest in northwestern Oklahoma again. Hitchhiking as usual, I started soon after daybreak and caught rides west all day before arriving at Alva and beyond in the high plains country where Walt and Edna Blevins lived past the Cimmaron River south of Freedom.

Once again, I frantically scooped wheat into the bins while the combine circled the huge fields. And again, after the first frantic week when I was sure I couldn't keep up, my muscles gradually hardened and I not only kept up, I exulted in emptying each fifty bushel pickup load before straightening up and taking a breather.

After the wheat was harvested and stored, my job changed to plowing under the wheat stubble with a long, one-way disc. Day after day, from sunup to sundown, little interrupted my six days a week work of manhandling the cumbersome WD-40 Allis Chalmers tractor. I'm not sure what motivated me— breaking the monotony was part of it—but frequent sightings of doves on nests in the machinery's path caused me to stop countless times and carefully transport the flat, flimsy nests with their fragile eggs to safety on the freshly turned ground. I learned to mark a place near the relocated nests in order to better spot the doves on my subsequent rounds, but the demure gray birds soon blended into the vast stretches of alkali soil.

Considerably more exciting than doves were the big rattlesnakes I occasionally ran up on. With hardly a rock anywhere, I depended upon a four foot sharpshooter, a narrow shovel built for digging postholes, as my weapon for killing every rattlesnake I could corner or outrun. I felt no compunction about

239

killing the beautiful, brutal looking rattlesnakes then cutting off their rattles and flaunting them as coups.

Killing a rattlesnake with the sharp bladed shovel was ordinarily fairly easy, but once when I crossed a depression filled with tall cane—an old buffalo wallow, Walt called it—I saw the biggest rattlesnake I'd ever seen, bigger around than my forearm and longer than the six foot one I'd killed and measured. Stopping the tractor and grabbing the shovel, I jumped down and delivered what I thought was a killing, or disabling, blow to the back of the writhing snake. But my best shot didn't faze it at all. Instead, it instantly turned on me and, without coiling, struck heavily several times from its waist high position on the matted cane, narrowly missing my head and chest. I managed a weak flurry of ineffectual blows, nothing damaging, but enough to cause the snake to slither away while I climbed to safety aboard the tractor. I didn't think my confrontation with the huge rattlesnake was life threatening, but I've since wondered if a bite on the head or neck might have not only been dangerous, but perhaps deadly, especially since I was plowing in a remote area more than two miles from the nearest phone, a considerable distance on the slow tractor.

I convinced Walt and Edna that I'd get along fine batching and plowing while they took their usual midsummer month's vacation in Colorado Springs. After they left I discovered they'd taken the keys of their fast '41 Ford pickup, leaving me no transportation to Freedom on Saturday nights. I had my thumb and shank's mare, of course, but a hamburger at the cafe followed by a pint of walnut ice cream at the drugstore, tasty as they were, seemed small reward for a ten mile trek each way.

I hadn't learned to drink or dance, but in order to make my rare Saturday night jaunts more interesting, I took to stopping at the legion hall near the Cimmaron River at the edge of town where Bob Wills and his Texas Plowboys wannabes played and sang their repetitive, plaintive tunes while courtly young cow-boys fresh from the rodeo performed their shuffling two-steps with their beautiful, expressionless dates.

The languor of one such dance was suddenly and violently interrupted as two young women who'd been alternately dancing with the same cowboy squared off. Instead of the usual predictable tactics in men's fights, a mixture of shoving, wrestling, and boxing, this far more elemental catfight was an eye-opening spectacle of toe-to-toe hair pulling, scratching, biting, and clothes tearing, all punctuated with hoarse squalls, high-pitched screams, and vile curses. For violence and high drama it beat anything I'd ever seen, including much maligned cock-fights in Missouri. The fight in the dance hall ended when one woman ripped the other's dress from top to bottom, showering buttons all over the place. One hit me in the chest. Someone more modest than the exposed woman wrapped her in a checkered oilcloth from a table in the hall and led her away.

When I looked in at the dance hall the following Saturday night there was no sign of the combatants, and I soon left and headed for the ranch. On the way, I decided against telling Walt and Edna, who were due back any time, about going honky-tonking. Walt was broad-minded and most likely would have laughed, but Edna was straightlaced: she might start in on me again about driving her to church and getting saved.

One evening, before Walt and Edna returned, I was walking from the barn to the house with a bucket of milk when I heard an ominous, familiar whirring sound near the garage. A large rattlesnake lay coiled, rattling away a few feet ahead of me. A short distance in front of the snake, the family cat lay flat on her belly, her tail slowly twitching. Each animal's eyes locked on the other, ignoring me. Although I'm not a cat lover, I located a hoe and killed the spellbound snake. Later I wished I'd retreated a few steps and watched the well matched enemies fight. Their battle might have been more exciting than the cat-fight I'd seen at the dance hall.

* * *

When Walt and Edna got back from Colorado, they seemed pleased with the amount of work I'd done. They didn't ask about what I did in my spare time on Saturday nights and Sundays; maybe they thought I spent all of my free time sleeping. My food improved considerably with Edna's return, and I enjoyed the late evening conversations on the front porch as Walt reminisced about his early life cowboying in the rugged gypsum hills in the same vicinity where Dad had hunted, trapped, and cowboyed as a young man. Although Walt had only a fuzzy recollection of Dad, he vividly recalled working on a ranch one summer with Dale, Dad's middle brother.

During the last month of my summer's stay in Oklahoma, I increasingly made preparations for the upcoming football season in Missouri. At Edna's daybreak call up the steep stairway, I quickly dressed and climbed down on my way to the pasture where a large colony of prairie dogs sitting erect on a wide mound watched my daily mile run. The cow trail I methodically jogged on cut through big patches of thickly matted buffalo grass, a short grass well suited to the carefree yards on many surrounding homesteads. Randomly interspersed throughout the pasture, I saw thousands of scrubby green shrubs, the same sage brush Zane Grey raved about in his western novels. Examined up close, the pesky plants were no more romantic than the sumac and sassafras Dad made us grub out in our pastures back home.

Following my morning run, I'd do my regular early morning business in the old horse barn rather than go to the toilet near the garage where my first day's job had been to dig a fresh six foot hole in the sandy soil, wrestle the toilet in place over the hole, then heap the extra dirt over what was left of a year's worth of groceries. Although the lime in the toilet effectively kept down the stench, I was much more comfortable going to the barn where I squatted in private the good old fashioned way.

I disliked running every morning, but I didn't want to be unprepared for football when I returned the first of September, a full two weeks after practice started. I'd played enough—this would be my fifth year of high school—to know that the first and second teams were likely to be set before I had a chance to try out.

Finally, on a Friday when my work was finished and it was time to go, Walt told me to get the calendar off the back porch where I'd marked off each day's work, and figure up what he owed me. The six dollars a day times six days a week for ten weeks, minus a few rainy days, came to well over three hundred dollars. Recoiling in feigned horror, Walt said, "How could it be that much?"

"You offered to pay me every week, but I took twenty dollars before you went on vacation, and that was it. Here, figure it out yourself."

"I'm just kiddin'," Walt smiled. "You're worth every penny of it. But tell me, how'd you learn to save like this?"

"I'm not sure, " I said, "but I read something once about the importance of deferred gratification. It must've stuck with me."

"That's a new one on me," Walt exclaimed. "All I know is, out of all the dozens, maybe hundreds, of hired hands I've had over the years, you're the first one who didn't spend most of his money as quick as he made it. Keep it up," he said, "and you'll amount to something."

"Thanks," I said. "Well, 'bye. See ya later."

Getting back to Missouri in time for school the following Monday was the only deadline I was worried about, so instead of going straight home I detoured north to Wichita where I planned on staying in Pap and Lottie's basement a couple of nights. Saturday morning I ambled downtown, on the look-out for old pool halls, movie theaters, and eating joints my friends and I once frequented instead of going to school. On east Douglas near the train station I entered a used shoe store, the same one where Mama had hunted bargains. Looking around, I spotted a good looking pair of oxblood colored wingtip slippers. The 7½ D shoes were a full size too small, but with the aid of a long handled shoe horn an energetic salesman managed to wrestle them on me.

"Walk around and see how they feel," he said.

"They're plenty tight," I said, after a few steps. "How much do you want for them?"

"Five dollars," he said. "That's a bargain for Florsheims."

"Throw in that old belt on the rack down the aisle, and I'll trade with you," I said.

"Which belt are you talking about?"

"That one," I said, picking up a supple belt with the maker's name worn off, but with an address, Miles City, Montana, clearly visible.

"All right," he agreed. "What else do you need?"

"I'm not sure," I hedged. "What's the story on that muddy pair of football shoes on the top of the shelf back there?"

"A boy brought them in a few days ago; he said he wore them once and didn't have any more use for them. I took them off his hands."

"What size are they?" I asked.

"It says 8 1/2 D on the box. Try 'em on."

I tried to not shake as I laced up the same as new, perfect fitting, high-topped shoes. "What's your low dollar for them?" I asked.

"I'm going to take a beating, but I'll let you have them at the same price you agreed to pay for the slippers, five dollars."

"You've got yourself a deal," I said. "Here's your ten dollars."

"Do you want to wear your new slippers?" he asked.

"No, I'd better break them in gradually," I said. "I'll wear my old ones."

Pap and Lottie invited me to go with them to the big Assembly of God church where all our family once went, but I declined with the excuse that it sometimes took all day to hitchhike to Missouri. As it turned out, my excuse was valid; it was well after dark Sunday evening when I dragged in at the

Parvin Place. The folks had gone to evening services at White Oak, giving me enough time for a refreshing nap on the davenport before they got back.

TWENTY-FOUR
FOOTBALL AT AURORA

Early on Monday morning, Jay and Wanda and I walked a mile north to the bottom of the red hill west of Osie where we caught the school bus to Aurora. My first half day's work at Leonard Bisby's machine shop on the square across from the Farmers' Exchange was uneventful, as were my afternoon classes.

"Howdy. I'm Wayne Holmes," I said to Jeff Neal, the burly young coach at the armory. "I'd like to go out for football."

"Where've you been?" he asked. "We've been practicin' hard since the middle of August. Most of the slots are filled."

"I've been workin'. Am I too late?"

"Maybe, maybe not," the big man said. "It'll be accordin' to how experienced and how tough you are."

Afraid I might be ineligible if I admitted having already played four years, I mumbled something about playing the previous year at Marionville.

"What position do you play best?"

"Defensive guard."

"That's too bad," he said. "We already have plenty of good guards."

"Well, I'm still a guard," I repeated. "You'll give me a shot at it, won't you?"

"Yes, I will," he said. "In about thirty minutes we'll find out what you're made of. I see you have your own shoes. The manager'll fix you up with everything else you need."

Following a short round of calisthenics, Coach Neal directed the first offensive team into position, then barked off the names of defensive players.

"Holmes," he said, "get in there at right guard."

The mean looking bucktoothed youngster across the line from me, Grover Phillips, Patches everyone called him, was about my size, maybe 150 pounds wringing wet, but he was taller, rangier, and a whole lot uglier. At each snap of the ball, the two of us slammed into one another as hard as we could, with first one and then the other delivering the more punishing blow. Finally, imperceptibly at first, my three year age advantage and longer playing experience paid off. The sixteen year old junior never gave up, but when gouts of bloody snot flew out of his nose, his loud sobs were drowned out by Coach Neal's sharp whistle and gruff command: "You two men change positions. Johnny Bill," he directed the big center, "you'll have to give Holmes his blocking assignments."

Patches was angry for a long time after I beat him out of his starting position, but he gradually warmed up after Coach Neal began substituting him for me on offense, where he was an excellent blocker, better than I ever was. Occasionally he'd come bounding in to give me a much needed breather playing defense the way I found most pleasurable and effective: pell-mell and oblivious to everyone's safety, including my own. Few players got badly hurt, but when our starting quarterback fractured his left elbow in a non-conference game against Mountain Grove, his high-pitched scream sounded eerily like a scared rabbit being pulled out of a hollow log. Porky Sullivan suffered a mean diagonal gash across his nose and face during a scrimmage, but after it healed he laughingly wore the long scar as if it were a badge of honor. Because the tight leather helmets we wore weren't equipped with face masks, and only sissies and pretty boys used mouth pieces, many of us sported swollen lips, black eyes, and abrasions galore. I'm not sure whether ill fitting helmets or my in-your-face style of play caused it, but during the several years I played, I proudly wore a scab on the bridge of my nose all season long.

As much as I relished playing football at Aurora, getting home after practice was a problem. Unlike the three and four mile jaunts Hosie Gold and I had made after practice at Marionville, it was eleven miles from the armory to the Parvin Place, and I didn't have Hosie for company. After stopping at Hughes' Drug Store for a pint of ice cream and a few minutes of flirting with the friendly girl who worked at the counter, I often caught a ride with someone off work headed my way south on 39. When one ride played out, others generally followed, sometimes with people I knew.

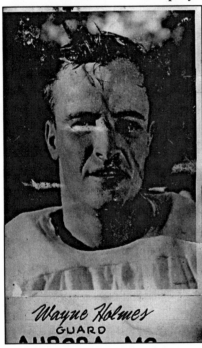

Wayne Holmes
GUARD
AURORA, MO.

Football picture with my scab nose

I didn't exactly know Norma Jean Burk the first time she stopped as I walked east on the county line, but I knew who she was. Diffident and socially inept as we were, the two of us had a hard time keeping a conversation alive at first, but as time passed I looked forward to the all too short rides when Norma dropped me off at Sage Hill where I went south and she drove on east. Later, I wished I'd ridden most of the way home with her to the bottom of the hill north of the Clanton Place, where I would have been a short two miles from home. When practice lasted longer than usual, past the time when people who worked in town were still on the road, I sometimes failed to catch a ride. It's hard to imagine now, with all the cars whizzing by on the blacktop covered roads, but few people travelled those dirt and gravel roads after dark many years ago.

One evening following an extra long football practice, when I'd caught few rides and had to hoof it most of the eleven miles home in the dark, I'd come in the back door and was eating leftovers at the kitchen table and talking to Jay when I heard a voice I didn't recognize coming from the girls' bedroom.

"What's all that chatter about?" I asked him.

"I'm not sure," he said, "but it's been goin' on ever since Mary Lou Wiley's folks dropped her off on their way to town."

"Well, I'm headed to bed," I told him. "How about doin' me a favor and askin' 'em to hold down the noise?"

"Sure," he said.

I'd taken off my jeans and shirt and was fast asleep when I heard someone at the foot of the bed. Cranky at being awakened, I asked, "What's goin' on?"

"After Jay told us you'd gone to bed I told him you'd sleep like a baby if you heard me sing," the girl I'd heard of, but never before met, bragged.

"Maybe, maybe not," I said, "but now that I'm wide awake and you're so sure of yourself, why don't you give it a try?"

"I'll just do that," she said, and to my surprise and amazement the fetching and precocious thirteen year old girl sat down on the bed next to me where she unabashedly and flawlessly lulled me into the sweet by-and-by of never-never land with her rendition of "Too-ra-loo-ra-loo-ra."

* * *

The worst part about dragging in late way up in the night was seeing the cows lying down chewing their cuds in the moonlight when I passed the barn lot, and knowing that Dad waited, red faced and ready to explode because I hadn't arrived home in time to do my share of the milking. Not that he had to milk any extra cows himself. Mama always milked my four when I was gone; but I guessed that the reason she milked them was not because she favored what I was doing—she opposed football as much as Dad did—but because she and Dad remained locked in their own scoreless game of dominance. Although I sullenly ignored much of Dad's diatribe, I couldn't block out his favorite conclusion: "If you'd work half as hard out here on the farm as you play football in town, young man, you might amount to somethin'."

* * *

For one of our last home games of the season, someone came up with the bright idea that the senior players' fathers should be honored by inviting them to sit on sideline benches where they could root for their sons and be recognized at halftime. A big spread in the *Aurora Advertiser* hyped the upcoming event, but since the folks didn't take the paper, and I kept my mouth shut, I thought they wouldn't get wind of it. I felt fairly safe because, even if Dad did find out about it, he wasn't likely to have anything to do with something he openly despised. But if he decided to go, I'd be embarrassed by his faded overalls and pale blue chambray shirt tightly buttoned at the neck. To top it off, he'd be wearing his usual disapproving frown and the same old shiny coat from his blue dress suit he'd bought with the five dollars Pap and Lottie had given him several years before to make sure he had something decent to wear at Uncle Willie Eller's funeral.

At the last minute, I asked Leonard Bisby at work if he'd represent me at Friday night's observance. "Sure, I'll be glad to," he obligingly said.

Although I felt sheepish about my subterfuge, I have to admit I felt good when, just before the second half kickoff, the announcer called out my name followed by Dad's, and Leonard, wearing a nice pair of khaki pants and a gabardine jacket, smiled broadly as he stood and waved to the crowd.

School was dismissed at noon the following Friday when a carnival came to town as part of the festivities connected with the Tri-County Fair. Little besides a motley dressed, white-faced clown with his oversized shoes caught our attention as Herb Cox, Jackie Muench, Ralph Shomer, Jack Halterman and I circled the square. As we ambled along in front of the Farmers Exchange, we stopped abruptly at the sight of several scantily dressed beauties swaying provocatively in front of the hootchy-kootchy show while a barker made his persuasive pitch.

"I've gotta see this," Herb said, and he headed for the entrance.

"Hold on," Muench said. "Fifty cents is high. Let's sneak a peek and then if it looks like it's worth it, we'll see the show."

"That sounds like a good idea," I agreed.

"Let's go around to the back of the tent," Halterman said. "Herb, you and Shomer are stout. Muench and I'll get up on your shoulders and look over the top."

"Okay, okay, but hurry up," Herb said.

While the two lucky ones peered over the top of the canvas from their precarious perches, I, kneeling on the ground, hiked up the bottom of the tent. Before I could spot even one bare breast I heard a sharp whistle followed by a rallying cry from an adjoining stand, and looked up in time to see Muench jump from Herb's shoulders and land on his feet running while Herb lay sprawled on the ground. I didn't see what happened to Shomer and Halterman, but the high stepping clown with his extraordinarily long flip-flopping shoes grabbed Herb and began choking him. My first impulse was to follow Muench into the crowd, but Herb needed help. I knew it was a cheap shot, but while the clown continued to bend over, throttling Herb, I hit him with a sucker punch to the mouth, straightening him up. Shomer says to this day that I knocked the man a winding, but he's been known to exaggerate.

In the general uproar that followed, several carneys who'd heard the initial whistle and call grabbed and held Herb and me until a one-armed policeman hustled the two of us and the bleeding clown to the police station a short distance away in city hall. I was worried when the police chief asked the sad faced man if he wanted to press charges. "I ought to," he muttered behind a rag he held to his bloody mouth, "but I wouldn't collect no damages. I'm gonna pull out of this two-bit burg and head for the next stop."

"It's your decision," the police chief said, "Is there anything you want to say to these boys before I turn 'em loose?"

"I don't have nothin' to say to them iggernunt hillbills."

Following a stern lecture of his own, the officer released us. As we walked down the outside stairs, Herb and I saw workmen busily taking down the hootchy-kootchy tent.

News of our ruckus on the square spread quickly, including a wild version, a version I never totally denied, from Bill Mason at work on Monday describing how I'd knocked out four of the clown's front teeth. It's unlikely I knocked out any of his teeth; he'd probably lost them in an earlier fight. All I remember seeing for sure were his bloody gums. It was a good thing no charges were brought against us. I don't know about Herb, but if the school authorities or the police had brought Dad in on the matter, my football career would have ended right then and there. Besides that, I would have had to quit school and go to work full time, something I wasn't ready for.

TWENTY-FIVE
SUNDAY JAUNTS

I ordinarily confined my Sunday walks to places closer than
the Swartzfeger Ranch. Going south with one of my hounds a
short distance to where the skinny but increasingly striking
Fern Hartin lived, I turned down the rocky road past the Allman place. Even though I knew Eva Allman had married Jack
Eubanks, and was living in Aurora, I always slowed in hopes
of catching a glimpse of the beautiful young woman. Of all the
good looking girls I ever saw in Barry County, Eva Allman
took the cake. I wondered if this vivacious young woman I'd
known earlier was content living in town and working at the
cap factory. On the infrequent Saturday afternoons when I
went to town, I looked forward to seeing Eva, always alone,
walking along in that peculiar sliding gait of hers up and down
the sidewalk of the main street, window shopping. Eva spoke
first, prompting me to speak, but a conversation was unthink-
able. Dressed simply, with a flair that set off her trim figure
and long, thick black mane and pale complexion, Eva's direct

and unwavering look, along with her increasing lack of facial expression, made me recall the time when, already married, she joined all of us at White Oak for a play day on the last day of school.

At a jog in the road, I stopped fantasizing about Eva and concentrated on where I was going. Instead of taking the main road, I preferred a narrow trail south where, after climbing over a wire gate, I proceeded down a long, steep and narrow road that led to an empty clapboard house on a knoll overlooking a spring in a corner of the yard. Surrounded on three sides by wooded hills, the houseplace and its surroundings reminded me of one of Zane Grey's descriptions of a box canyon, but instead of being in some far off place in the west, it was here within walking distance of home, practically in our own back yard. Why, I thought, would anyone ever leave such an idyllic location?

After eating my food under a tree near the spring, I followed the small stream some distance down the narrow valley where another similar sized branch came in from the east. After following this second stream a few hundred yards, I came to its source, a small spring with especially cold water tumbling off the hillside in a waterfall. Wilder and even more picturesque than the place I'd just come from, this had to be Cold Spring and Cold Spring Holler near where I'd heard Gearl Lemaster say his dad had once built a log cabin the French way, placing the logs upright like a palisade fence instead of in the conventional horizontal fashion. But though I searched for signs of where the unique cabin might have stood, I found only a few clumps of iris and daylilies planted by some woman trying to domesticate the wilderness. Given the rough terrain and the inaccessibility of the spring, drinking water had been carried a considerable distance up the steep path to a flat place suitable for a house.

Wherever I went on Sundays, I kept an eye on the sun so I would be sure to have enough leeway to return home and help with the evening chores. Once, when I barely got back in time, Dad roughly asked, "Where've you been all day?"

"Nowhere in particular, just here and there," I answered.

"Don't give me that here and there business, young man. I want to know exactly where you've been."

"I went past George Hartin's and then cut across Cheney's to Parker Cave. After I ate my sandwich and rested awhile, I tried to find the cabin Dewey Garoutte told me he built when he squatted on the Hartin Ranch during the depression, but I couldn't locate it."

"That didn't take all day."

"No, it didn't. When I got to the east side of the ranch, I dropped down to the Seitz Place, and then on to Cold Spring. What was wrong with that? I didn't see anybody or bother anything. Why do you ask?"

"No special reason," Dad said. "I just wondered. If you're not careful you'll turn into your great granddad Eller."

"How's that?"

"When he lived in a log cabin west of Leann, near Liberty, it wasn't uncommon for him to be gone hunting for several days, up to a week at a time."

"What did he eat, and where did he sleep?" I asked.

"He ate small game he shot, and nuts and berries, whatever he could find. He slept wherever he could, under a bluff or in a dry cave with his dogs."

"That wouldn't be too bad a life," I ventured.

"No, not bad at all," Dad said, and instead of receiving a harsh reprimand, I ended up gleaning one of the few bits of information I ever heard about my grandmother Holmes' diminutive Irish father, Josh Eller. Also, for the first time, I thought I partially understood what lay behind that preoccupied far away yearning look in Dad's eyes when he thought no one was looking.

* * *

One Sunday morning when I was in the mood for company, instead of packing my lunch and taking a dog along, I slipped through the woods alone across Sand Ridge to the west a mile away where Houston lived. An only child, the oversized teenager was given a free rein by his doting parents. When I knocked on the front door, Houston's lanky, sharp faced mother welcomed me inside with a wry smile. "Howdy, he's still in the bed back there."

"Yeah," his huge, powerful looking dad agreed from where he sat sipping his coffee out of a saucer at the kitchen table. "He was out tomcattin' most of the night. Go ahead and roust him out."

Inside the small bedroom, Houston lay asleep on his back on a three quarter size wrought iron bed decorated at the head and foot with elaborate curlicues. Crowded on a relic of an earlier generation when most people and their beds were short, the fully seven foot tall giant, his arms akimbo, stretched from the head to the foot of the bed and beyond where his bare feet, ankles, and bony legs stuck out like rusty stovepipes. A tied comforter stretched from Houston's chin to his mottled shins, and a sly grin played at the corners of his wide mouth. With my limited experience, but active fantasies, I could imagine why he'd be cranky at having his dream interrupted. Just as I expected, when I shook his shoulder, he growled, "Go away. Leave me alone."

"Get up," I said, "It's late. Get up and tell me about last night."

"Not yet, not until I've had some coffee," Houston replied, slowly extricating himself, first one foot and then the other, from the iron snares at the foot of his ancient bed. "Tell Mom to pour you a cup, and get one for me while I shake the cobwebs out. Okay?"

"You know I don't drink coffee," I said, "but I'll go get you some."

Wordless, we sat on the edge of the thin sagging mattress while Houston slurped coffee out of his saucer before we went outside where his nondescript yellow shepherd joined us as we headed for the nearby woods. Old Shep was no good as a stock dog, and he wasn't much of a squirrel dog, but he was tops at baying terrapins. Some few people in the community ate snapping turtles as well as the less common leatherbacks—Mama cooked turtles right along—but I never heard of anyone hungry enough to eat terrapins, not even part Indians such as Mama or Houston's family whose ancestors reportedly ate them in great numbers.

Anytime Houston and I were out in the woods during the spring and early summer, we kept a sharp lookout for crows' nests in hopes of catching young ones. We'd heard that crows made good pets, and that if we split their tongues with a straight razor, they could be taught to speak as well as any parrot. But our tree climbing efforts resulted in nothing more than empty nests and unhatched eggs.

"What about last night?" I asked him while we rested on a big moss covered sandstone ledge. "Did you do any good?"

"Yeah, I did," Houston said, grinning. He gave no details, but his smile was convincing.

"I need to know somethin'," I said. "How come someone as good lookin' and smooth as I am rarely gets to first base, while to hear you tell it, you almost always score?"

"That's easy. It's cause I'm longer legged than you are," Houston said, laughing. "Besides, looks don't count in the dark. Another thing," he continued, "You're way too picky and I don't cull nothin'." As I mulled over my lesson, I thought it must be close to noon, time to head for home, when Houston changed the subject. "You want to see Old Shep climb a tree?"

"Sure, if it doesn't take too long."

The few times I'd watched Houston urge his eager dog a few feet up apple or peach trees with their low limbs, I was not all that impressed, but this time when he slapped the base of a straight black oak and whistled, the small brown dog quickly

257

ran to the base of the tree and catapulted himself upward eight feet or more to the first limb, where he awkwardly proceeded higher and higher, limb by slow limb, until he was close to fifteen feet in the air. There, despite Houston's half whistling, half kissing entreaties for him to go higher, the trembling, wobbly dog lost his hold and fell hard to the ground. Houston sometimes caught Shep when he fell, or at least helped break his fall, but this time the dog whined in pain as he limped toward the barn. "Whatta ya think of that?" Houston asked. "He's some climber, ain't he?"

"He sure is," I agreed. "But how do you get him to climb after he's been hurt like that?"

"I'll letcha in on a little secret. A dog's a lot like a girl. Both of 'em'll do almost anything for you as long as you're patient and pet 'em. You know, rub their bellies and sweet-talk 'em."

"That makes sense."

"I've learned that I can almost always get 'em to go as far, or farther, than they've ever been before."

"Well, I've gotta go. 'Bye, come see me," I said, and as I retraced my steps across Sand Ridge toward home, I wished I'd thought to ask more questions. I wondered if a girl or a dog had ever quit Houston for good after he'd expected too much or been too rough? If so, did he feel any guilt or responsibility for his actions? And what about his reputation? Did he worry about his reputation as much as I worried about mine? Probably not.

* * *

Raising and fighting gamecocks was commonplace among the boys and young men in the Osie community. We'd raise, buy, or trade for young stags, trim their combs and wattles while they were young so they wouldn't bleed too much, and make sure that an opposing fighting cock wouldn't have much to hold on to with his beak later on while he was spurring. Then we'd build a four by eight foot rectangular walk enclosed in chicken wire big enough for a cock and two or three hens to ensure that the natural pecking order was never established and the cocks were always fit and aggressive. We kept the natural spurs on the cocks instead of sawing them off and replacing them with curved steel gaffs or, more rarely, razor sharp blades that more serious betting cockfighters used. We'd

Houston taking it easy while Mary Lou cops a
feel on the loading chute

ordinarily pit our cocks in short two to three minute long bouts. When two older cocks of considerable reputation were being matched, we would sometimes let them fight to the death, but we didn't bet on them. Gambling was strictly forbidden around our place.

Houston was one of the main promoters of cockfighting in the community. After we'd gotten our several walks set up between the house and barn at our place, he'd often appear with a rooster tucked under his arm. Seven foot tall by now, with his father's wide shoulders and a roguish smile on his lips, he was always itching for a good cockfight.

Houston was also regularly involved in bigger bouts meant to satisfy greater itches, if his own stories and growing accounts by others who went out with him were to be believed. Stories about his sexual exploits with the ugly and the beautiful, the single and the married, and the skinny and the fat became commonplace. And invariably the stories revolved around how well-hung he was. For some baffling and unfair reason, Houston's tallywhacker had grown disproportionately longer than his legs had. And whatever he did, I never heard of him darkening the door of a church.

Houston and I gradually grew farther and farther apart. The truth is, I got too good for him. He didn't seem to realize that he couldn't be totally promiscuous without serious penalty from the upper crust at Aurora High School. Part of our estrangement came as a result of my football playing and as a result gaining a measure of acceptance and respectability, while he refused to quit smoking and conform to the standards required for the basketball team.

In addition to enjoying our increasingly infrequent cockfighting and Rook games, Houston and I sometimes squirrel hunted and possum hunted together, and I'd occasionally go slumming with him on a week night to Crane, where no one from Aurora was likely to see us. We nodded and spoke in the halls at school, but we both understood that we ran in different crowds.

* * *

Many of the same people who'd lived around Osie when we'd moved into the community ten years earlier still lived in the area in 1948, and the folks were better satisfied than they'd been on Honey Creek. Instead of driving to Aurora on Saturday afternoons, Dad resumed his earlier practice of shopping at Osie. Cow feed and the few staples on Mama's short list cost more at Osie than they did at the Farmers' Exchange at Aurora, but Dad thought a chance to visit with the neighbors more than made up for the extra cost.

Lacking Dad's quick wit and easy familiarity, Mama was stiff and uncomfortable with the friendly banter at the crossroads store, and she usually stayed home on Saturdays. Much more to her liking was the usual routine staidness of a church service, and she limited her few friends to women who shared her tight-lipped sense of decorum and piety. Outside of church, Mama's main enjoyment was working in her flowers. Early and late, she wielded a mean, man sized pick as she prepared the poor rocky soil for hundreds of flags. Gradually, imperceptibly, both ends of her pick became dubbed off nubbins. She liked to sweeten and improve the soil with lime, fertilizer and bone meal, but when Dad objected to their cost, she made do with tow sack after tow sack full of leaf mulch she packed or dragged out of deep draws in the woods.

Most people in the community weren't as single-minded or as work brittle as Mama was; many folks liked to get together on Saturday nights and play cards. By cards I don't mean wicked face cards: Rook was the game of choice. Although Mama allowed us to play Rook, she never played it or any other game, not even Hide the Thimble. Saturday night gatherings rotated amongst half a dozen or so neighbors, but everyone understood that

Mama ready for church

some houses, including ours, were off limits. Even so, Dad's presence at a party added enough extra spark to insure that he was always invited, and he in turn invited us older kids to go

261

with him. Not that he wanted any of us to be his partner. He preferred someone as accomplished as he was who'd help better his odds of being on the champion team for the evening.

Another reason why Dad invited us to go with him, a reason never mentioned but understood, was because Mama knew how much everyone—men, women and kids—liked him, and she was jealous. Never mind that Dad and Mama had long since ceased enjoying one another's company; both of them knew having some of us kids along made Dad's irrepressible behavior in company less damaging.

Going to the Rook parties and helping chaperone Dad reminded me of stories passed down in Mama's family about how Grandpa Green often accompanied his three oldest children, courting age daughters, to play parties in western Oklahoma where he initially begged off repeated requests to sing. He invariably weakened, allowing he'd sing if his girls  "Wouldn't tell Birdie," their dour mother at home in bed. Once Bob Green started singing there was no stopping him and, by his own account, he could sing the night through without repeating himself. Late in life, before old age finally got him, he still led the spirited singing, now exclusively hymns, at the yearly family reunion back in Oklahoma. But he never forgot the early ballads, cowboy songs and occasional bawdy tunes he once sang. "If I ever

Dad's best Rook party manner

262

heard a song once, it was mine," the high-spirited wheelchair bound old man laughingly told us.

Fragments of songs Grandpa Green sang when I was a child still surface in my head, especially when I'm feeling light-hearted. Fugitive bits and pieces of tunes he sang in his high tenor, include:

> *Oh, Johnny dear, dear, dear,*
> *Why did you come, come, come,*
> *Down here, here, here,*
> *Upon the gra-ra-rass,*
> *Come a rattle*
> *Come a do di do?*

* * *

> *I did not like my Papa,*
> *I did not like my home.*
> *I had two beautiful sisters*
> *Who wept and prayed for me.*

* * *

> *She caused me to weep,*
> *She caused me to mourn,*
> *She caused me to leave my home.*
> *And when you see that girl of mine,*
> *There's somethin' you must tell'er...*

The number of people attending the parties around Osie and White Oak determined how many tables were set up on any given night. Only a few families had more than a kitchen table, but flimsy folding cardboard tables were pressed into use, as were stools, milk cans and upended tomato crates for extra seating. Once at Howard and Bernice Robbins' house, benches on both sides of a bed made good seats for the low improvised table. Whichever side made 250 points first was declared the winner and got to play the winners of another table. Likewise, losers played losers all evening long. Ultimately, around midnight, the couple who had won the most games were announced winners, and the party broke up.

Of course there was absolutely no drinking of liquor, inside or outside the house. The water bucket with the dipper on the washstand provided the only refreshment anyone expected or received. Some men smoked, but no women, and before the evening was over cigarette and pipe smoke added to the haze and stench of the guttering coal oil lamps and unwashed bodies.

Several teenagers, mostly boys, often gathered at our house on Sunday afternoons where we played game after raucous game of Rook in the kitchen on our big round table. Mama stayed out of sight in the front room, noncommittal and grim, listening, while Dad joined in the rowdy fun. Skilled and highly competitive, he and his partner won more than their share, but when their luck ran out, Dad wasn't above stacking the deck, reneging, discarding illegally, or failing to follow suit. None of us had the nerve to confront him, but some of us decided if he could cheat and get away with it, so could we.

Once, when Dad was absent, one of the older boys flagrantly dealt himself a choice card off the bottom of the deck. "I saw that, you cheatin' son of a bitch!" Jack Lemaster squalled, bringing Mama, her dark eyes flashing, into the room.

"Sorry, Mis Holmes, sorry," Jack muttered. "I forgot."

"Don't let it happen again," Mama warned. "Another outburst like that'll end card playin' around here."

TWENTY-SIX

THE SUMMIT CITY
OF THE OZARKS

I increasingly ran around with curly headed Herb Cox, a recent transplant from California. He was the first person I knew who was honest enough to talk straight about how condescending the south town kids in Aurora were to many of the kids from north town, and to virtually all of us who lived in the country. "Holmes," he began, as we sat in a booth nursing our cherry cokes in teen town one evening. "Look at us; then look around. There's not another guy in sight as handsome or as witty as we are. Let's face it, we're as low as a snake's belly in this so-called Summit City of the Ozarks. Not one person here would give us the time of day if we didn't play football."

"You're wrong about that," I protested.

"No, I'm not," Herb said. "And they barely tolerate us as it is."

"You don't know what you're talkin' about," I replied. "Either one of us could take out any girl here."

"Yeah, right. How many times of being turned down flat would it take before you wised up?"

"I bet the first one I ask'll go out with me," I said.

"How much'll you bet? I bet a dollar no one here'd be caught dead with you. Look around. See for yourself."

After scanning the crowd, I turned to Herb. "Let's get out of here. Maybe there'll be more action at the skatin' rink."

As we walked down the stairs, Herb held out his hand. "Pay me my dollar."

"Whatta ya mean? I didn't ask anyone."

"From the look on your face, it's just a matter of time," he said. "You might as well pay me now instead of later."

"We'll see about that," I said.

* * *

After a Friday night football game, Herb and I sometimes stayed in town in a private home a couple of blocks from the high school where for a dollar each we slept in a fresh bedroom and ate breakfast with the old couple who owned the house.

This early bed and breakfast arrangement, the first I knew of, worked well for us. Even the obliging old woman's warning on our first night added some shivery anticipation to our stay. "Wedge the back of a straight chair under the doorknob when you're ready to go to bed," she said matter-of-factly. "My husband is losing his mind, and he sometimes wanders around in the night. He wouldn't hurt you if he came in on you, but he might not remember you."

About the middle of football season we heard an announcement over the school intercom saying Corydon Lenhart would be taking senior pictures the following Tuesday, and everyone should be dressed up. Dressed up meant a suit and tie, which Herb and I didn't own. Both of us had money—Herb had worked all summer in California picking fruit and I, of course, had worked in Oklahoma—so we skipped school on

266

Monday and hitchhiked to downtown Springfield where someone in the know had steered us to Rubenstein's, a men's clothing store west of the square. Herb knew what he was looking for.

"What about your silent friend here?" the short, gnomelike salesman said. "What does he have in mind?"

"I don't know. Ask him," Herb said.

But I didn't have a clue. After showing me several suits I didn't like, the bullet headed little man rubbed his hands together and his face brightened. "I think I may have just the ticket for someone discriminating," he said. "I'll go get it."

I liked the mix of brown and green colors in the hard worsted wool suit he brought out. "Let me try it on," I said. The long, upturned legs looked weird, but the size 30 waist was right. "I don't care for these pleats in front," I complained. "Can somethin' be done about 'em?"

My new suit

"Not very easily," the man said. "Besides, they're the in thing this year."

"The coat fits, but I'm not sure I like the shoulder pads. My shoulders are broad enough as they are."

"We can fix that when we make the alterations," the man said, patting me.

"All right, I'll take it," I agreed. "When can we pick 'em up?"

"Give us an hour," the pleased man said. "By the time you look around the square and eat lunch they'll be ready."

Herb was feeling cocky when we picked up our boxes and left Rubenstein's, but the uneasy feeling in my belly grew into a hard knot when I spotted all the sharp looking single-breasted suits on manikins in the window. No wonder the double-breasted old man's suit with the wide lapels the store's owner unloaded on me was in the back of the store. It had to be one of the last double-breasted suits sold in Springfield for over forty years.

The school day was over and it was time for football practice when Herb and I walked down the armory steps carrying our new suits. A mouthy rich kid who was a poor student and a sorrier athlete announced our arrival with a loud snicker and question: "What did you guys do, go out and rent you some suits?"

Out on the field a few minutes later, I lined up across from the unsuspecting boy for our rugged one-on-one drills. Saying nothing, I made him pay dearly for his smart remark.

Some forty-five years later at a reunion of sorts, the ignorant young man turned mainstay of the community laughingly said, "Wayne, you hurt me something awful in football practice,"

"You deserved to be hurt," I wanted to say, but instead I smiled weakly, shrugged, and let it go.

* * *

The house at the Parvin Place was crowded, especially in the 8 by 10 west bedroom where Joyce, eighteen, Wanda, going on fifteen, and Lottie Jean, now Jean, ten, shared the same bed. Joyce was still moping around, red eyed and pallid, over having been left in the lurch by her first boyfriend, but when Fred sent her the money for a train ticket to Sacramento where he was making good money stocking produce in a grocery store, she left home wearing her shabbiest clothes in order to lessen the likelihood—Mama's words—that she'd be violated along the way.

The cause of Freddy Wright's suddenly cooled ardor wasn't altogether clear, but I thought Mama had pushed way too hard, especially after she proclaimed that Freddy's ecstatic behavior after being saved at the Rocky Comfort revival was a sure sign that he had gotten the Holy Ghost and had been called to preach. Mama may have decided that because none of her three sons seemed promising as preachers, her best prospect was a son-in-law. Anyway, she was right in the middle of promoting the marriage when, without a word, Freddy suddenly dumped Joyce and immediately started dating one of Otho Black's nieces from Verona, a quiet girl he soon married.

Before the marriage, while Joyce still had hope, she offered Jay a quarter if he'd ask Freddy why he'd spurned her. The quarter loomed large in Jay's eyes—he'd rat-holed his quarter a week allowance for nearly two years in Wichita until he had accumulated eighteen dollars and seventy-five cents for a war bond which matured to the twenty-five dollars he later paid for a heifer calf that grew up to become a fine cow—but as tempting as the quarter bribe was, Jay wouldn't demean himself by asking Freddy, and Joyce never knew for sure why she had received such a damaging blow to her ego.

Even with Joyce and Fred both gone, the six of us were considerably more cramped in the house at the Parvin Place than all eight of us had been on Honey Creek, but with the coming of April, Jay and I moved an extra bed out to the empty smokehouse where we'd have six to eight months to enjoy our boars' nest before cold weather drove us back inside the house.

We'd barely got settled in at the new place when the Model A started smoking and using a lot of oil. From the way the Madewell boys hot-rodded the Hupmobile up and down the road, I thought they'd done the same with the Ford. When Dad asked Lee Kelley, a mechanic in north town, to listen to the engine run, Lee said, "That motor's shot, Clay. If it was me I'd get another car. This one's on its last legs."

"My dad always said Henry Ford couldn't improve on a Model A. He was wrong, wasn't he, Lee?"

"Yeah, he was dead wrong. They're pretty good cars, an improvement over Model T's and better than the B models that followed them, but they can be improved."

"What do I owe you," Dad asked.

269

"Not a thing," the accomodating man replied. "I didn't do anything but look and listen and give you some advice."

"Well, much obliged," Dad said.

A few days later Dad followed Gearl Lemaster to Springfield where Gearl traded for a good late model Buick sedan, and Dad traded for another Model A, giving a hundred dollars to boot.

I couldn't believe my eyes when he drove up in a bright canary colored Model A Ford coupe highlighted with shiny black wire wheels. "Whatta you think of that?" he asked with a foolish grin as he opened the back and popped open a poor fitting rumble seat. The younger kids oohed and aahed while Dad showed off his gaudy toy. All I could think of was the ridiculous looking spectacle we'd make wherever we went, and how exposed those of us riding in the rumble seat would be.

"What's that miss in the motor?" I asked Dad when he took us for a short ride.

"I'm not sure," Dad said. "When I first heard it on the way home I had Gearl listen to it. He said it sounded to him like a cracked block. I'm afraid I've been skinned."

"It looks good," I said. "Maybe we can trade it for somethin' better."

Later, while riding the school bus home, I spotted a '36 Ford sedan parked in front of Chester Bowling's house with a For Sale sign on the windshield. Dad perked up when I told him and, to my surprise, he suggested that I drive the Model A over to Chester's and hit him up for a trade. "You'll have better luck tradin' with Chester than I would," he said. "If his car looks all right and runs to suit you, offer to trade even up."

"All right," I said.

Chester had little, if any, formal education, but he was mighty sharp, and I expected him to pick up on the knock in the motor right off. When he ignored the miss, I felt no obligation to call it to his attention.

"How'll you trade?" Chester asked, after he'd examined Dad's car.

"Oh, I don't know. Yours is a later model, but the front seats need to be upholstered, and the dash is rusty. Our car is a little older, but it's got a new paint job and it's a lot sportier lookin'. How about tradin' even up? We can change 'em here and now."

Chester grinned. "You sound like a trader, just like your dad, but I'm gonna take a chance and trade with you anyway. Maybe that miss is from a bad spark plug."

"I'm not sure," I said. "You know a lot more about cars than I do."

Dad didn't say anything when I drove up in the dull black sedan, but he seemed relieved that I'd gotten rid of the lemon the used car salesman in Springfield had foisted off on him.

Jay and I spent the following Sunday afternoon sanding the badly pitted dashboard and then applying a half pint of dark blue Western Auto paint with a tiny watercolor brush Wanda loaned us. It took us most of the afternoon, in shifts, to finish the tedious job, but we were well pleased with the result. Mama jumped in and fashioned dark blue denim slipcovers for the shredded front seats, then laced them in a snug fit with a stout trotline cord strung on Great-Grandpa Nate's curved three-sided needle Dad ordinarily used to sew up a ruptured pig.

When Mama had finished her sewing Jay and I admired her handiwork, and ours, in the oddly harmonious two-toned blues. Maybe our work was amateurish, but anything was better than that outlandish looking canary colored Model A coupe with the cracked block.

TWENTY-SEVEN
MARY JANE

The first time I saw Mary Jane may have been in study hall, as she remembered it, but my first distinct memory of her was during a lull in a ballgame when she was one of several cheerleaders on the sidelines performing a routine meant to rouse the crowd's flagging spirits. Unlike the other girls with their self-conscious smiles and wooden efforts, the short acrobatic girl with the wide, gap-toothed grin enjoyed herself immensely as she kicked higher than her head while cavorting on the sidelines.

Later in the evening, I saw her out on the dance floor at teen town, still laughing, jitterbugging with anyone who imagined he might be able to keep up with her. Several guys tried, but only one was her match.

"Who are those dancing fools?" I asked Herb from our safe booth.

"That's Lum Fulp and his sister Mary Jane," Herb replied. "Don't you wish you could dance like that?"

"Yeah, I do," I admitted. "She looks kind of familiar. Do you know if she has an older sister, a black headed knockout named Ramona?"

"I don't know if she does or not. Ask her if she ever stops dancin'."

When Lum, exhausted, went downstairs for a cigarette, I approached the smiling, sweating girl.

"Hi, I'm Wayne. Are you any kin to Ramona Fulp?"

"I'm Mary Jane. Ramona—we call her Mocho—is my older sister. Do you know her?"

"Ramona and I picked strawberries together at Old Sprando's for a week the summer I turned twelve, and I've never forgotten how pretty and friendly she was."

"That sounds like Mocho, all right. You'll have to go to California if you want to see her. She left for Pasadena last year right after she graduated."

"Too bad I missed her," I said. "But I bet I could be consoled by her little sister. Anyone who enjoys cheerleadin' and dancin' the way you do is bound to be fun."

"Maybe," Mary Jane said. "Are you a dancer?"

"I'm afraid not."

"Oh," she said. "Well, I might teach you a few steps."

"I doubt it," I said. "I'm clumsy. Real clumsy."

Our conversation was interrupted by Lum's return, but before Mary Jane rejoined him, I asked her: "How about if I walk you home later tonight?"

"Sure, why not?" she said. "See ya at closin' time."

As I walked over to where Herb sat I extended my hand. "Pay me. I told you the first girl I asked would go out with me."

"You lucky dog. Knowing her sister was what did it."

On our first walk down Washington toward her house I was struck by how easy it was to talk to Mary Jane. But what bowled me over was her smell.

After several hours of strenuous activity, I always smelled like a boar hog. But not Mary Jane. Not by a long shot. She smelled better than anyone I'd ever smelled before, something like a dead ripe muskmelon crossed with blooming lilacs and a dash of Grapette pop thrown in for good measure. Mixed in with the sweet aromas, I detected a faint suggestion of crushed possum grapes and a compelling hint of far away skunk. Mary Jane's accommodating lift to her tiptoes, her quick thanks, and our short kiss left me with a taste as sweet as her smell.

On our first real date a week later I recall her mom's friendly "Come in," at my knock and seeing several young children scurry to a back room in the cramped little house. A piled high ironing board dominated the small front room, but Mary Jane and her mother ignored the general clutter. Another thing that impressed me about Helen Fulp was her direct manner and her firm handshake. Most women were reluctant to shake hands, if they shook hands at all.

"Try to behave yourselves, but have a good time." Helen told us. "Remember, Jane, I'll be workin' late at the Bank Hotel tonight. Don't wait up for me."

Mary Jane and I saw a movie at the Princess that night, but as we continued going out it became clear that she preferred something more active, such as going to the B & V, the Belch and Vomit as everyone called it, a place on Highway 60 with a beer joint in front and a teen hangout in the rear with a jukebox in the corner. Pansy and her sister Gladys, proprietors of the B and V, maintained strict control over both ends of their small establishment, and as a result only the most unreasonable parents objected to their children frequenting the place.

Most parents did everything in their power to keep their children from going to the Cockatoo, a honky-tonk located about a half mile east of Aurora. As good a place as the Cockatoo must have been to drink and dance, few high schoolers, especially girls, dared risk ruining their reputations by being seen there. Nondancer and strict teetotaler that I was, the only attraction the infamous roadhouse held for me was as a rumored den of iniquity. Although I was drawn to depravity and violence, the death of a young neighbor at the hands of a man wielding a beer bottle outside the Cockatoo a few years earlier had put a damper on my inclination to go there.

Whether she was at the B and V on weeknights, or at teen town on the square on Saturday nights, Mary Jane danced anytime she could find a willing partner. When Lum was around the two of them put on a show jitterbugging, but when he wasn't there she made do with whoever she could coax out on the floor. Bob Lear liked to slow dance with her, but as often as not she and one of her girlfriends danced fast numbers together.

She always beat me when we went bowling. Worse, after I repeatedly failed to return her blistering serves at Ping-Pong, she easily won even after she'd shifted to playing left-handed. Oddly enough, as competitive as I was playing football, it didn't bother me for Mary Jane to trounce me in games requiring coordination and finesse. Once, when I pouted, Mary Jane said, "You don't care."

And I didn't. What mattered was simply being near the highly charged, upbeat girl. Whether we were meeting briefly in the hall at school, walking to or from a movie or teen town, sitting close in the front seat of Dad's fume filled '35 Ford, or necking late at night on the couch in her front room where the acrid unvented gas heater sputtered, all I had to do to make my day or night was lean over, pull her to me, breathe deeply, and fill my swelling chest with her sweet essence.

* * *

Near the end of the school year graduating seniors took an aptitude test, the Ohio Psychological, and teachers discussed our scores with us. Mr. McDaniel was surprised to see that Neil Graf and I, both lackadaisical and sorry students, had come in first and second in our class. He was amazed that we'd achieved higher scores than the valedictorian and salutatorian, Irma McConnell and Norma Lee Barker had, or, for that matter, Ethyl Jean Medlin, who at sixteen was not only the youngest and most voluptuous girl in the class, but likely the smartest.

275

"Have you thought about going to college?" Mr. McDaniel asked me.

"No, I haven't," I said, laughing at his absurd question.

"Well, you ought to," he advised. "The results of this test indicate that if you'd apply yourself you could do well in college."

"Does the test say where I could get the money I'd need?"

"Don't get smart, young man. Of course not."

"My folks don't have any extra money, Mr. McDaniel, and even if they did they wouldn't spend it on somethin' as foolish as college."

"Well," he said. "There's always the service for someone like you. By saving your money for four years and then using the G.I. Bill, you could manage college fairly easily."

"I'll think about it," I said. "But four years in the service and four more years in school is a long time."

"Maybe so, but the eight years will pass, no matter what," Mr. McDaniel observed.

"Like I said, I'll think about it. Thanks."

Mr. McDaniel's advice made me think of one of Mama's younger brothers, Reuben, who had obtained a wrestling scholarship at the University of Oklahoma. In addition to cutting other students' hair at fifteen cents a head, Reuben had ridden his bicycle sixty miles home every month or so, supplementing the food he got at the training table with sow belly and an occasional ham as well as boxes of raisins and oats Grandpa and Grandma Green gave him. But as much as I admired him for his perseverance, I wondered if going to college would turn me into a stuffed shirt like Reuben. It was bad enough that I was almost a dead ringer for him in looks.

On the night of my graduation I was surprised and a little pleased, but mostly apprehensive, when all the folks, including Dad, got ready to go. We were late, as always, and as we neared town on Highway 39, our left rear tire blew out. Since I was dressed up in my new double-breasted suit, and Dad was wearing his overalls, he changed the tire. Highway 39 was a narrow gravel road in 1949, and while Dad stretched halfway across it trying to get the balky jack in place, a speeding Model A with weak headlights narrowly missed running over him. Rex and Wilma Wilkin, even later than we were on their way to graduation with Bobby Lynn, stopped long enough to give me a ride.

I don't recall the ceremony, but when the folks entered the auditorium, I saw that Dad had enough sense to stay outside in the dark where no one could see him in his dirty overalls.

Although I had a standing offer to return to western Oklahoma for the summer and work for Walt Blevins again, I briefly looked for work around Aurora.

When nothing materialized, instead of heading to Oklahoma, I bought a bus ticket to Wichita, where I hoped to find work. On the day I left, Mary Jane and I spent a long time sitting hidden on the basement stairs of the post office across from the bus station waiting for my departure.

"Are we going to write?" I wondered.

"Let's not," Mary Jane replied. "I'm a poor hand at writin' letters. But I wish you didn't have to leave, and I'll be thinkin' of you."

"Okay," I agreed.

In Wichita I caught a city bus to Lottie and Pap's place where, in their one bathroom house, Lottie rented out rooms to as many as a dozen people.

It was hard to read Pap—gruff but kind like his father before him—but Lottie cheerfully directed me to a dusty bed in the open basement where sheets for walls separated me from paying customers.

The next morning I took a bus out to Boeing where I was immediately hired. A union representative was turned loose on me, but I withstood his hard sell and threat that I'd be ostracized by my fellow workers if I showed up for work without a union pin.

After I'd been picked to attend a school for riveters, I got acquainted with an older man, George Toothaker, who was working and saving his money in order to become a dentist. Seeing I was having trouble with the specialized jargon and the exact figures of the close tolerances we were expected to know, George drilled me repeatedly in what he thought would be on our final test. Apparently he knew what he was doing because the two of us made high scores. To George's chagrin and my surprise, I edged him out.

A week later, tired of the incessant noise and tedium of bucking rivets, and annoyed at having to act busy when there was no work to be done, I called Walt Blevins in Oklahoma.

"Walt. This is Wayne Holmes. Do you still need a hired hand?"

"I sure do. Can you come?"

"Yes. I can be there ready to go to work Monday morning."

"Good. We'll be lookin' for you."

"Okay. Well, 'by."

When I arrived at Walt's the frantic and exhausting job of combining and storing the wheat was almost finished, leaving me with the familiar and comfortable routine of plowing several hundred acres of ground twice in preparation for the fall planting of the following year's wheat crop. Besides keeping my eye peeled for rattlesnakes to kill and mourning dove nests to save while driving the big tractor pulling the wide one-way disc over the prairie, I pondered my future. Should I go to college? And what about Mary Jane?

* * *

At the end of the plowing season, with considerably less money in my pocket than I'd made the previous two summers, I returned to Wichita where, after agreeing to pay Lottie five dollars a week for room and board, I enrolled at Wichita State. By claiming Pap and Lottie's address, and saying I'd graduated from nearby North High, I avoided paying out-of-state tuition. At first I wanted to play football for the Shockers, but after a couple of weeks of holding dummies for freshmen, I turned in my gear and took a job throwing newspapers for the *Beacon*.

My paper route was within easy walking distance, and after I'd memorized my customers' addresses the cumbersome canvas sack filled with newspapers steadily lightened as I got the hang of folding and tossing the compact square missiles against screen doors. Saturday mornings, when I collected for the previous week's papers, I was often invited to step inside. I especially liked collecting when exotic black haired girls with a Spanish lilt to their voices shyly at first and then boldly flirted with me.

College itself was only so-so. For one thing, I found it impossible to adjust my microscope satisfactorily in my biology laboratory. Instead of the clearly delineated reproductions of my lab partner, I had nothing to show beyond chaotic shapes resembling fuzzy Rorschach tests. In my English class, on the other hand, the witty young woman perched on the edge of her desk led our small group through exhilarating discussions, and when she promptly returned my papers their margins were filled with encouraging words. I despised Reserve Officer Training Corps. Once a week we wore our ill fitting government issue uniforms to school where we practiced our rudimentary lessons in close order drill and military history at the hands of officious instructors bent on eliciting lightning quick responses of "Yes, sir!" and "No, sir!"

Although I blamed ROTC for my increasingly disenchanted outlook, the main reason I was unhappy was because I longed to see and smell Mary Jane, and I hadn't got well enough acquainted with the girls I saw in college to ask them out. Once I saw a girl I recognized in an orientation meeting. "Aren't you Betty Baumchen from Planeview?" I eagerly asked.

"My maiden name was Betty Baumchen, and I once lived in Planeview, but I don't believe I know you," she said.

"You don't remember me? I'm Wayne, Wayne Holmes. We used to date."

"Yes, of course. But it's been four years and you've changed. How did you know me?"

"The distinctive curve of your mouth," I said. "And I couldn't forget those one-of-a-kind kisses."

"Oh. Well, thanks, I guess," the flustered young woman said. "I'll tell my husband I ran into you. Maybe I'll see you again."

"I hope so. 'Bye."

Shortly afterward I made an appointment to see the president of the college.

"Sir, I'm here to drop ROTC."

"What's wrong?' the young administrator asked. 'You're not disabled are you?"

"No, but I hate ROTC."

"ROTC is compulsory for all able-bodied young men. "

"Can I get a refund if I quit school?"

"Our policy varies," he said, "but if you're set on leaving I'll try to get you a 60% refund."

"Fair enough," I said, "I'll be back shortly."

TWENTY-EIGHT
POSTGRADUATE CLASS

I felt relieved but anxious on the all day trip hitchhiking back to Missouri.

Once I got to Aurora, instead of going home, I spent a dollar for a room and breakfast in the house where Herb and I had sometimes stayed the previous year. After breakfast the following morning, I walked to the square where Leonard Bisby and his small crew worked.

"How's business?" I asked Leonard.

"Good. We're real busy. Too bad you graduated. We could use you."

"I sure liked workin' here," I said. "Well, I'm goin' over to the high school. See you later."

When I checked in at the principal's office, Mr. McConnell seemed glad to see me. "Why, if it's not Wayne Holmes. I thought we got shed of you."

"Maybe not," I said. "I've got a question for you. Is it possible for someone who has already graduated to return to high school for post graduate work?"

"I've never heard of it," Mr. McConnell laughed. "You're not thinking about coming back, are you?"

"Yes, I am," I said. "Leonard Bisby will hire me to work in the mornings again and I'd like to take a couple of classes in the afternoon, maybe history and English, and then help Coach Neal with football."

"This sounds like a crazy idea," Mr. McConnell said. "But the more I think about it the better I like it. You'd be a good influence here at school and I'm sure Coach Neal would like to have your help. I'll go talk it over with the superintendent." Mr. McConnell was all smiles when he returned. "Mr. Leitle said he didn't see any reason why not."

"Thanks," I said. "I better go see if I can catch Coach Neal."

Coach Neal smiled in his lopsided, bemused way when I told him my newly hatched plan. "Sure," he said. "Maybe your style of football will rub off on some of this year's players."

Although I wanted to see Mary Jane, I decided against looking for her until the next day when I'd officially enroll.

I expected the folks to be surprised after I showed up with Wanda and Jay on the school bus, but they were noncommittal. "What are your plans now?" Mama asked.

"Leonard Bisby will hire me at Armo again, and Mr. McConnell has arranged for me to take a couple of post graduate classes in the afternoon, and then help Coach Neal with football."

"Post graduate classes?" Dad asked. "I've never heard of such a thing."

"Me neither," Mama said. "But it sounds a lot like when Mama and Papa let me repeat the eighth grade. And," she reminded Dad, "we let Joyce do the same thing instead of goin' to high school."

"Maybe so," Dad grudgingly admitted. "Just make sure you do your share of the work around here, young man."

"I will," I said.

Wouldn't Mary Jane be surprised?

* * *

When I saw Mary Jane in the hall at school she was her usual chirpy self, but she seemed uneasy.

"What's wrong?" I asked. "I thought you'd be glad to see me."

"Mr. McConnell's secretary told me you'd enrolled in school again," she said. "Doesn't being here feel weird after you've already graduated?"

"Yeah, it does feel odd," I admitted, "But seeing everyone makes me feel good. I've missed you, Mary Jane."

"You should have listened to me and never left in the first place," she said. "Remember when you didn't think you could make enough money around here and you went to Wichita?"

"Yeah."

"Well, your name was picked for a hundred dollars at the drawing on the square one Saturday afternoon. If you'd 'a been here you'd 've had plenty of money, and we could've been seeing each other all summer."

"Maybe so," I allowed. "But I didn't know I'd win the drawing. Anyway, I left and now I'm back. Can't we get together the way we were before?"

"I've had a lot of time to think about it, and I'm not sure."

"Not sure? Sounds to me like you've got somebody else on the string,"

"Not at all," she assured me, "but I don't think we should go steady like we did last year. We were headed for trouble."

"Whatta ya mean, headed for trouble?"

"You know what I mean. When a couple's together all the time they always get too involved. We've both seen it happen, and I don't have to draw a map for you to understand what I'm gettin' at."

"Okay, okay," I conceded. "How about meetin' you at teen town Saturday night?"

"That'll be fine," she said. "And you can take me home afterward, like you used to. Now don't take anything I've said wrong. I'm glad you're back."

"That's good," I said. "Oh, there's one thing I forgot to tell you."

"What's that?"

I drew her close, took a deep breath, then slowly exhaled: "You smell as good as you ever did, Mary Jane."

* * *

During a break at the machine shop one morning, a machinist asked me if I knew how possums mated, and did I know how the tiny hairless young arrived in the sow's pouch? "No," I answered, "I guess not."

"Well, you know that an old boar possum has a forked dick, don't you?"

"No, I didn't know that, either."

"Well, he does. And he screws the sow with his forked dick through her nose holes up into her head." Was Nolan pullin' my leg? I wondered, but as he continued, his earnest manner left little doubt. "You do know how narrow a possum's head is?" When I nodded yes, he continued. "The little possums are conceived in their mother's head. But since there's not much room in her head, after while the old sow snorts the tiny bald babies out of her nose and into her pouch like she had a snotty nose. Each baby possum latches on to its own separate tit. Then each tit swells up and the babies can't turn loose until after their hair comes in."

Nolan ended his lesson and returned to his work. He'd be dead and gone long before a National Geographic Special showed a kangaroo, close cousin to the possum, give birth the good, old-fashioned way, with two hairless young on their slow squirming way to their mother's pouch.

Ah, folklore. Ah, education.

* * *

Since Mary Jane was the head cheerleader and I was helping Coach Neal with football, we were thrown together a lot, and before long we were as thick as ever. Besides going to the movies, bowling, and more or less hanging out together at the B & V and teen town, late at night we increasingly went parking, my favorite activity. Sometimes when her mom worked late at the Bank Hotel, and the younger kids were gone or asleep, we necked on the living room couch.

Our necking started as a result of Mary Jane's attempt to teach me how to dance. She'd made sure everyone else was gone and the lights were dim when she played "Stardust" on her old record player. Despite my best intentions, I didn't have a clue how to move my feet to the sweet music.

"Just move back and forth in place," she finally said.

"I can do that on the couch," I ventured.

"Well, all right," Mary Jane sighed.

Although I called what we were doing making out— hugging, kissing, and holding hands was as far as it went. Unlike some of my friends who, to hear them tell it, regularly got on first and second base and beyond, I weakly subscribed to something I'd read in Reader's Digest called delayed gratification, something supposedly high minded but suspiciously like an early version of Just Say No.

Of course Mary Jane and I were circumspect. For example, we never discussed, much less practiced, anything as exciting or as degenerate as the sloppy kiss attributed to the French. Like most of our friends, I suppose, Mary Jane and I practiced our chaste and hard little kisses we'd copied from our favorite actors. The girls I knew generally kissed timidly, without heat, but I pressed hard, compressing my lips into thin lines like Randolph Scott at his best.

One bitterly cold night in February, after Mary Jane and I had been parked on Lover's Lane longer than usual, she broke our embrace, turned to me, and asked: "When are you going to marry me?" I was so dumbfounded I was speechless. In the continuing silence I wiped off the steamed up windshield, started the engine, and drove the pale girl home. The instant the car stopped, she bolted inside the house.

It was hard for me to see the road on my way home. After my feet turned numb I stopped long enough to cross my legs, Indian fashion, then drove the rest of the way using the hand throttle instead of the foot feed. After barely grazing one of several galloping horses loose on the road near the curve at White Oak School, I recalled the previous Friday night when Mary Jane had been cheerleading at an out of town basketball game, and I had taken Jay to the annual White Oak pie supper.

Squandering my money on a high priced pie and then eating the whole thing with a giggly grade school girl had held no appeal for me, but as I was looking over the crowd I'd noticed that the new young teacher, Violet Hancock, a big bosomed Scandinavian looking natural blonde with wide-set eyes and high cheekbones, kept checking me out. Violet might be just the ticket, I thought, as I drove cross-legged down the icy road. She might help me cool off Mary Jane.

* * *

Since neither we nor the Hancocks had a telephone, I couldn't call Violet to ask if she wanted to go with me to the basketball game at Aurora on Saturday night. Rather than waste gas ahead of time on the long drive almost to Flat Creek where the Hancocks lived, I decided to risk going early Saturday evening.

It was still light when I forded Carney Branch before reaching my destination. At my knock, Vena Hancock opened the door. "I'm looking for Violet," I said.

"She and Glenna are out at the barn milking," she replied. "I'll holler for her if you want me to."

"That's all right. I'll find her. Thanks."

When I opened the barn door, Violet jumped up, upsetting her stool. "What are you doin' here?"

"How would you like to go with me to a basketball game at Aurora tonight?"

"I don't care if I do. Glenna, will you milk my last cow for me?"

"I don't mind," her younger sister said.

"I'll be ready soon," Violet said, and she dashed to the house. Within minutes we were on our way.

"Slow down so you don't drownd out your engine when we ford the creek," she warned me.

"I'll be careful," I said.

I was also careful about how I negotiated the hills alongside Carney Branch. I knew from experience that if I gunned the oil guzzling motor too hard, embarrassing foul smelling black smoke would billow up through the floor board, and if I failed to accelerate enough, I'd lose my momentum and have to downshift to second or even low in order to make it to the top.

Before we'd reached the worst hills, Violet reached over and took hold of my hand.

"You feel stout," she said.

"Thanks. You feel pretty strong yourself."

When I disengaged my hand to shift on the steep hill where Violet's aunt lived her furtive and isolated life, I caught a whiff of something familiar. It's hard to describe, but anyone who has ever milked a cow by hand is not likely to forget the distinctive and not altogether unpleasant smell caused by the mix of manure and milk along with bits of hay and straw and something like dandruff that flakes off cows' bags. Violet must have been in a bigger hurry to go to the ball game than I'd first guessed.

We were past Wheelerville when she started in on me.

"Have you been saved?"

"No, I haven't."

"Well, you oughta be."

"I tried hard to get saved when I was sixteen, but it didn't take."

"Whatta you mean, it didn't take? What church was it?"

"Southern or Hard-Shelled Baptist, I'm not sure which."

"No wonder," she said. "Even if you'd 'a thought you was saved, you wouldn't 'a been."

"What are you talkin' about?"

"There's only one way to be saved, and that's through the church," she said, whispering the last two words. Her lowered voice and emphasis on "the church" reminded me of the time several years earlier when a nun had sharply rebuked me for talking out loud while I was mopping the chapel at St. Francis Hospital in Wichita.

"Oh, I get it," I said. "You think the only way to be saved is through the Catholic Church."

"I don't think anything of the kind," she said in an extra loud voice. "The Catholic Church is a cult. I'm talking about the one and only means of salvation—the Church of Christ."

"Oh, I didn't realize you were a Campbellite."

"Only rude or ignorant people call us Campbellites," Violet sniffed. "Us true Christians attend Christ's church; we call it 'the church,'" and she whispered again.

"I think we'd better change the subject. How do you like teachin' school?"

"Not very good. I've decided I'd rather be a housewife."

While I busied myself shifting gears, our conversation lagged until I pulled up at the armory.

"Where do you wanta sit?" I asked, as we walked in front of the cheerleaders inside the gym.

"Anywhere. You decide."

"Let's climb up high so we can see all the action," I said. I hoped she didn't catch on that I wanted to make sure everyone saw how good looking she was, but not be able to hear anything she said.

The basketball game was long and boring. Although Mary Jane gave no sign she'd seen Violet or me, I thought her cheerleading was below par. After the game, Violet and I had little to say as I took her straight home. I drove faster than usual, especially on the mostly downhill last part of the way.

288

"You better slow down," she warned as we neared Carney Branch, but it was too late. The splashing water at Carney Branch Ford drowned out my car.

"You did that on purpose!" Violet screeched.

"On purpose? Why would I stall my car in the middle of the creek on purpose?"

"Maybe you thought you could take advantage of me."

"I'm not in the habit of taking advantage of anyone," I said, "and I don't appreciate bein' accused of it."

By carefully opening my door and then creeping sideways on the running board above the small stream, I managed to get to the front fender where I lifted the left side of the hood and wiped off the wet plugs and distributor with my handkerchief. To my relief, the engine fired right up. Minutes later, with the engine left running, I walked Violet to the back porch where we exchanged cool pecks.

After lunch at school on Monday I met Mary Jane in the hall. "Hi," I said, "How about a movie tonight?"

"I'm not interested," she replied.

"How about tomorrow night?"

"Not tomorrow night, either."

"Wednesday night?"

"No, I'm not going anywhere with you ever again."

"Why not?"

"Because," she said as she hammered me hard on the chest with both fists, "I hate you! I hate you! I hate you!"

* * *

Talk about cold, Mary Jane froze me out at every turn. Finally, in desperation, as I headed for her house on foot one night I spotted a Jim Beam bottle in the gutter. After swigging the few remaining drops of whiskey I'd pretend I was drunk then apologize and try to convince her to give me a chance. When Mary Jane refused to see me, her mother came out on the porch where we sat and talked.

Finally, Helen said, "I wish Jane would reconsider, but she feels betrayed. Unless I'm badly mistaken, she's through with you. To tell the truth, she's already found someone she says she likes better than she ever liked you."

Sure enough, Mary Jane had taken up with an older guy fresh out of the service, a lightweight named Leonard who could have passed for Charlton Heston. As far as I could tell, Leonard never took Mary Jane dancing or bowling, but he spent long hours skating with her at her aunt and uncle's rink across the railroad tracks. Once, hiding in the dark, I watched the two of them gliding effortlessly forward, backwards, every which way, smiling foolishly, arm in arm. Outside, looking in, I finally understood. I was beat.

Not long afterward, when the lilacs were at their best full bloom, I asked Tappy, Mary Jane's younger sister, if there was anything to the rumor that Mary Jane and Leonard were engaged.

"Yes," Tappy said. "They're gonna get married as soon as Jane graduates. Then they're movin' to Peoria."

"Peoria? Is he gonna work at Caterpillar?"

"No, Leonard has a good job lined up workin' in a salvage yard and sellin' used cars. By the way," she continued, "I haven't seen much of you lately. What's up?"

"Not much. The only thing exciting is Johnny Bill and Patches and I are gonna play spring football at Southwest Missouri State. Coach Neal thinks we can get scholarships."

"Good luck," Tappy said.

"Thanks. And much obliged for giving me the straight scoop on Mary Jane."

When Coach Neal told us he'd recommended us to Coach Fred Thomsen, he'd said we'd meet the former University of Arkansas head coach at the armory. Although I was impressed with the red faced man's courtly manner, I was uneasy when I saw that he mainly made eye contact with Coach Neal and Johnny Bill. "We need a good, big center like you," he told Johnny Bill, before turning to Patches and me: "The smallest and best defensive guard in the conference, Jim Somers, a senior, will be coaching you smaller guys these next two weeks. If you're as tough as Coach Neal says you are, maybe you can make it."

Patches and I immediately took to the short, burly blond with a drawl who demonstrated his bag of tricks while patiently instructing us in various defensive skills. On the final evening of practice, with only a few die-hard fans and a lone reporter watching from the sidelines, Patches and I found ourselves playing defense at the guard positions against the first string offensive team. Pumped up like crazy, we repeatedly raged back and forth delivering hammering forearm shivers and fending off blockers before tackling the runners for little or no gain. "Way to play defense!" Somers yelled as he slapped us on the butt when the simulated game ended.

Best of all, the newspaper reporter, pad in hand, sought us out. "What are your names and where are you guys from?" he asked.

"Grover Phillips, Aurora."

"Wayne Holmes, Aurora."

After we'd showered Coach Thomsen showed up. "All three of you are as good as Coach Neal told me," he said, and shook hands with us. "Come by my office and we'll discuss your scholarships." When my turn came, he told me to sit down. "There's one thing that concerns me, Holmes. How much do you weigh?"

"A hundred and fifty pounds. Why?"

"No bigger than you are, and the way you hit head on, I'm afraid you'll end up punch drunk."

"I've never been knocked out, and I've only seen stars once," I said. But I was careful to not mention I'd seen the stars after tackling his powerful fullback head-on that same evening.

"It still worries me," the coach said. "Why don't you consider switching to defensive back where you won't be taking so many direct hits?"

"I'll think about it," I said. "But I'm not sure I can cover a pass."

"We'll see this fall," he said.

The next day I drove to Aurora where I picked up a Springfield paper. There on the lower left hand side of the sports section was a short article about our final scrimmage. After more than fifty years I can't be certain, but if memory serves me right, the reporter wrote: "The best and most exciting part of the scrimmage was when two watchfob guards from Aurora, Grover Phillips and Wayne Holmes, shut down the Bears' first string offense with their defensive efforts." I didn't tell the folks, but I took the article out of my billfold and showed it to Jay and others who might well understand its importance. In fact, I showed it to so many people I finally wore it out.

I was working at Armo feeding sheets of metal into a power shear when a blonde I occasionally dated walked by the window. Distracted by the carefully controlled way she swung her hindend, I broke my rhythm and failed to pull my right hand back in time to clear the shear's blade. I felt nothing, but I quickly realized that the end of my middle finger was gone, and the spot of white I first glimpsed was bone.

The foreman growled, "Get back to work," when I approached him at his drill press, but at the sight of the bloody pulsing finger in his face, he turned off his machine and quickly took me down the street. The doctor thought he might be able to reattach the finger tip, but when he called the shop he learned someone had already flushed it.

Later, Leonard Bisby went with me to Mt. Vernon where I told a labor board that my on-the-job injury had impaired my ability to milk cows and type. I didn't mention that Miss Cox had told me long before the accident that I was the worst typing student she'd ever had. I felt lucky to get a hundred dollars, enough to pay my way to Crater Lake in Oregon with Roy Lee Nivens and Don Bisby after Don's graduation. I'd be on my way out west to an exciting job as a temporary forest ranger before Mary Jane was married and living in dreary Illinois.

TWENTY-NINE
THE GANG BANG

Profoundly saddened and shook up as I was over losing Mary Jane, and after a period of moping around and feeling sorry for myself, I decided that playing the field might be a good idea. The trouble was, of the many girls who would go out with me now that I'd made a name for myself, none of them smelled anything like Mary Jane. Most of them smelled all right, good enough in a pinch, but try as I might I found no one who even began to match Mary Jane's compelling, one-of-a-kind fragrance.

One of the more personable and promising of my prospects, a pretty natural blonde, dared to slip out her back bedroom window late one night clothed only in her night gown after I drove down the alley and scratched on her locked screen door. Little did she know that I'd spent the earlier part of the evening with her rival, the young, precocious daughter of uptight older parents who hoped their 10:30 curfew during the week might help keep their baby daughter's reputation unsullied. As much as I admired the daring blonde's behavior, and relished stroking all that smooth exposed skin, her lingering natural smell and taste made me yearn for Mary Jane.

Once when a friendly girl and I were well into the preliminaries of what I hoped would be a one-night stand in the back of an obliging friend's car at a basketball game, I suddenly stopped: "Harold's liable to come out here at half time. I'll run in and tell him we don't want to be bothered, and then I'll be right back."

"Okay, hurry. I'll be waitin' right here."

Once inside the tiny gymnasium, I crowded into the stands. Perhaps twenty agonizingly slow minutes later, the abandoned girl jabbed me hard in the back with her tight fist. When I turned around she muttered, "You chicken shit! I might have known!" I fully deserved her bitter barnyard outburst, but there was no way I could admit how green I was, and how surprised I'd been by her earthy arousal.

A neighbor girl I liked who'd graduated from high school ahead of me was left in the lurch by her boyfriend when she turned up pregnant. After the baby girl's birth, the mother and child were living with her folks when I, not wishing to be seen with her, sometimes took her to a late movie before we parked and necked on a country road for long spells. With the exception of Betty Baumchen in Wichita, this young woman was the best and most accomplished regular kisser I ever had anything to do with. Although she would tolerate light petting, she was not in the least interested in anything more. "I've tried it," she said, "and it's not any fun. Come on, let's kiss." Sometimes I thought she might have given in had I persisted, but I wasn't about to settle down with a wife and a ready-made kid.

There were others, but none suited me until Joyce Gardner moved into the White Oak neighborhood. The lovely, tall, unassuming, and long legged sixteen year old and I took a fancy to one another the first time the school bus stopped at the end of the lane leading up a steep hill where Mrs. Gardner, Joyce, and her younger brother had recently moved from Kansas.

Without either of us saying so, by the end of that first week it was clear that Joyce and I were seatmates. Not even the boldest brat on the bus had the nerve to sit next to one of us. In addition to being unusually good looking and friendly, it soon became apparent that Joyce was one smart cookie. And like many smart people I'd known, she possessed a lively wit and a good sense of humor.

The odd makeup of her family intrigued me. Why had she and her brother and their mother moved from Kansas to their remote eighty acre farm in Missouri? And how did her mother make a living? Besides a milk cow, a pony to ride to the store, a small flock of laying hens, and a garden, there was no other visible means of support for the small family.

As I got to know her better, Joyce filled me in on details of an older married sister as well as three older brothers in the Navy. "What about your dad?" I asked. "Is he dead?"

"No, what makes you think that?"

"You haven't said anything about him. I just supposed he's dead, or maybe your folks are separated."

"No, they're not separated either, if you mean divorced. But they're sort of separated, if you mean they're apart."

"Oh," I said. "What's the deal? What kind of work does he do?"

"He likes living in Kansas better than Missouri," she said. "He works at various odd jobs, whatever he can find, according to Mom. He recently made enough extra so he could pay cash for our farm here. He thinks it's a good place for Mom and us kids, and we like it. I especially like it since I met you."

"Oh, thanks."

Once we got over our initial awkwardness, Joyce and I spent as much of our free time together as we could manage. She seemed oblivious to how shabby our rented house and furnishings were when my sister Wanda invited her over, and I felt increasingly secure as I squired her hither and yon in Dad's rough, smoke belching '36 Ford sedan.

Joyce was a bubbly conversationalist, and little was off limits in our bantering exchanges. She sometimes attended church, but unlike most of the girls I'd taken out, she felt refreshingly free to poke fun at religion, especially after the latest preacher at White Oak made blatant advances toward her.

Naturally, the more time Joyce and I spent together, the more involved we became, leading to serious frustrations. One evening, when we spent the entire time parked near Wise Spring instead of going to church as we'd said we'd do, Joyce's actions seemed to belie her insistent but weakening, "No, no."

Joyce Gardner

When I drove over to see her a few days later, Joyce was crying when she came out to the car. "Dad was here last night. He said he's moving us to Aurora."

"Why? What for?"

"He said he's moving us to town where we'll stay until he can sell the farm, then we'll all move back to Kansas."

"Did he say why?"

"No, but he was real nervous, kind of scared looking, I thought."

"So when do you have to move?"

"Right away. He's rented us an apartment on Jefferson Street. We'll be out of here as soon as a truck comes for our household things. He's made arrangements to sell our horse and cow."

"What's your dad's big hurry?"

"I'm not sure, and Mom won't say, but I have my suspicions. I'll tell you later. Here's our address. We'll be upstairs. I've got to help Mom move and get settled in, so I can't see you

296

for a few days. Well, 'bye," and she slipped me a soft kiss before she turned toward the house.

During the next few days, I pondered my predicament. If things continued at the rate they were going, I'd soon be in the same fix I'd been with Mary Jane. Joyce's resolve was steadily giving way, and with this latest turn of events, I feared she'd want to stay in Missouri and get married instead of going to Kansas with her family. Of course I still stuck to my quaintly principled ideal: I should never have intercourse with anyone I wasn't ready to marry.

When I drove to Aurora and climbed the outside stairs to the old apartment and knocked, Mrs. Gardner came to the door. "Hi Wayne. I'm glad you came. Joyce needs to be perked up. Wait here and I'll call her out."

When Joyce walked out on the landing she was pale and distraught. "It's a done deal," she said. "The realtor already has a buyer for the farm, and as soon as school's out we'll be moving to Kansas."

"Where in Kansas? Is it far?"

"Hutchinson. You know where that is?"

"Yeah, Hutchinson's a long ways out. It's north of Wichita."

"Maybe you can come visit me," she said. "But I'm afraid a visit won't be anything like the wonderful times we've had here."

"I'm afraid you're right," I said. "But maybe somethin' will work out in the meantime. Have you met any town kids yet?"

"Not really."

"Don Bisby lives a couple of blocks from here. I'll run by and tell him he needs to take you around town so you can meet more people. With your personality, you'll get acquainted in no time."

"Yeah, right," Joyce said. "In no time I'll be Queen of the Summit City of the Ozarks."

"Okay, okay," I said, "I deserved that. Sounds like I better get outta here. See ya later when you're in better spirits. 'Bye."

Before I went home I stopped by Don's house and told him the situation.

"Yeah, I know Joyce Gardner," he said. "In fact, I have a class with her. If you're sure it's all right with you, I'll be glad to drive her around and show her off."

"There's no need to overdo it," I said. "She's hurtin' bad right now."

"You know you can trust me," he said. "Since Barbara threw me over, I've been needin' someone to have fun with, you know, someone I can just be friends with."

My stupidity caught up with me fast. Within a week Don and Joyce were seen here, there, and everywhere in Don's dad's souped up '36 Chevy pickup; soon, with Don's bragging going full blast, they were widely regarded as an item.

Although I was peeved at Don's behavior and cockiness, I had no one but myself to blame. The situation was further complicated by the plans Don and I had made about going to Crater Lake in California, where we had a good chance of becoming summer forest rangers.

* * *

Nineteen, going on twenty, my virginity hung over me like a pall. Having held on to the strange notion that screwing out of wedlock was unwise, if not sinful, I'd become a laughingstock. Now, with Mary Jane married and Joyce gone, it was time to discard my scruples and get laid.

After a movie eight of us, country boys all, loitered at Ruckers on the outskirts of town. Tiny Joy waited tables there, all the while longing for midnight when Houston, seven feet tall and double hung, would pick her up. All of us were bored. "What can we do for fun?" someone asked.

One of the older boys knew. "Let's go over in north town and pick up that Miller girl. We'll have to take both cars cause she'll balk if we're all packed in one. Another thing," he said. "We've got to be careful when we get her out to Bonham by the railroad tracks. Houston gets to be first. They'll be in the back seat of our lead car. When he's through, he'll slip out the left side, and I'll slip in on the right. My brother'll be next, then on down the line. It'll go smooth as silk unless somebody gets loud or tries to crowd in. Let's go get her."

Houston honked the thirteen year-old blond girl out and she jumped in the back seat with Joe while we, the five first timers, kept our discreet and fearful distance in the second vehicle.

With the pecking order already established among the veterans in the lead car, the hard job of determining rank for the rest of us had to be done during our ten minute ride. "Age," I said, "ought to be the criteria."

"No, no," said Newt, snickering. "We'll go by size. That way I'll be the first one of us." We voted and Newt won. And so it went: Houston first, Bill, Joe, then Newt, and I, beat out, with homely Jack nudging rowdy Mac by a single vote, while fourteen year-old little Toshie bore no malice for being relegated to the tail end.

The plan ran smoothly. Houston short stroked her a few minutes, then eased his long frame out the left side as Bill entered on the right; with Bill's quick thrusts and spasm soon finished, Joe climbed in and on, and came. Newt, shaking hard, climbed in next, while I, tense, waited my turn. Five minutes turned to ten, then twenty. Houston's vaunted prowess was in question as we marveled at Newt's staying power. As time slowly ground on, curiosity overcame discretion; we left our places and crowded around the rear of the steamy front car where we hoped to learn and copy Newt's fine techniques. Unable to see, we carefully listened. With his freckled good right ear planted against the back glass, Toshie suddenly laughed and shouted, "Boys, Newt's fallen in love! He's busy sweet talkin' her!" Our loud whoops and hollers at Newt's naivete broke up the party. As the chagrined boy emerged, still tightly buttoned, the sounds of the girl's bitter sobs rose. While she wept in the back seat, the three who'd scored shook out their cigarettes then chatted and laughed in the front seat as they drove her home. The rest of us drove straight to Ruckers where we had time for a bottle of pop before Houston arrived all set for Joy.

Both disappointed and relieved, I mulled over my dilemma as I drove home. And all this time, since ever so long, I'd imagined a gang bang would be fun.

While I shopped absentmindedly at Walmart several decades later, I fumbled for my billfold and ID when a new clerk reassuringly said, "Never mind. I know you."

Embarrassed and dumbfounded, but remembering well, I thought, "That's that Miller girl, the same compliant girl of long ago." Now, when I see her from time to time she nods and smiles, friendlier than Walmart's paid greeter, while I, tongue-tied but also friendly, wonder how she has the grace to acknowledge me at all.

THIRTY
CRATER LAKE

After Roy Lee backed out of going to Crater Lake, he pulled out his billfold and handed Don a piece of paper. "Here's the number of the secretary in Portland you'll need," he said, and waved as we pulled out of the driveway in Don's newly acquired black '39 Ford sedan. Somewhere on Highway 54 in the Flint Hills, after much of our initial excitement had worn off, Don pulled over and we stripped off and went swimming in a deep pond. Several miles down the highway, we stopped again to investigate a recently wrecked Wonder Bread delivery truck. As we pilfered through the vehicle, Don spotted a large Kroner harmonica in a leather case behind the visor, which we agreed might help while away the time on lonesome stretches of our trip. We rationalized that from the looks of the wreck, the driver wasn't likely to be playing an instrument any time soon. Besides, other people passing by would likely strip the abandoned truck.

We stayed in Wichita at Pap and Lottie's long enough for my cousin Ben to talk his folks into letting him go with us following his graduation a few days later. On our way out of town, we stopped at the dog pound where we hoped to find a dog suitable for big game hunting in the far west. "I don't have any hounds," the attendant said. "But I have as mean a dog back there as I ever saw." As we neared a large compound filled with barking dogs, a fight broke out, but it quickly ended when an unlikely looking dog asserted his dominance. "That's him," the man said, pointing to a stocky, growling, menacing liver and white dog. The bobtailed boss of the pen, weighing forty pounds at the most, reminded me of a big Cocker Spaniel.

"What breed of dog is he?" I asked.

"I'm not sure, but I think he's a Springer Spaniel."

"I don't know anything about bird dogs," I said, "but I like the way he acts. Let's take him." Don and Ben agreed, we paid the small adoption fee, and we were soon on our way, loaded for bear.

"What are we gonna call him?" Ben asked from the back seat as he petted the now friendly dog.

"Let's call him Cougar," Don suggested. "If anyone asks we'll say he's our cougar dog." The name stuck.

That evening we reached Alton in northern Kansas where Ben had formerly lived. Before we went to his Grandma Johnston's place downtown in the back of an old store building, we stopped out in the country where Ben flirted several hours with a red headed girl he'd dated before he moved to Wichita.

The next day we bought a case of dog food at the grocery store and a case of oil at cost from Ben's Aunt Sally's husband, who delivered gas and oil to local farms and ranches. Before we took out we counted our money. Altogether, with Don's hundred and twenty-five or so, my hundred dollar blood money finger settlement, and Ben's graduation gifts, we had right at three hundred dollars; but since we were going all the way to Portland before swinging south to Crater Lake, we calculated we'd have to be careful or we'd run out of money.

"Let's drive straight through," Don said. "We can drive in shifts and not spend anything on motels."

"Yeah," Ben agreed. "Breakfasts are cheap, and hamburgers will do for our other meals."

"Sounds good to me," I said.

Somewhere in Colorado we stopped at a bank in a little town where we traded our paper money for silver dollars which we placed in a slit Don cut in the headliner above the windshield. From then on, anytime we bought something, we simply reached overhead and thumbed silver dollars out of our common stash. We loved the look and feel of the slick silver coins. Although the price of gasoline hovered around a quarter a gallon, it was still a big expense. Don, more daring than Ben or me, said out loud what we'd all been thinking: "How do you guys feel about gettin' a hose and a couple of five gallon cans, and doin' some midnight requisitionin'?"

"You mean siphonin' gas?" Ben asked.

"Right. We all know how, don't we?"

"Yeah, and we've all done it at one time or another," I said, "but I'm afraid if we're lookin' over our shoulders all the time, it'll ruin our adventure. I vote against it."

Before Ben had time to say yea or nay, Don conceded, "Okay, okay."

Not that we were totally honest, as our persistent but futile efforts to make music with the harmonica reminded us. Somewhere in Utah, after we decided our dog was lonesome and needed a traveling companion, I spotted a border collie gyp which I whistled up and coaxed into the back seat I was sharing with Cougar. Ben and Don were surprised and disappointed when the standoffish female rebuffed our eager dog, but they seemed to understand after I explained how a female dog's heat cycle worked.

I'm not sure when the car first started backfiring, but the farther we drove the worse it got, causing us to pull over any number of times while Don adjusted the carburetor. "I think the timin's off," he finally said. "And I'm afraid to tackle it with these tools."

"This reminds me of when I was a kid and we went to Aurora in a wagon behind a jill-flirted mare," I began.

"Oh, no," Don said to Ben. "Your cousin's about to tell another one of his country stories. Have you ever heard of such a thing as a jill-flirted mare?"

"I can't say that I have," Ben admitted.

"Me neither," Don said.

"Just because you guys haven't heard of somethin' doesn't mean it's not so," I asserted.

"Go ahead with your story. Not that anyone could stop you."

"As I started to say, when I was a kid Dad had a mare that farted a lot. It wasn't too embarrassin' way out in the country like this, but the closer we got to town, the louder she sounded."

"What was wrong with the mare?" Don asked.

"I'm not sure," I said. "When I asked Dad what made her do that, he said he thought she'd been pasture bred, but that didn't mean any more to me than when you say the carburetor needs adjustin', or maybe the timin's off," and I paused.

"Are you finished?" Don asked.

"Maybe."

"What's your point?"

"I've already told you. As a kid I was embarrassed by Dad's mare, and now I'm embarrassed by your car."

"Poor baby," Don said. "If you're that sensitive I'll stop at the next town and have a mechanic take a look. By the way, Ben, what do you think about namin' the car?"

"Why would anyone want to name a car?" Ben asked.

"Wayne just told us why. I vote we name her Jill."

"I second it," Ben laughed.

"Jill it is, two to one," Don crowed, while I sulked in the back seat.

When we stopped at a garage in Green River, Wyoming the mechanic agreed with Don. "Yes, it sounds like the timing. I can tell you ahead of time it'll cost you at least $20 to fix it."

"We can't afford that," Ben said. "Let's just keep on rollin'."

A more serious problem arose after we'd mounted the last of the four bald spare tires we'd started out with. Increasingly short on money, we searched ditches and right-of-ways for castoff tires. Surprisingly, we found enough tires to keep going. Once when Ben was driving, Don and I were awakened by a loud blast from an approaching truck.

"What's all that honkin' about?" Don asked.

"Maybe because I was driving on his side of the road." Ben admitted. "Haven't you guys noticed that the left side of the road is always smoother than the right side?" Ben knew what he was talking about, we decided. From then on, especially on remote stretches, all three of us habitually drove on the wrong side of the road. When Don was at the wheel and he got stuck behind a slow driver in a no passing zone, he often impatiently pulled over and passed on the right. Alarmed drivers would glare and yell at us, but we laughed and half belligerently shook our fists at them. We were kings of the road.

On and on we sputtered and popped through the surprisingly high and dry country of eastern Oregon toward the mighty Columbia, a river far bigger than Crane Creek, Honey Creek, Flat Creek, James River and White River combined. The highlight of our trip was riding a ferry below The Dalles across the roiling Columbia and then driving alongside it toward Portland. At an out of the way turnoff, we stopped beside a waterfall long enough to shed our clothes and take a quick and exhilarating shower, the first bath we'd taken since we'd left Wichita. Refreshed and elated, we stopped on the outskirts of Portland where I was elected to call Roy Lee's contact for summer jobs at Crater Lake.

"Meet me downtown in the morning at ten o'clock," the woman said, then gave directions. "If you make a good impression, my boss is sure to give you good recommendations."

"Okay, thanks. 'Bye."

Don called Joyce Gardner. "Joyce said for us to come on over; we can stay in her brother's empty apartment. Oh, she also told me she's wearin' an engagement ring, and I shouldn't get any ideas."

"What did you say?" I asked.

"I told her I'd see about that," he laughed. And see about it he did. During the long evening while Ben and I lounged around and catnapped in the apartment, Don and Joyce got reacquainted.

I was awake when Don came in after midnight. "How'd it go?" I asked.

"Good, real good," he replied. "She's no longer wearin' that ring."

"Does that mean you two are back together?"

"You could say that," he grinned.

The three of us spruced up the best we could the next morning in preparation for our all-important meeting with the head of the Park Service. When we arrived at our destination downtown, our fears were quickly put to rest by the friendly secretary, as well as by the big man himself with his easy manner and nonthreatening questions. "You boys'll make good summer forest rangers," he said. "If you'll step out in the waiting room, I'll dictate a letter for you to present to the superintendent at Crater Lake. That should take care of it. Good luck."

We were pleased at the reception we got at park headquarters in Portland, but when we returned to the apartment we couldn't locate Gypsy, our border collie. "Looks like we'll have to leave without her," I finally admitted.

"Yeah," Ben agreed. "If we can pry Don and Joyce apart, we'd better get goin'."

"It's already too late to go today," Don argued. "Let's start in the mornin'. Joyce says we can make it in a day."

"Okay," I said. "But we're leavin' early."

Gypsy was still gone the next day, but we left in time for Ben to finish his driving by noon, when we stopped to gas up before I took my four hour turn. Don and Cougar slept in the back seat. When Don's turn came, he decided he could save gas by shutting off the motor, shifting into neutral, and freewheeling down the mountains. It was only after several headlong flights almost ended in disaster before he reluctantly agreed to put the car in gear soon enough for the engine to act as partial brake on our wild rides. When we finally climbed the winding slope into Crater Lake Park, we saw walls of snow higher than the car along the sides of the road. The only signs of life on the rim of the beautiful green lake were two uniformed men in a patrol car.

"They'll know where we need to go," Ben said.

"Yeah," Don agreed. "I'll pull over."

"We're lookin' for the superintendent of the park," I told the men.

"Mr. Shockley's gone. May we help you?" the driver asked.

"Maybe. We have a letter for him."

"I have his home number," the officer said. "Follow me and I'll call him."

Mr. Shockley soon drove up, and invited us to his office. "That's a strong recommendation," he said, "and I happen to have three slots left. But there's a slight catch, boys."

"What's that?" Don asked.

"As you can see, there's still a lot of snow on the ground, and there's little activity in the park. Fact is, you're here too early. But if you'll come back a week from Monday, I'll put you to work. Okay?"

"Okay, we'll be here," I said. "You can count on it."

"Now what?" Ben asked in the car.

"Don't you have an older brother in Sacramento?" Don asked me.

"Yeah, he does, and Fred's a nice guy," Ben said. "He'll take us in."

Fred was outside ready to go to work when we pulled up in his driveway the next morning. "What are you guys doin' out here?" he exclaimed.

"We've got jobs at Crater Lake, and we need a place to stay for a few days," I said.

"You're welcome to stay here if you don't mind sleepin' on the floor. Lois gets bored stayin' alone all day. She'll be glad to show you the sights."

"Thanks," I said, and Ben and Don chimed in.

Lois liked having us there to talk to and feed exotic avocado sandwiches while Fred worked long hours at a grocery store. She offered to take each of us on a tour of any place in the area, even China Town in San Francisco. I'm not sure where she went with the other two, but on my day she took me through the nearby capitol building, followed by a drive along the Sacramento River where she pointed out a makeshift houseboat.

"We lived there after the folks split up and Mom and us kids had to go on public assistance."

"Was that like the relief we got in Missouri?"

"I think so. Anyway, Mom had to be sterilized before she could get help, and since I was old enough to have a baby, I was supposed to get fixed, too. But while I was on the table, I talked the doctor out of it."

"You must have been some talker."

"I was," she replied. "On our way home I'll show you where Mom and her new husband live. She's at work, but he's usually home." When we stopped at a small, neat house, Lois jumped out of the car, ran up the walk, and rushed inside. On her return, she held on to the arm of a man, perhaps thirty-five, who looked like a dissipated version of Jack Palance.

Eager to get to work, Ben, Don and I left for Crater Lake Saturday morning. Although we drove steadily, it was almost dark before we arrived.

"Mr. Shockley's not here," Ben said.

"Let's see if we can get in the dorm," Don suggested.

The door was unlocked, and when we turned on the lights, we saw empty bunkbeds in the big room.

"I'd better call Mr. Shockley," I said.

"Good idea," Ben agreed. "There's a phone."

"Hello, Mr. Shockley? This is Wayne Holmes."

"Who?"

"Remember the three guys from Missouri you talked to last week?"

"Three guys with a dog?"

"Yes. We're at the dorm and we'd like to get settled in."

"What's your name again?"

"Wayne Holmes."

"Wayne, I've got bad news. After you left last week, I got to worrying that you guys wouldn't come back, and when three reliable boys I knew came by, I signed them up. I'm sorry, but it's a done deal."

"Listen, mister, you made a deal with us first, and where we come from a man's word means something. You need to talk to us face to face."

"Face to face wouldn't change anything," he said, and hung up.

Ben and Don had heard enough to know that our Crater Lake dream was over. "Now what?" Ben asked.

"I don't know about you guys!" I raged. "But I'm for finding out where that gentleman lives! I'm ready to call him out in the road and work him over!" They nodded in agreement, but a patrol car cruising by changed their minds.

"We're liable to get arrested or shot," Ben said. "We better leave."

"Yeah," Don reluctantly agreed. "Let's go. We've got enough money to get back to Portland. Whose turn is it to drive?"

"It's Ben's," I said. Whipped, I crawled into the back seat with Cougar.

THIRTY-ONE
HEADIN' HOME

Deeply disappointed over losing the jobs we'd been promised at Crater Lake, Ben and Don and I were barely civil on the drive back to Portland. To make matters worse, the car's intermittent backfiring turned constant.

Joyce was glad to see us, but her mother was cool. "Here's the key," she said. "I think it's all right for you boys to use Bob's apartment again, but we expect him back any day now."

"Thanks, Mrs. Gardner," I said.

"Yeah, thanks," Ben said.

Don and Joyce had already disappeared.

After taking our belongings and Cougar to the apartment, Ben and I slept. "What are we gonna eat?" he asked later.

"I don't know. Maybe we can scrounge up something." We knew the icebox was empty, but we hadn't pilfered through the cupboard. The only edible thing we found in it was a box of bad tasting instant potatoes.

310

"We've gotta get outta here," Ben said. "At least we'll have plenty of bread and avocadoes in Sacramento."

"I'm ready to go," I replied.

Not surprisingly, Don didn't want to leave Joyce. "Listen, " he said. "Before the car quits running altogether I'm gonna sell it for whatever I can get. I'll share the money with you guys if you'll stay a little longer."

"Fair enough," Ben said. "But how'll we get to Sacramento?"

"Remember how Wayne's always talkin' about how much fun hitchhikin' is?"

"Yeah," Ben said. "We'll hitchhike."

"I didn't say it was fun; I said it was cheap."

The next day Don, as good as his word, handed over ten dollars each to Ben and me out of the thirty dollars he'd received for his car. A few days later Ben told me he was broke.

"Broke? How can you be broke?"

"It's easy. How much money do you have left?"

"Not much," I said, counting it out. "Thirty-seven cents, to be exact."

"We'd better pack up and be ready to go when Don comes."

Don didn't argue about leaving, but he was reluctant to say how much money he had. "Four bits," he finally said. "And I'll bet that's more than you guys have."

"You're right," I admitted. "Let's hit the road."

The sight of three scruffy, swaggering young men standing alongside the highway with cocked thumbs caused many drivers to accelerate instead of stop, especially when they saw a dog sitting on top of six stacked suitcases.

Sometime after noon, disheartened, we stopped for lunch. Don figured three hamburgers would take most, if not all, of our money.

"A box of crackers and a quart of milk'll be cheaper," Ben said.

"Good idea," Don replied. "We can count the crackers so nobody'll get cheated, but how'll we measure the milk?"

"Like this," I said, grabbing him by the throat. "Anyone who tries to take more than three swallows at a time gets choked."

After our measured lunch, a sporty coupe with a rumble seat pulled over on the right of way and stopped. Don and Ben and Cougar, all fast runners, were almost up to the car when the driver peeled out, throwing gravel. I, lagging behind, smelled a rat. As the car accelerated and the jeering boys in the rumble seat stood up, I peppered them with rocks.

All afternoon we hiked more than we hitched. "Let's stop at a farm and trade work for our supper," Ben suggested.

"Yeah," Don said. 'Wayne can milk and we can shovel shit."

We picked out a dairy down a long lane where a barking dog announced our arrival. "What do you guys want?" a man in the barn lot asked.

"We're hungry," I began, "and we thought you might let us do chores for our supper."

"No."

"I'm a good milker and my friends are hard workers."

"We don't need any help," the man said, turning away.

"I'm still hungry," Don said, as we walked back toward the highway, "Do you suppose anyone ever eats butterflies?"

"I doubt it," Ben said. "Why?"

"On our way down the lane I saw several flyin' around a mud puddle. Let's catch one and sample it."

"You mean raw?" Ben asked.

"Yeah. Why not?"

"Count me out," Ben said.

"I'm game," I said. "Who'll eat what?"

"I'll eat the wings if you'll eat the body."

"Suits me."

Butterflies are fast, but Ben caught a plump, crippled monarch. "Here you go," he said. "Eat up."

It's difficult to describe the exact sensation of chomping down on a struggling butterfly, but it was far worse than baked possum, fried mountain oysters, or boiled screech owl had ever been. I don't know how much of his part Don swallowed, but after rolling the squishy, disgustingly sweet body around in my mouth, I spit it out. Don said the wings tasted like lacey edges on eggs fried in a hot skillet, then sprinkled with talcum powder.

It was almost dark by the time we got to the next town where we saw several empty railroad cars, including one with narrow metal cots down the middle. We had unstrapped our blankets and were settling in when Cougar growled and a big man with a long flashlight appeared.

"You guys can't sleep here," he informed us.

"We've had bad luck, mister," Don said. "We lost our jobs and I had to practically give away my car. Now, no one wants to pick us up, and we haven't had anything to eat all day except crackers and milk early this morning."

"All right," the bull said. "You can stay if you'll promise to keep that dog quiet and be out of here by daybreak."

"We promise," Ben said. "Thanks a lot,"

We were almost asleep when Cougar growled and the man reappeared. "Call off your dog," he said. "Here's somethin' for you. Remember, be out of here early or we're all in trouble," and he was gone. Inside a cardboard box we found three half-pints of milk and six big, juicy hamburgers.

Cougar was quiet the rest of the night and we made sure we were up and gone early the next morning so we wouldn't get the watchman who befriended us in trouble. All three of us, including easy going Ben, were irritable as we stood alongside the highway trying to look optimistic and respectable while we halfheartedly stuck out our thumbs to occasional approaching cars.

"I'd feel better if I had somethin' in my belly," Don said.

"Me too," I said. "I get a headache when I don't eat on time."

"A big stack of pancakes washed down with cold milk wouldn't be bad," Ben said.

"We don't have enough money for crackers, much less pancakes," Don said. "Talkin' about it will only make matters worse."

"I don't know about that," Ben replied as he removed his left shoe. "Look here," and he lifted the insole and pulled out a wrinkled dollar bill.

"What are you doin' holdin' out on us?" I demanded.

"I put it back in case we really needed it," he grinned. "Let's stop at the next cafe. With that dollar and what little change we have left, we'll splurge on a short stack and a small glass of milk. Maybe that'll hold us till we get to Sacramento." As good as the pancakes tasted, the extra butter and heavy syrup I slathered on mine upset my stomach. I didn't throw up, but I felt queasy all day.

While studying the California map in the late afternoon, Don recognized Redding, California. "Redding is where some of my folks' friends live," he said. "We're sure not goin' to make it to Sacramento tonight." It was dark before we reached Redding, and while Don made a phone call he turned and whispered that we were invited to have supper and stay all night. After the former Missourians had picked us up and taken us to their house, they asked about various people they'd known, including someone whose name I recognized.

"Yeah, I know Clay Judd," I said. "He lives south of Aurora past the C. P. Church, and a couple of miles west toward Pleasant Ridge."

"That's right," the man said. "Clay Judd and I went fox hunting together many a time."

"We mostly hunted possums around White Oak," I said. "But one of my favorite pastimes was listenin' to hounds circlin' a fox." I didn't see any point in telling him how strongly Mama disapproved of fox hunting. "Maybe you know Howard Robbins," I said. "Before he moved to Aurora, he kept runnin' dogs. I remember he used to talk about goin' to school and growin' up with Clay Judd."

314

"Howard Robbins? A big man with a booming voice and a hearty laugh?"

"Yeah, that's him."

"Go help yourselves to some more hamburgers," he said. "I can tell you boys are hungry." It was embarrassing to see how much food we put away, but not embarrassing enough to make us stop before we made pigs of ourselves. Even Don's normally rock hard flat belly bulged. After we'd stuffed ourselves, we naturally began to yawn.

"Feel welcome to take a bath," his wife said. "There are plenty of clean towels in the closet."

"Much obliged, but we're gonna pass on the baths, "I said. "We've been on the road roughin' it so long we don't have any clean clothes to change into. We'll sleep on the floor just like we are if it's all right with you."

"That'll be fine," she said. "I'll get you some pillows. You're bound to be tired." The accommodating man had left for work before we stirred the next morning, but his wife fed us a big breakfast before we were up and on our way again.

After we arrived in Sacramento and located Fred's place, a young stranger met us at the door. "Is Lois Holmes here?" I asked.

"Yes, she is," the teenaged girl replied. "May I tell her who's here?"

"I'm Wayne, Fred's brother. This is Ben and Don."

"Oh, yeah. Hi. Lois has talked a lot about you guys. I'm her baby sister."

Lois was glad to see us, but Fred seemed nervous. "Lois's sister has dibs on the couch," he told me privately. "She and her husband are separated."

"She doesn't look old enough to be married."

"She's fifteen goin' on sixteen, two years younger than Lois," he said. "To tell you the truth, I'm not sure Lois is old enough herself."

"We'll try to not stay too long," I said. "As soon as we find work and get paid, we'll be out of here."

"The railroad's been hirin'. Why don't you try that?"

A long line of us waited a long time outside a gate at the railroad office before a spokesman appeared and announced that no applications would be taken that day. Instead of leaving with the others, I hung around until two men carrying a heavy beam started to enter the gate. "Here, let me help you with that," I said, shouldering a good part of the load while the gate swung open. Once we were well into the compound, I excused myself.

"Thanks for the help," one of the men said.

"You're welcome. Where can I find the employment office?"

"Right over there in that brick building."

"What are you doing in here?" a man at a desk asked. "We're not taking applications today."

"I can't believe you don't need a machinist."

"You're not a machinist."

"Well, I'm not exactly a machinist, but I've worked in a machine shop for two years."

"Since you're here, go ahead and fill this out," he said. "We're not hiring today, but sooner or later we will be."

"Okay," I said, "Thanks."

Increasingly desperate after hearing nothing from the railroad, I agreed with Ben and Don to enlist in the Army if we were assured we'd be paratroopers in the same outfit. "You'll get to stay together through basic training," the recruiter assured us. "After that, I can't guarantee anything."

All three of us easily passed the written tests, but Ben, totally flat-footed, couldn't pass the physical. "You guys go ahead," he said.

"No, we're in this together," Don assured him. "We all go, or nobody goes."

"That's right," I said. "All or none."

Things turned sour back at Fred and Lois' apartment. Don's smooth manner and winning ways may have had something to do with him remaining in Lois and her sister's good graces; but Ben and I noticed they acted more and more indifferent, and

316

then increasingly hostile, toward us. "This is a bad situation," I told Ben one morning. "We've gotta get outta here."

"I know it," he said. "Whatta ya think about headin' home?"

"We're broke, or close to it," I said. "But we'll get along somehow. Let's go tell Don we're leavin'."

Fred didn't say much, but I could see he was relieved when I asked him if he could take us out to the east edge of Sacramento before he went to work the next morning. "Yeah, I'll be glad to," he said. "The sooner you get on the road, the better chance you'll have of catchin' a ride." After shaking hands all around, reckless as always, he cut a cat's ass in the middle of the highway, burning rubber with his fast little Ford.

If you've ever stood in one place for seven hours straight you know what I mean when I say the topography of a place can be permanently etched in a person's mind. In all of the considerable hitch-hiking I've done – more than ten thousand miles – I've stood in one place only three times so long I can never forget how it looked. Two of the times were on opposite ends of Kansas, and the third, the most vivid, was that interminable day outside Sacramento.

After lunch, when we ate the avocado sandwiches Don had helped Lois pack, we reluctantly agreed we'd have to give up our dog. When I walked back to a pay phone and called him, Fred was dead set against taking Cougar, but he gave in when I told him we'd all be back to stay at his house if we didn't catch a ride by nightfall. "Okay, I'll take him," he said, but after he picked him up I could tell how angry he was from the sensible way he turned around.

Some two hours later, still standing in the same spot, we faced up to the inevitable: we'd have to split up. "We'll flip for it," Ben said, "odd man out."

"Yeah," I agreed. "But whoever loses gets half of the money."

"That sounds fair to me," Don said. "Let's count our money and divide it into two piles before we flip. That'll lessen the chance of the one losin' the toss backin' out. It's gettin' late."

317

"Okay," Ben said. "Ever'body empty his pockets." The two little stacks of change totaled almost two dollars. Each of us took a penny, flipped it into the air, caught it, and turned it upside down on our left arms where it remained hidden until we simultaneously uncovered the coins.

Ben and I had heads, Don tails. Don pocketed his half of the money, shook hands with us, and said, "See you guys back in Missouri," and quickly hoisted his suitcase to his shoulder. Without looking back, he walked with long determined strides down the side of the road a few hundred yards where in a few minutes a fast car pulled over and picked him up. A second car soon stopped for Ben and me, and we were on our way.

I have blocked out much of what followed the next couple of days, but I clearly remember being let out in downtown Reno that first night and seeing the garish signs of the casinos before we walked past well lighted used car lots on the east side where we failed to find an unlocked car to sleep in. As nearly broke as Ben and I were, we feared we'd end up in jail if the police caught us loitering. We walked way out of town before spreading our blankets in a ditch near a junction and bedded down for the night. Before we could get to sleep we put dirty tee shirts over our heads to keep off swarming mosquitoes. We walked across the junction east of Reno early the next morning, but before we stuck out our thumbs we went to the restroom in a nearby service station, got a drink of water from the outside hose, and spent a little more than half of our remaining dollar on ten candy bars we stashed in Ben's suitcase. Before we'd finished eating our first shared breakfast candy bar, a middle-aged couple in a sedan pulled over. "Where are you boys headed?" the friendly man inquired.

"Southwest Missouri," I replied.

"Well, get in. We'll take you as far as Denver."

"Much obliged," I said and we piled in the back seat.

Gently at first, the woman started in on us. "Are you boys saved?"

"I'm not," I said. "I tried to get saved when I was sixteen, but nothin' happened."

"What about you?" the woman asked Ben.

"Not yet," he replied. "But I aim to get saved some time." Encouraged by Ben's polite manner, the woman droned on hour after long hour in her attempt to convert him. Sleepy and surly, I sulled up like a possum in my corner.

When the couple stopped for gas and food, they asked us to join them, but we begged off. "We have food with us," Ben said. When they stopped at a roadside motel that evening, there was an awkward moment when it was clear that Ben and I couldn't afford to pay for a room.

"You boys are welcome to sleep in the car, and then ride on with us to Denver tomorrow," the man said.

"Much obliged," Ben said.

"This is a good ride, but I'm not sure I can stand another day with that woman," I told him as we spread our blankets in the car.

"Remember when the man followed me outside at the gas station?"

"Yeah, why?"

"He took me aside and told me he could tell we were sick of hearin' all that religious malarkey, but if we'd ignore it as best we could he'd buy our supper tomorrow evenin' when we get to Denver."

"We better take him up on it," I said. "These Baby Ruth candy bars are gettin' old."

The second day was similar to the first, and Ben and I, homesick for Kansas and Missouri, had a hard time appreciating the Rockies. The man stopped and bought us a good supper of hamburgers and french fries before taking us to a likely looking spot on Highway 40 southeast of Denver where we'd try hitchhiking at night. "Now don't wait too late to be saved," the woman called as she and her kind husband drove off.

We had been standing on the side of the highway only a short time when a man in a small white car, a Morris Minor, pulled over. "Where are you headed?" he asked, when I opened the door.

"Wichita and beyond. What about you?"

"Just over into Kansas. You're welcome to ride along if I can depend on one of you stayin' awake. I need somebody to talk to."

"We'll do that," I said, and first Ben and then I kept up a steady stream of talk with the lanky driver as we bumped over the rough road toward western Kansas. When we reached Sharon Springs, the man's destination, it was early in the morning and still dark, but after scouting around we found that the door of the railroad station was unlocked. The long wooden benches with their cast iron partitions designed to deter vagrants kept us from stretching out, but we catnapped sitting up.

When I looked myself over in the restroom mirror in the daylight, I was appalled. "Man, we'd better shave." I told Ben. "We look like somethin' the dogs drug in and the cats wouldn't eat."

"We still have some old razor blades," Ben said. "But our soap's long gone."

"That cafe down the street'll be open, and we've still got enough money for two glasses of milk. I'll check out the restroom while you order."

"Any luck?" Ben asked on my return.

"A little," I grinned, showing him a sliver of dark soap. "Let's go."

The scrapes and cuts from the combination of cold water, rusty blades and Lava soap made us look worse than ever, and we feared we'd be taken for escaped convicts as we walked out of town. Occasional approaching drivers, who seemed to speed up instead of slowing down when they saw us, made us think everyone viewed us with suspicion. At any rate, the sun was straight overhead and we'd eaten our last two candy bars before a driver, hell-bent for Wichita, pulled over.

When Xerpha, Ben's mom, first saw us she was aghast. "You boys look awful. When was the last time you had a bath?"

"About a month ago," Ben admitted. "We took a shower alongside the Columbia River just before we got to Portland." I was afraid he'd mention that we were buck naked in full view of everyone driving by, but he didn't.

Xerpha's face clouded up when Ben asked her where his dad was. "Maybe he's workin' late again," she said. "He'll turn up sooner or later. You better go call your Grandma Holmes. She's been prayin' you'll make it home safe."

"Grandma wants us to sleep over at her place," Ben said, after he got off the phone.

"That'll be fine," his mom said. "Maybe you'll get to see your dad tomorrow night."

Pap was his usual reserved and gruff but kind self as he swung on the dark porch, but Lottie babbled with unabashed joy and relief at seeing her darling Bennie George, her favorite grandchild by far. She'd taken care of him for weeks and months on end when Vincel was out of work. Ben enjoyed being petted and made over, but on the second day when I told him I was ready to go home to Missouri, he seemed interested in going with me. "What'll we do when we get there?" he asked.

"I'm not sure what all," I said, "but by the fourth of July the blackberries are generally beginning to get ripe. We can pick and sell enough berries to keep us in gas and spending money for a couple of weeks. After that, who knows? We just might join the Navy.

"Yeah," Ben agreed. "that Army recruiter in Sacramento thought the Navy would take me, flat feet and all."

While we were at Pap and Lottie's, Ben and I washed our grimy clothes in the basement, then carried them outside and were in the awkward process of hanging them on the clothes line, when two friendly girls from across the street showed up. "That's not the way," a ripe looking thirteen year old girl wearing short shorts said.

"Here," I said, handing her my underwear. "I bet you know how it's done."

"I certainly do," she said, and lightly patted the bulging crotch of my wet briefs. "Just like that," she said, smiling. "Is there anything else you'd like help with?"

"Yeah, plenty of things," I said. "But I guess we'll have to pass for now. We're headin' for Missouri as soon as these clothes get dry."

"That's too bad," she said. "Well, if you ever come back, just whistle and we'll be right over."

Our fresh haircuts Xerpha paid for may have helped us look more reputable after all. At any rate, we got several quick rides to Missouri, including a long ride with a man driving a fast '34 Ford sedan outfitted with a police siren that he proudly showed off on a remote stretch in eastern Kansas. The black car with its distinctive suicide doors was a duplicate of the car Mr. Farley had offered to let me have instead of the hundred dollars he owed me at the end of my first wheat harvest five years earlier.

As we walked the last mile after being dropped off at the crossroads north of the Parvin Place, I grew increasingly anxious because I remembered Mama had always thought Ben was a bad influence on me, and she made little attempt to mask her feelings. As I expected, Dad put on his jovial company face when he saw Ben, and Mama looked sour. There was no sign of a handshake, and the closest thing to a hug was when Jay and I awkwardly bumped shoulders and grinned. "How you been?" I asked him.

"Okay, I guess."

"Take your suitcases out to the smokehouse," Mama told Ben and me. "There's room for the three of you out there where Jay sleeps."

"That'll be just fine," Ben said.

"And there's a pot of beans and plenty of cornbread and milk left over in the kitchen," she said. "Help yourself."

"Okay," I said, "That sounds good."

After Ben and I finished regaling Jay with our Wild West stories out in the smokehouse, he filled us in on what he'd been up to since he'd recently started running around with Houston. Jay said Houston was bigger than ever. Landing a full time job shoveling cans at Carnation had enabled him to buy a few acres east of the Cockatoo roadhouse where he kept and broke spotted western broncs.

Jay, who was six foot tall himself, said he felt dwarfed standing next to the seven foot giant decked out in his high-heeled cowboy boots and a high-crowned, wide brimmed felt hat. I was astounded to hear that the once shy youngster cut didoes for hours on end dancing at Yonkersville, an infamous rough-as-a-cob Polish tavern near Pulaskifield.

Bill Reavis chimed in one afternoon with an account of his own. "Me and maybe half a dozen others was ridin' single file on the right of way east of the Cockatoo the other evenin' when Houston, in the lead as usual on one of his little paints, guided his horse off the grass and onto the middle of the highway. All of a sudden two cars, one goin' one way, one another, headed straight for him. We thought he was a goner for sure," Bill said. "But he wasn't. Cool as a cucumber, Houston dropped his legs out of the stirrups, put his feet flat on the blacktop, and with a mighty heave he moved the horse sideways off the highway and over to the shoulder and out of the way."

Later, Ben and I were at Madry selling blackberries for gas money, when Velma, who owned the store, asked me if I'd heard that Houston was in the hospital.

"No." I said. "What's wrong with him?"

"I heard he had a heart attack. But I doubt it. He's too young for a heart attack."

"I think you're right," I agreed, "but from what I hear he's been overdoin' himself in more ways than one."

"Come to think of it, I've been hearin' that too," she said with a smile. "But I've never heard of anything like that killin' a man, especially a young man."

"Me neither," I said. "I may go see him."

"Good. Let me know what you find out. Okay?"

"Yeah, okay."

Sure enough, Houston said he'd suffered a light heart attack. Suffered didn't seem to be the right word given his bright and bushy tailed appearance as he suggested we go to the lounge where he could smoke and we could shoot the shit in private. We laughed and talked about many things, including our grade school plans to have a goat ranch together. After swapping stories about what we'd done since graduating from high school the year before, we switched to our more recent experiences. Although Houston was interested in hearing about the faraway and exotic places I'd visited, it was clear that my accounts didn't hold a candle to his graphically related adventures with the eighty-some girls and women he'd carved notches for in the headboard of the new seven foot bed his grandma had given him when he'd graduated from high school.

When I visited him two days later, Houston, dressed in his cowboy outfit, nervously awaited his release from the hospital. "Thanks for comin'," he said, as we shook hands. "Let's keep in touch."

"Yeah, let's do," I said. "Well, here come your folks. See ya."

Houston's picture and obituary were in the paper the following Wednesday, giving me plenty of time to get around early for his funeral on Saturday. Given all his friends and admirers, I knew there'd be a big crowd, and I wanted a good seat near the coffin. At the start of the service I felt low and out of sorts. And when the preacher stood I felt worse when I saw that he was Houston's Uncle Ed. While it was true that Ed was the only Friend in the area who went to church, I thought it was inappropriate for him to preach Houston's funeral. This was confirmed when Ed began preaching him into hell. For thirty minutes he ranted and raved. The only difference between this sermon and the ones I'd heard so many times before was that the usual hypothetical sinner had been replaced by the real example and corpse of Houston before us. Ed said, "We all know what kind of wicked and unrepentant life Houston lived, and unless we get down on our knees and get right with the Lord, we'll all end up in the same place."

But that wasn't enough. As I sat there disconsolate, sliding lower and lower in my seat, I realized that something more, something worse, was wrong. Why, I wondered, was Houston's mouth drawn down, with no trace of his usual roguish grin? And why were his hands clasped in that phony, pious pose? While I stared at his big head and nose and saw him once more in his old familiar position, I finally understood that the ancient iron bed from long before answered my questions. Of course Houston wasn't smiling; they'd crammed his seven foot frame into a six foot coffin.

* * *

Ben and I helped Dad and Jay with the milking morning and night. In between times, we picked and sold enough berries to keep us in gas and pocket money for our evening jaunts into Aurora, where we soon settled into dating two girls who lived on opposite sides of Porter Street, Mary Nivens and Nellie Langwell.

The two eighteen year old recent high school graduates— apparently stuck in dead end jobs for thirty five cents an hour at the garment factory—amused Ben and me as well as each other with their caustic zinging remarks. Mary, Ben's date, seemed to have learned her scathing disapproving banter from her mother, but Nellie's readiness to lash out may have been caused in part because her father had carried her as a nine month old baby with a bottle while he hitchhiked two hundred miles to his obliging mother who took over and reared the willful child. I liked the fearless and fiery cranky girl with her pouty lips, hooded eyes, wonderful tits, and quick wit, but at this point I didn't want to risk getting tied down with her or any other girl.

While the blackberry season steadily wound down, Ben and I discussed our options. Although I was confident I could count on Coach Thomson's football scholarship offer at Southwest

Missouri State College, I didn't relish having to scrimp by on the small monthly stipend he said I'd get in addition to room and board, books, and tuition each semester.

The more Ben and I talked, the better joining the Navy sounded, especially since we'd been told no other branch of service would take someone totally flat-footed like Ben. Sick of hitchhiking, we bought train tickets with our final week's berry money and rode to St. Louis, where we passed our exams with flying colors. Upon our arrival in San Diego for boot camp, we were assigned to separate companies. Following boot camp Ben was sent to the Philippines, and I went to radar school across from San Francisco in preparation for boarding a destroyer escort bound for the east coast, Florida, and the Caribbean Sea.

THIRTY-TWO
FINAL LEAVE

While hitchhiking home on emergency leave, I couldn't understand why it took so long to get from Key West to Missouri. In all my over the road experiences, from California to Missouri and back again, when I stuck out my thumb sooner or later someone pulled over and picked me up. But in the deep south not a single one of the many black people traveling my way would give me a ride, nor would any of them meet my curious gaze. Though I considered myself a worldly traveler, I didn't have a clue about what was going on during the fifties.

Final Leave

When I finally made it home, Dad lay in an unfamiliar position on his side on a hard pallet in the front room. His knees were drawn up to his chest, and a small, noisy fan played back and forth across his thin frame. His normally red face, now pale as ashes, gaunt and drawn, was highlighted by black bristles. He nodded: "How've you been?"

"All right, how about yourself?"

"Not good," he said. "Not good at all. We need help. You think you can shoe Jay's saddle horse?"

"I don't know. I've never shod a horse. You always did it, remember?"

"Yeah, but I can't now. I'm too weak. We're out of grass here at home and we've rented Smalley's Place. It has grass but no water, so we have to drive the cows back and forth twice a day on horseback. Old Dan's thrown both of his front shoes and he's lame. Whatta ya think? Can you shoe him?" Exhausted from his monologue, he looked away.

"I'll try," I said, as I thought, "He's too poor to pay and too proud to ask any of his friends." While I gathered horseshoes, nails, rasp, pinchers, and hammer, I tried to remember which direction the nails went. One way meant quicking the horse's hoof, drawing blood; the other, success. I remembered right, but what would have once been an easy thirty minute job for Dad took me all morning.

Finished, I led the horse to the front door where Dad, propped up on his elbow, looked out, smiled wanly, and asked, "How'd you know how?"

"From watchin' you all those times,"

Dad rallied, but not enough to ride Old Dan. Sometimes Jay rode him. Sometimes Mama.

Shortly after I shod Old Dan, Dad told me, "There's another job needin' to be done."

"What's that?" I asked.

"I don't suppose you ever cleaned a cow?"

"No, I never did. I helped with the horseshoein' right along, but you didn't act like you needed help the few times I remember you cleanin' a cow."

"Well, it can be a messy job," he said, "especially when the cow's been carrying the afterbirth as long as this one has."

"What'll I need to do?"

"You'll have to find her first, but that'll be easy. She'll be humped up, strainin', trying' to pass the afterbirth, and you'll prob'ly see a cord hangin' out of her hindend."

"I remember seein' you clean a cow out in the barn lot once."

"Yeah," he said, "Sometimes you can ease up close to the cow when she's strainin', get a good grip on the cord, then gradually pull it down and out somethin' like the way you pull a calf. But that won't work with this cow."

"Why not?"

"'Cause it's been in her too long. The cord'll break off and the main part will stay inside, poisonin' her."

"How'll I get it out?"

"Toll her into a stout stanchion with a can of shorts. While she eats, take off your shirt and wash your right arm and shoulder with warm, soapy water, then gradually work your hand and arm into her slit. Use the cord as a guide."

"Then what?"

"Now's the hard part. Once you're inside her you'll likely find that the sack is still attached."

"Can't I just pull it out?"

"Not at first," he said, "It's not that simple."

"Whatta you mean?"

"You'll feel raised places about the size of a boil or warble scattered here and there, workin' like suction cups or leeches, holdin' the afterbirth in place. Press in on 'em with your thumb and pry 'em up and pretty soon you can pull out the whole kit and caboodle. Think you can do it?"

"Maybe," I said, "I'll try."

"I'm gonna have to lay down and rest," Dad said. "You oughta be finished by dinnertime."

"Okay," I said, "See ya then."

Dad apparently forgot to tell me the worst part: the smell would've gagged a mule. The only way I could keep from puking as I slid my hand and arm into the cow was to turn side-

329

ways and breathe through my mouth. Even so, I had to back out a couple of times and fill my lungs with great gulps of fresh air in order to finish.

When I got through, Jay turned the cow loose and watered her before he drove her to Smalley's where he'd taken the rest of the cows. As he rode past the west window Dad looked out long enough to see that the cow's tail still stuck out, but she no longer stopped and strained every few steps.

Meanwhile, I took a shower under the fifty gallon barrel Jay and I had rigged up on the north side of the garage. Drawing water out of the cistern and then climbing a rickety ladder on the side of the open barrel was tiresome, but water warmed by the sun beat taking a bath in a galvanized tub. I ordinarily enjoyed taking a shower, but in spite of all my efforts, including using Mama's homemade lye soap, I couldn't get rid of an occasional unmistakable whiff of stinking afterbirth.

When Mama hollered, "Dinner's ready," at twelve o'clock sharp, I hurried inside. Dad, already at the table, asked, "How'd it go?"

"All right, once I got the hang of it," I said, "but I don't think I'd like to do it for a livin'."

Careful to pick up my bread and fried chicken with my left hand, I also made sure I touched nothing except the handles of my utensils. I managed fairly well, but as I turned to the right to respond to Dad's occasional questions, a familiar putrid smell turned my stomach. When Mama passed the food for seconds, I said, "I better not. Maybe next time." Nobody let on when I excused myself and went outside. As sharp as Dad's sense of smell was, he may have known why I left the table, but if he did he was good enough not to mention it.

A few days later Dad asked Jay and me if we had enough gumption to butcher the stocky two year old Jersey-Guernsey cross bull he'd raised for his herd bull.

"I thought you meant to keep him," I said.

"Sometimes you have to change your mind," he said. "We need meat and we're short on money. You boys ain't butchered a beef before," he continued, "but remember to slit its throat sideways instead of stickin' it, and skin the hide instead of scrapin' it. Otherwise the butcherin's pretty much the same as it is with a hog."

"Wayne, my single-shot 22 might do the job, but if it was me I'd shoot him with your 30-30 Winchester. The first shot'll prob'ly drop him like he's been poleaxed, but if it don't that lever action'll give you a quick backup."

Dad knew what he was talking about. When the seven to eight hundred pound bull dropped, Dad stepped up and grabbed him by the balls and managed to cut them off and throw them in the direction of his waiting dog. "I don't want to risk taintin' the meat," he said, then slowly headed for the house.

As I quickly moved to grab a horn, Jay picked up Mama's sharpest and longest butcher knife and began working on the downed animal's throat. The deeper he cut the more trouble I had holding the jerking head, but when he neared the neck-bone a bright gush of blood spurted out, and with a final spasm the steer lay still. Jay had blood smeared on his hands and arms and red spray on his face, and his eyes glittered as he turned and asked, "Whatta ya think?"

"Good job!" I said. "Too bad the Old He wasn't here to see it."

"Yeah," Jay said. "We fooled him."

It took most of the afternoon to saw and cut the carcass into manageable chunks which we rubbed with salt and packed into a wooden barrel in the smokehouse. After I'd left and be-fore the meat had time to turn rancid, Jay supplied the man-power for turning Mama's powerful grinder while she pre-pared and stuffed hamburger meat into quart jars placed in her big pressure cooker on the kitchen stove.

During the days' long hours Dad and I got acquainted in the shade of a white oak tree in the back yard where he lay resting on his rusty iron cot and I sat on a stool. We talked of sundry things, both weighty and of little matter. One day he paused and said, "You're not ashamed of us anymore."

"No, I'm not," I said.

When my leave had almost expired, I got ready to go. Dad stood, awkwardly; and for the first time in memory, we hugged. "I won't see you again," he said. "I wish I had somethin' to give you." Then, smiling, he pulled his good Case pocketknife out of his left front pocket, placed it in my open hand, and turned away.

Dad was right. He didn't see me again. I saw him once more, clean shaven, stretched out straight on his back. Instead of his comfortable worn overalls, he wore his dark blue suit and black tie reserved for just such an occasion.

Clay Holmes

ACKNOWLEDGEMENTS

Shortly after my retirement in 1990 from teaching at Drury College in Springfield, Missouri, Kate Staley Marymont, a former student who was editor of the Springfield *News-Leader*, talked me into writing an every other Sunday column about growing up on a number of rented and sharecropped hillside farms in the Missouri Ozarks during and immediately following the Great Depression. The ensuing columns, including much but not all of what follows, appeared in the *News-Leader* over a three year period in the early nineties.

While I used the actual names of people and places for the most part in my memoir, I reluctantly made some changes. For example, as fond as I was of the original title, *The Jill-Flirted Mare*, it apparently confused many readers and listeners. The more I considered various new titles, the better I liked *Rocky Comfort*, the name of a small and remote farm community a few miles southwest of where my family eked out a living on various hillside farms. I trust that the people who live in or near Rocky Comfort in McDonald County don't mind that I appropriated their name. And I also hope that no one thinks I was writing about the McDonald County community when I changed the name of the Lawrence County Dover Baptist Church my family attended to the Rocky Comfort Baptist Church. In addition, I don't want readers to think I'm bad-mouthing anyone except the auctioneer turned evangelist from Springfield who, after I tried but failed to get saved, proclaimed I had committed an unforgivable sin against the Holy Ghost. By the way, traumatic as the damning proclamation initially was, as time passed I decided the preacher's dire words were nothing more than a cock-and-bull story meant to frighten gullible people.

The main reason for naming one of my characters Houston was because his mother was still alive and I didn't want to hurt her feelings. That was false reasoning on my part, of course, because she would have known from start to finish who I was writing about. Now that she as well as the other close members of her family are dead, perhaps I should use her son's real name; but I'm so used to Houston I've decided to stick with it. Not that there's anything wrong with the name Dallas.

Although I changed the names of several characters in a column published in the *News-Leader* during the early nineties, the irate sister of the main character called and scolded me at length for divulging information kept secret by the family for over fifty years. The woman calmed down after I'd apologized, and I recall that she hoped her brother, who was also a main character in what I'd written and who lived in a nursing home, didn't read the column in his Sunday paper. I also remember the woman's final words: "You don't have any idea what all went on in that house back then." While she didn't elaborate, her obscure words added to the mystery of an unsolved death.

I also omitted or markedly changed a half dozen or so additional names of persons who might have been embarrassed or offended had I used their real names. Although changing names may have occasionally protected the guilty, I have bent over backwards in an effort to give my characters the benefit of the doubt when it came to matters of integrity.

While I strongly oppose hearing racial slurs that were common parlance in the communities where I grew up, I feel that to maintain authenticity they are necessary.

A former high school student and longtime friend, Jeffery Viles, suggested I send the first chapter, "The Jill-Flirted Mare," to Speer Morgan, editor of *The Missouri Review*, who highlighted it in a early 2001 issue entitled "Hard Times."

Looking back, I must acknowledge the crucial role Mr. Lloyd Shelton, my high school English teacher from 1946 to 1948, played in turning me around after I'd refused to diagram sentences and flunked eighth grade English twice, going on three times. The ordinarily mild and unfailingly fair little man with a bobbing Adam's apple expected us to behave as well as study our assignments and participate in lively class discussions. Mr. Shelton's personal example, including his wide ranging observations and willingness to share his forthright and sometimes iconoclastic views, helped me understand the absurdity of the commonly held view that anyone with a lot of book learning never had a lick of common sense.

I also wish to extend my thanks to a number of football coaches, especially Mr. Jay Hunter and Mr. Jeff Neal, who encouraged my scab nosed aggressiveness as I explored and pushed the parameters of this dangerous and exhilarating game. Paradoxically, as much as I enjoyed Mr. Shelton's English classes, the prospect of knocking heads on the playing fields more than once tipped the scales in favor of staying in school rather than dropping out the way my more compliant and harder working older brother and sister had done once they finished grade school.

After graduating from high school and joining the Navy in 1950, I went to boot camp in San Diego and then attended radar school on Treasure Island, across the bay from San Francisco, before going on board a destroyer escort in Los Angeles. Although I was appalled at all the nit-picking rules aboard ship, the cramped quarters promoted feelings of camaraderie. Anytime we were in port, which was often, some few of us who rarely went on liberty got in the habit of hanging out in the radar shack, where we spent long hours taking turns sharing our stories about who we were and where we came from. Initially unsure and ashamed of my poor background, I gained confidence when I saw that my often more knowledgeable and sophisticated shipmates from various parts of the country looked forward to hearing my accounts of growing up in the Missouri Ozarks during the Great Depression.

I also thank Dr. and Mrs. Richard Bushman for their support in the Summer of 1977 when the two historians taught "Plain Life in Early America," a National Endowment for the Humanities course which I attended. Mrs. Bushman strongly encouraged me to write an account of my rural life in the Ozarks, an account which closely paralleled the lives and circumstances of many New Englanders some two hundred years earlier.

I was awarded a similar NEH fellowship at the University of California, Berkeley, three summers later. The American history course was broader in scope and much more recent than the Boston course, but Dr. Levine, my main teacher, encouraged me to continue writing about my life in the Ozarks. I was surprised and delighted when a visiting folklore lecturer said that Vance Randolph's lifelong work on the Ozarks was the best ever.

Shortly after retiring from teaching at Drury in 1990, I began a stint of storytelling for the Missouri Humanities Council. My wife and I drove throughout much of the state to schools, churches, and various places where civic organizations gathered as I spoke and read about growing up in the Ozarks. My accounts often evoked anecdotes from listeners who spoke in the give and take following my presentations.

In addition to our close family members, a coterie of friends have provided encouragement over the years. Supporters include my younger brother Jay and his wife Carol and their extended family; Joe and Wanda Valentine; Charley and Rosa Robbins; Charley and Joan Collins; Steve and Mildred Rutan; Donna Lemaster; and Marjorie Hoss. I appreciate many others who have been helpful, including Don and Judy Weber, Bill and Joyce Pyle, Harvey and Sandra Asher, Fred and Faye Pfister, Steve Wiggenstein, Sharon Buzzard, Karen Buzzard, Judy Baughman, Kathy List, Leon Combs, Price Flanagan, Carol Webb, John Holmes, Jeffery Viles, Patty Viles, C.W. Gusewelle, Lynn Morrow, Diana Ross, and Donna Baker. And I'm happy to acknowledge many hundreds of former students. Much obliged to you all.

I thank Stephen and David Trobisch, my publishers; Kaitlyn Ramsey, who designed the book's cover; Sheila Perryman, copy editor; and Karen Schaefer, publicist. I especially appreci-

ate Stephen and Kaitlyn's support when a more genteel read
took offense at some of my graphic accounts.

I wish to thank Speer Morgan, editor of the *The Missouri Re
view*; and Fred Pfister, editor of *The Ozarks Mountaineer*, for
their kind words; and thanks to Frank McCourt who gave me a
big boost when he told me "The Jill-Flirted Mare," which he'd
read in *The Missouri Review*, was extraordinary.

Most of all, I am indebted to Mary Lou, my companion and
helper over the past fifty-five years. I am also indebted to our
four children and their companions: Laura and Gerald, Clay
and Becky, Marty and Kevin, and Karen and Lee, along with
their children: Jackson, Lacey, Emily, Cody; Nathan, Chris and
Steve; and our great grandchildren: Lilah Jane, Sophie Lou, and
Aiden.

Finally, as much as I've been helped, I, and I alone, am responsible for any and all of the mistakes, omissions, half-truths,
outright lies, and anything else disconcerting that readers of
Rocky Comfort happen to run up on.

Wayne Holmes

Breinigsville, PA USA
02 February 2010
231741BV00003B/1/P